THE LOGIC OF SOCIAL
ENQUIRY

INTERNATIONAL LIBRARY OF SOCIOLOGY AND SOCIAL RECONSTRUCTION

Founded by Karl Mannheim

Editor: W. J. H. Sprott

A catalogue of the books available in the INTERNATIONAL LIBRARY OF SOCIOLOGY AND SOCIAL RECONSTRUCTION, and new books in preparation for the Library, will be found at the end of this volume.

THE LOGIC OF
SOCIAL ENQUIRY

Quentin Gibson

LONDON
ROUTLEDGE & KEGAN PAUL
NEW YORK: THE HUMANITIES PRESS

First published in 1960
by Routledge and Kegan Paul Ltd.
Broadway House, 68–74 Carter Lane
London, E.C.4

Second Impression 1963
Third Impression 1966

Printed in Great Britain by
Lowe & Brydone (Printers) Ltd,
London

220134

ACKNOWLEDGEMENTS

MUCH of the groundwork for this book was laid while I held a Travelling Research Fellowship from the Australian National University. I wish here to register my thanks to that institution for the assistance so given towards its production.

Since that time I have been continuously assisted by discussions with colleagues, students and friends, more numerous than it would be possible to mention here. I will do no more than single out for mention those who have given their time to read the whole of the manuscript, Professor L. J. Russell, Mr. B. S. Benjamin, and my wife. Their comments and criticisms have brought about considerable improvements in the final version, though these may not of course be to their satisfaction.

QUENTIN GIBSON

Canberra University College,
November, 1959.

CONTENTS

CONTENTS

PART TWO

THE LOGICAL PECULIARITIES OF SOCIAL ENQUIRY

CONTENTS

I

INTRODUCTION

THROUGHOUT the centuries, men have been concerned to enquire into the structure and the changes of the society of which they form a part. In the last century or so, however, these enquiries have gathered momentum, have become more systematic and more detailed, and have been split up among various specialists—economists, political scientists, historians, anthropologists, sociologists, and so on. The word 'science', which tended to be used only for men's investigations of their natural surroundings, has come to be used quite freely for these social investigations as well.

As the subject-matter of these social enquiries is so different from that of the natural sciences, and as, moreover, the social enquirer is in the peculiar position of being part of his subject-matter, it is not surprising that controversy has developed about the ways in which such enquiries should be conducted.

. Those who have engaged in this controversy have of course recognized that there is a swiftly growing body of social theory already in existence. They have not supposed that historians, economists and the rest must wait for their conclusions so that they can be told how to proceed in their particular enquiries. The controversy has arisen rather out of reflection on the differing presuppositions about method which have been implied, or have been thought to be implied, in the conduct of these enquiries, and out of the differing expectations which ordinary people have about the character and extent of their results.

It is with this question of the proper procedure in social enquiries and the controversies to which it has given rise that we shall be concerned.

We shall not, however, be concerned with everything that is involved in this question. In deciding how one should proceed in any enquiry reference may be made to considerations of two different kinds, which we may call considerations of logic and considerations of economy. On the one hand we may ask whether a procedure satisfies logical requirements—on the other we may ask whether it enables us to get results with the greatest speed and the least trouble. It is possible to adopt a pro-

1

cedure which is logically unexceptionable and still waste time—for example by collecting irrelevant material, or by setting out results in a way which cannot be easily understood. It is important that people should consider how to conduct their enquiries with economy, and valuable advice may be given, especially by those with experience in research. But this will not be our concern. Our question will be not about the technique but about the logic of social enquiry.

Since the procedures of the natural sciences are more familiar and less subject to dispute, it is natural for the question about procedure in social enquiry to be framed with a reference to these. Hence the two questions arise:

(*a*) Are the procedures of the natural sciences applicable in a social enquiry?

(*b*) Are there alternative procedures, available to the social enquirer but denied to the natural scientist?

Those who deny that the procedures of the natural sciences are applicable, those who assert that there are alternative procedures, and, *a fortiori*, those who do both these things in combination, may all be said to hold anti-scientific views about social enquiry. Our thesis will be that these views are mistaken, and in Part One scientific procedure in social enquiries will be defended against criticism. At the same time it will be admitted that there are logical peculiarities which the subject-matter of the social enquiries forces upon us. These will be examined in Part Two.

This division of the subject, however, implies a definite use of the word 'science' which must be made clear at the outset. It is notorious that it is a word which can be used in various ways in different contexts. It is this which accounts for the futility of so many disputes about whether some branch of enquiry —psychology, for example, or economics—is or is not a science. If anyone wishes to apply the word only to an enquiry which has *all* the features of the procedure of the natural sciences—including, for example exact measurement and experimental control[1]—we would agree at once that it cannot be applied to much social investigation. On the other hand, if the word is given a very broad meaning, any social enquiry might be counted as a science, so long as it could be carried on at all, and all differences could be considered as modifications of scientific procedure.

It is clear, then, that we are assuming a use of the word which falls between these two extremes. What we must do now is set out explicitly the use we have in mind. What features must a procedure retain if it is still to be entitled 'scientific'?

Actually there is one set of fairly general features which people seem

---

[1] I am neglecting here very considerable differences between the natural sciences themselves.

frequently to have in mind when they disagree about the scientific character of social enquiry. These may be set down as follows:

1. A 'scientific' procedure is one which involves what in its broadest sense may be called abstraction—one in which we distinguish the properties and relations of things, and make statements in which we attribute properties and relations to these things—that is, describe them. (This may seem a very elementary feature, but it is, as we shall see, one which needs separate mention.)

2. It is one in which we seek not only to describe particular things, but also to make *general* statements of one kind or another, usually including what we call scientific laws.

3. It is one in which there is empirical evidence in support of the statements we make, this consisting in the last resort of our sensory observations and our awareness of our own mental processes.

4. It is one in which we are concerned with facts, our study of the facts being unaffected by considerations about what is good or what is valuable or what ought to be done.

5. It is one in which there is objectivity; that is to say, in which no one is prevented by the general circumstances of the enquiry from basing his statements on a consideration of the evidence.

It is these five features—those of abstraction, generality, reliance on empirical evidence, ethical neutrality, and objectivity—which we propose to adopt as the defining characteristics of a science. They are commonly accepted not only as essential for correct procedure in the natural sciences, but also as essential for the gaining of knowledge about anything whatsoever. Yet it is sometimes held that in social enquiries a procedure which has one or another of these features is either ineffective or impossible. And it is also sometimes held that for social enquiries there is an alternative procedure, both possible and effective, which does not have one or other of these features. It is these views which we speak of as anti-scientific views about social enquiry. Admittedly there are features other than those here listed which are often associated with the name of 'science';—for example, the requirement that all general statements take a quantitative form. But a denial that such features are possible or effective in a social enquiry will not be considered as an anti-scientific view; it will be spoken of rather as a modification of scientific procedure.

The anti-scientific criticisms which have been levelled at one time or another against the admission of each of these five features in a social enquiry, have taken a great variety of forms. Often they have existed only as common but unformulated tendencies of thought, or as presuppositions which social enquirers appear to have accepted, rightly or wrongly, as lying behind their practice. Where they have been put forward explicitly by particular writers, they have rarely been separated clearly from one another. For this reason, we will make no attempt to do justice to the views of any individual or to meet his criticism as a whole. Instead, we will take each of the five features in turn, attempt to state in our own way the main lines of criticism which have been directed against it, and see how it withstands the attack.

PART I

Anti-Scientific Views about Social Enquiry

II

THE CRITICISM OF ABSTRACTION

SUPPOSE that, wishing to find out about the political institutions of a country, I ask you to describe to me a parliamentary debate you have recently attended. You say, 'The Prime Minister spoke for an hour on the importance of reducing taxation. The Chamber was crowded and there were many interjections. The idea behind the speech was clearly to influence voters in favour of the Government in the coming elections.'

In saying this, you have presented me with the result of a simple—and, of course, small-scale and unsystematic—piece of social enquiry. This has taken the form of a description of a particular social situation. In order to give such a description, you must have distinguished certain features of the situation—the presence of a Prime Minister, the delivery of a speech on a certain subject, the crowdedness of the Chamber, and so on.[1] It is this distinguishing of features, on which all description depends, that we have called abstraction.[2]

Though abstraction, in this sense, seems a fundamental feature of any investigation, its value in social enquiry has nevertheless been questioned on various grounds which are not often properly distinguished. We will examine these in turn.

The Multiplicity of Features

The first ground of criticism is that the features of any social situation

[1] Note that the Prime Minister, his speech, the Chamber, are not being considered here as features of the situation;—they are rather its elements, or parts. For the word 'feature' we might if we wished substitute the words 'characteristic' or 'property'. A situation may be characterized by—that is, have among its features—the *presence* of parts of various sorts, but the parts could not themselves be said to characterize the situation. On the dangerous consequences of confusing features, as here understood, with parts, see pp. 10–11.

[2] Note that the word 'abstraction' has other uses. Thus when people speak of abstraction in science, they often have in mind the formulation and use of what we will call 'theoretical laws' or 'tendency statements'. To abstract, in this sense, is to consider separately the effects of different factors and to construct theories based on 'unrealistic assumptions'. For a discussion of abstraction in this sense, see Ch. XIII. We will not be concerned with it at this stage.

are very large in number, and that it is therefore not possible for anyone to distinguish more than relatively few of them. This multiplicity of features is one of the main things which people have in mind when they speak of the complexity of social life.

The question here is not whether it is possible to give a *complete* description of any social situation. For the critic may admit that we can never be sure whether we have distinguished *all* the features of *anything* we are trying to describe. His point is rather that we fall much *further* short of complete description in social inquiries than we do elsewhere, and that this is because of a *special* multiplicity of features which is not present elsewhere. If, for instance, a fossil or a combustion engine were carefully examined, a description might be given which was relatively exhaustive. But in the description of a parliamentary debate the possibilities for distinguishing further features open out almost indefinitely.

Whether all social situations are more complex than all physical situations is something which is open to dispute. But let us admit straightaway that there is some point in drawing the contrast, and concentrate on noticing what follows from it.

It clearly does not follow that the results obtained by abstraction are of no use at all. When you have described the debate to me, no one questions that I have found out something about it. What is complained of is that I have not found out enough and could never find out enough about it by having its features enumerated. This implies that the critic has in mind a certain standard of sufficiency—a standard which is modelled on what he believes possible in other enquiries. What he is saying is that it is impossible in practice[1] to describe social situations fully enough to measure up to that standard.

If it is now asked why he insists on such a high standard, we come to the real point behind this kind of criticism. The normal procedure of scientific description can only be condemned as inadequate to cope with the complexities of social situations if there is an alternative procedure which avoids its defects. The crucial question therefore is whether there is such a procedure.

As this question is crucial for other criticisms also, we will examine these before considering it directly.

---

[1] It should be noted that he is not saying it is impossible in *principle*,—still less that it is *logically* impossible. To say that it is logically impossible to achieve results in a given way is to say that there would be a breach of logical rules in supposing it done. To say that it is impossible in principle would be to say that it is never in fact done because of the general nature of the subject-matter being studied or because of the general relation in which the enquirer stands to it. Whereas to say that it is impossible in practice is to say that it is never in fact done because of the limitation of human capacities. We will find that it is important to keep in mind these different grounds for asserting the impossibility of gaining knowledge in one way or another.

THE CRITICISM OF ABSTRACTION

The Uniqueness of Social Events

It is sometimes said that in describing social events we miss what is unique, or individual, about them. When an event is called a parliamentary debate, it is immediately classified as one instance of a kind— that is, of parliamentary debates in general. And, however many of its features are described, what is stated is still only what it has in common, or may have in common, with other events. Similarly, to describe the French Revolution as a revolution, as a revolution in which all social classes were involved, as one in which such and such types of people came to power, and so on, is to miss its status as a unique event in human history. The chemist or the biologist may be satisfied when he has classified his specimens into kinds, but social events cannot be so classified. Each has to be treated in its unique individuality.

This criticism, unlike the first, seems to rest on a simple verbal confusion which can be cleared up without much difficulty. What, after all, is meant by those who insist on the uniqueness of a social event? They are hardly likely to mean merely that such an event is a *particular* event, numerically distinct from others. For in this sense every event is unique, the swing of a pendulum as well as the French Revolution. And, anyway, the particularity of events of whatever kind is not something which we could be said to miss when we describe them. In giving a description we do not merely name features, what we do is to attribute those features to the particular event in question. Abstraction of features and reference to particulars may clearly go along together.

Perhaps what they wish to emphasize in speaking of a social event as unique is not merely that it is a particular event, but rather that it is *not exactly like* any other event—that it is distinct from others qualitatively as well as numerically. If so, the same two comments may be made. Firstly it is safe to assume that every event is unique in this sense as well as in the previous one. There are no exact repetitions in nature any more than in the history of human society. Minute investigation would no doubt show that any one rotation of the hands of a clock is no more *exactly* like another than one social revolution is exactly like another. Secondly, the qualitative difference of any one event from another is not something we miss when we distinguish its features; on the contrary, it is best brought out by pointing to those features which it alone possesses. To show that the French Revolution is unique in this sense, the thing to do is to point out *in what respects*—that is, in which of its features—it is unique. It is true that the features we distinguish by abstraction are what it *may* have in common with other events, and scientists commonly select those which various events do in fact have in common, so that they can classify them into kinds. But the selection of features may be for the purpose of bringing out differences as well as likenesses.

9

But usually what is meant is something less stringent than exact similarity—something that could perhaps be best expressed by saying that no social event is *very* like any other. On this meaning it is admitted that 'uniqueness' is a matter of degree, and at the same time point is given to the suggestion that there is a certain uniqueness about social events not to be found in other cases. There is, it will be said, very much *less* repetition in social life than in the life of animals or plants or in the inanimate world. The differences are as prominent as the likenesses, and that is why the social enquirer cannot afford to treat debates or revolutions or social systems as mere specimens to be classified into kinds.

On the face of it there seems some truth in this, though the special variety of social situations, like their special complexity, has been open to dispute. But even if it is so, nothing whatsoever follows from it which will help the critic of abstraction. If the failure of the French Revolution to be exactly like any other event is best brought out by distinguishing those features which it alone possesses, its failure to be even approximately like any other event may best be brought out in the same way also. Admittedly in this case it will have a greater number of features which differ from those of other events, and if we were to bring out its uniqueness in a complete way, we would have to distinguish all these features. But it remains true that the distinguishing of features is an effective way of finding out, in a greater or lesser degree, what is unique about an event.

To avoid this, the critic might suggest that every social event was unique in the sense of having some inner core or individual essence which could never be revealed by description, however complete. But this leads us on to other criticisms.

The Abstract and the Concrete

The next criticism is that in describing a situation, however exhaustively, we mention its features separately, whereas in reality they are not separate. The ultimate object of our study—the parliamentary debate say, or the French Revolution—is always the concrete situation, but, by considering its various features in abstraction from one another, we can never get a view of it in the concrete. Science, it is said, dissects what is in fact all of a piece, and in doing so must necessarily distort it. In giving an account of the Prime Minister's speech, for example, one may quote his words verbatim, describe his tone of voice and his gestures, even perhaps his assumptions, feelings and intentions, but, however thoroughly one does this, one will never reproduce what actually happened.

It should be noticed that an analogy is being used here. It is the analogy between the *features* of a thing and its *parts*. To dissect is literally to cut something up into its parts as you might cut up a picture with the scissors to make a jig-saw puzzle. No one, of course, supposes that, in abstracting, a scientist dissects a situation in this sense, literally separating its features one from another. But he considers the features separately in the same way in which someone might consider the parts of a picture separately, and this, it is suggested, gives rise to an analogous difficulty. No one will ever see a picture by considering its parts separately, even if he has all of them. Similarly, no one will ever understand a situation by considering its features separately even if he considers all of them.

Once it is made clear that the criticism rests on this analogy, it loses a great deal of its force. This is because the analogy is a bad one. There is undoubtedly a sense in which it is true that the whole is more than the sum of its parts. When we consider the parts of a picture separately, there is something which is left out—the pattern they form—the way the parts are related to one another in the whole. But if we consider the features of a situation separately there is nothing comparable left out at all.

Following the analogy, we might say that what was left out was the way the features were related to one another. But what exactly could this mean? The features of a situation do not form a pattern in the same way that the parts of a whole do. When we speak of a situation, it does not make sense to say that its features are in fact arranged in a certain way, but might have been arranged in another. All that we can say is that they are jointly features of the situation.

We must conclude then that to abstract is *not* to distort. When we select only certain features, we may at times be charged with giving a distorted picture of a situation. But if we were to mention all the features the picture would automatically become complete.

There would of course be a considerable advantage gained if we could get a view of a situation 'in the concrete', in the sense of getting it before us all at once without having to abstract its features and pay attention to them separately. And those who make this kind of criticism undoubtedly have such an alternative in mind, claiming that a social enquirer, unlike other enquirers, has some special way of understanding concrete situations.

But this raises once again the question whether there is such an alternative procedure. Let us postpone this further while we consider the final criticism.

The Outside and the Inside

This criticism uses a different analogy, and in this case the analogy is made explicit in the words in which the criticism is usually expressed. In abstraction, it is said, we approach things from the *outside*, whereas to gain an adequate knowledge of them we would have to approach them from the *inside*. Describing a situation in various ways is likened to looking at a solid object from various points of view, all of them external to the object itself. However many points of view we take, we

11

get no nearer to observing the object's internal constitution, and similarly, however many features of a situation we notice, we get no nearer to an inner understanding of it. Or again, to get away from the specifically spatial reference this illustration gives to the analogy, the description of a situation may be likened to what an outsider can discover about a club if he is not able to become a member and join in its activities. In the positive sciences, as Henri Bergson put it, 'we move round the object, we do not enter into it'.[1]

On the face of it, this criticism seems to have an obvious special application to social enquiries. For the social activities of human beings appear to have an inner side in a different sense from the movements of ordinary material objects, and hence it would seem something is lost by scientific description in the former case, which is not there to lose in the latter.

Human beings think and feel, do things on purpose, experience pleasure and pain, love and hate, and so on. It is common and not unnatural to regard these experiences of theirs as constituting the inner side of their activities—an inner side which is conspicuously lacking in the case of everything else in their surroundings except perhaps animals. Their behaviour may be observed from various external points of view, but it is only when we understand what they think and feel that we can be said to have gained an inside knowledge of their activities.

Here for the first time mention has been made of what is clearly a very fundamental peculiarity of the subject-matter of social enquiries. It is only in so far as human beings are aware of each other and adopt certain attitudes towards each other—in fact are experiencing or conscious beings—that there can be said to be any social relationship between them at all.[2] And since this fact of experience is such a distinc-

---

[1] See the opening passage of *An Introduction to Metaphysics*, pp. 1–7 (tr. T. E. Hulme, Macmillan, 1913) for Bergson's general criticism of scientific pretensions in these terms.

[2] I pass over the question whether in the conduct of a social enquiry, one need refer to experience at all. The view has sometimes been held that a scientific social enquiry is concerned only with the study of the behaviour of human beings in relation to their environment. Their experiences, insofar as these cannot be defined in terms of their behaviour, are held to be something which we can afford to ignore, and which for various reasons we should ignore. This view is, roughly, what goes under the name of behaviourism. If it were accepted, many of the objections to scientific procedure which are discussed in Part I of this book would be very easily met. I propose throughout, however, to show that these objections are unfounded without resorting to this—as it seems to me—untenable view.
I also pass over the question whether experience and behaviour belong to distinct 'worlds'—the inner and the outer—or whether they are to be regarded rather as two sides—the inside and the outside—of the one thing, the human action. Cf. R. G. Collingwood—*The Idea of History*, Part V, sect. 1, pp. 212–14, for the use of the 'inside-outside' terminology to refer to the distinction between thought and behaviour and an insistence that these are the inside and the outside of the one thing—the action. Collingwood does not appear to draw the conclusion that the thought, which is the inside, cannot be described. Hence his view does not come under consideration in the discussion of this objection.

tive feature of human beings, we should not be surprised to find that it makes a very great difference to the procedure of any social enquiry.

It is a further question, however, whether the reference to experience as the inner side of social action does really help the critic of abstraction. It would undoubtedly do so if it were the case that experience could not be described. For we could then say that knowledge of the inner side of an action—what the agent thought or how he felt—could only be obtained, if at all, in some other way. But we know very well that people can describe what they and others think and how they feel. Experiences can be characterized just as much as can bodily movements, and we can indicate their various features. Otherwise we could give no sense to statements like 'I was angry' or 'The Prime Minister felt elated when he noticed the effects of his speech'.

Psychological descriptions may of course be hopelessly inadequate. It may well be argued that the complexity and subtle variety of states of mind is such as to make even a relatively exhaustive description impossible, and it may be said that it is this complexity and variety which is mainly responsible for that special inadequacy in the description of social situations, which we found suggested when we discussed the first objection. But as long as states of mind can be described at all, this is sufficient to show that the 'inner' side of human action is as susceptible to abstract treatment as the 'outer'.

The point which is here made about experience might be stated in more general terms. The analogy of outside and inside is in fact quite as deceptive as that of whole and part. The picture which is conjured up is that of a crust or covering which is wrapped round something else—the contents or the core. And we are left with the impression that, because of the wrapping, a special non-descriptive technique, like a sort of X-ray photography, is required for revealing the contents. But there is no real basis for this impression. The difference between the surface and what lies beneath it is not sufficient to justify such a radical difference in procedure. In describing an apple, we can describe not only its surface but also its internal structure. In describing the activities of a political party, we can include the 'inside story' as told us by its members. And in the same way when we describe human actions, we can describe the thoughts and purposes which are said to be 'behind' them, or constitute their inner side.

It might still be, of course, that while there was no indescribable inside core in the objects of social study, we could yet, as experiencing beings, approach these objects in a special 'inner' kind of way which made description unnecessary. And this, it might be said, is the real point of the criticism. It is not that people's thoughts, feelings and actions cannot be described from various points of view; it is rather that underlying any such description there is an inner understanding which takes us beyond all points of view.

If this is the point of the criticism, however, it becomes dependent, like others, on the view that there is an alternative procedure which makes abstraction unnecessary. Hence once again we are faced with the question whether there is such an alternative procedure.

The Alternative

We can now sum up what is required of this procedure by saying that it must give us a knowledge of social situations which is complete, concrete and internal, or at least has one or other of these characteristics. In principle the possession of any one of them would be sufficient, but in fact what critics of abstraction have in mind is the supplanting of descriptive knowledge by a procedure which combines all three.

This procedure is sometimes spoken of as 'intuition'.[1] It is essentially a matter of grasping a situation by living through it, instead of merely noting various features of it and piecing them together. The central idea here is that if we can *be* something, we can understand it completely there and then and without further fuss. This is why the obvious case that is pointed to is the understanding we have of our own thoughts and feelings by simply living through the experience of them. In simply being ourselves, we know ourselves, and from the inside. From this we can pass on to those cases where we find out about other people and the social situations in which they are placed by identifying ourselves with them. Though we cannot be the people concerned, we can put ourselves in their places and so appreciate what they feel. Since we use the word 'sympathy' for that form of social contact which consists in feeling not only for, but with, other people, it is natural to speak of this procedure as one of 'sympathetic understanding'.[2]

Thus it will be denied that the report which you have brought back about the parliamentary debate can be counted as the real result of the enquiry. It is merely obtained by abstraction after the event. What has happened is that you have participated in a social process in which a number of thinking and feeling beings have acted and reacted one with the other. You have not merely observed it or inferred facts about it as you would if it had been an empty Chamber or an engine-room. By participating in it, you have gained an understanding of it which you could not convey to others at the time, though you could convey some of it—at length—afterwards. And in fact, the best way for you to give me this understanding is not to launch into a detailed description, but to use language in such a way that I can re-create the scene for myself and live through it in imagination.

The question at issue is whether this process of understanding pro-

---

[1] As for example by Bergson, op. cit. p. 6.

[2] Cf. Bergson, op. cit. 'By intuition is meant the kind of *intellectual sympathy* by which one places oneself within an object in order to coincide with what is unique in it and consequently inexpressible.'

vides a genuine alternative to abstraction. It will be realized, however, that if there were such an alternative it would at the same time enable us to avoid other characteristics of scientific procedure as we have defined it. Closely associated with abstraction are generality and reliance on empirical evidence. It is impossible to generalize without abstracting, and for the most part impossible to draw conclusions from empirical evidence without generalizing. It follows from this that if there is this way of achieving social understanding without abstracting, it will enable us to by-pass generality and prevent us from having to rely solely on evidence derived from sensory observation and awareness of our own mental processes. The question thus has wider implications and a good deal can be made to hang on it.

Yet precisely because of the close association between these three characteristics, it will be difficult to answer the question until they have all been discussed. We find that what has been put forward is a proposal for an alternative procedure in social enquiries which might replace all three. In order to pass judgment on the proposal we should therefore have all three, and not merely the first, before us.

Let us recognize then that the objections to abstraction cannot be finally answered in isolation. This must wait until we are able to consider the notion of sympathetic understanding in its full setting.

III

THE CRITICISM OF GENERALITY: FREEDOM AND CHANGE

IN any social enquiry we rarely rest content with the description of particular situations. We are interested also in what features of what situations regularly occur together. And to express this we need general statements.

Thus from describing a particular Prime Minister in a particular situation as trying to influence the electorate, we quickly pass on to making such general statements as that Prime Ministers in such circumstances *always* try to influence their electorates. Similarly, an historian, after stating that the repeal of the Corn Laws in 1846 was followed by a period of agricultural prosperity in Britain, is likely to add that the threat of foreign competition *frequently* leads to an improvement in home technique.

This tendency to introduce general statements extends throughout all social enquiries. Our business is to consider whether the introduction of such statements is effective in enabling social enquirers to achieve their ends, and whether there is not some way in which they can achieve their ends without it.

But first we must ask: How is the making of general statements supposed to enable social enquirers to achieve their ends? What purpose are such statements intended to serve?

To this the defender of scientific procedure will answer that without general statements there could be no inductive reasoning, and without inductive reasoning we could not learn anything about anything, social life included, except within the narrowest limits. About some things we can learn merely by observing them with our senses; about others— some of our own mental processes—we can learn simply by living through them. But for statements we make about anything else, whether past, present or future, we must have evidence of a less direct kind. In the last resort, of course, it must be the same—the evidence of our sensory observations and our awareness of our own mental processes.

16

But in order to bridge the gap between what we have observed and what we have not observed, we must have general statements. The general statements are often not explicitly formulated. But unless we could formulate them if challenged, and could show that they were sufficiently supported by what we have observed, or become aware of in ourselves, on various occasions, we would be unable to verify any conclusions about what we have not observed.

How, for example, might we learn that there was social privilege in Ancient Egypt? We might point to the ruins of large tombs and monuments, and say this is the evidence. But it would only be evidence of social privilege if we presupposed, as already established on the basis of much other evidence, the general statement that tombs and monuments of this kind are built only by or for privileged people. In reality, the procedure is much more complicated than this illustration suggests, but it brings out nevertheless the essentials of the inductive way of discovering new facts.

Further, it will be said, the aim of an enquiry is not merely to discover facts, it is also to explain them. We want to know not only what happens but why it happens. And without general statements there could be no explanation, any more than there could be discovery. In explaining any event, we refer to another event, as when we say that the price of a commodity rose because of a rise in costs. But this explanation clearly presupposes that we already accept as established the general statement that wherever, in given conditions, there is a rise in the costs of producing a commodity, there is a rise in its price. Once again a general statement is required to bridge a gap.

Finally, as well as enabling us to discover and explain social facts, general statements are held to be required if we are to put our social knowledge into practice. Social enquiries are frequently carried on not for their own sake, but in order to help us to decide what to *do*. We have practical ends to achieve such as making profits or preventing wars, and we wish to know how to achieve them. For this we must know what will happen *if* we perform certain actions at particular times and places in the future. And in order to establish such conditional statements, the defender of scientific procedure will maintain, we require general statements about the consequences of various possible kinds of action in various possible kinds of circumstances.

Any critic of generality would admit that if we had general statements which we could regard as established by the evidence, it would be possible to use them for discovery, explanation and practical application in the way that has been indicated. But, while granting this, he could still assert either that it was impossible to establish such statements in social enquiries, or that it was possible to discover and explain social facts and guide social practice in some other way. It is these assertions which the defender of scientific procedure has to call in question.

17

Types of General Statement

It will avoid confusion if we begin by drawing two distinctions between types of general statement: first, between general statements which are universal and those which state chances or relative frequencies; second, between general statements which are unrestricted or open, and those which are restricted, or closed.

The simplest form of universal statement is one in which it is asserted that whenever some feature, a, is present, some other feature, b, is always present without exception. Someone would be making such a statement who said that in any social group, power always becomes concentrated in a few hands.

There is, however, another very common form of universal statement which cannot be fitted within this formula, because it is accepted as holding only under certain conditions not specified in the statement itself. If, for instance, I make the statement that when the supply of a commodity falls, its price rises, I recognize that there are conditions in which this does not hold and could add under my breath, 'So long as no interfering conditions are present.' These statements may therefore be expressed in the form: 'Whenever a is present, b will also be present in the absence of interfering conditions.' We might call these universal statements 'theoretical' to distinguish them from the straightforward ones, which have sometimes been called 'empirical'. Or we might call them tendency statements, since they are often expressed in the form: 'Whenever a is present, there is a tendency for b to be present.'

Universal statements of both these types are commonly called laws. And to speak of causal laws is commonly to refer to a sub-class of either type, namely, to those laws which are concerned with the features of events occurring in temporal succession to one another.

In contradistinction to these laws are statements about the chances of some feature, b, being present when a is present, or about how often b occurs when a is present. Such statements have sometimes been called relative-frequency, or statistical, generalizations, sometimes probability rules, but fewer dangerous ambiguities occur if they are called statements, or rules, of chance.[1] The chances stated in such rules may vary from very high to very low, and they may be stated with greater or with less precision. It is when the chances are stated somewhat vaguely to be towards the upper, or the lower, end of this scale that we speak of making approximate generalizations, or saying what generally, or usually, happens. Thus falling within this class are statements like 'Tariffs frequently have a bad effect on productive efficiency', or 'In

---

[1] We will not discuss here the further question as to the meaning of 'chance'. Statements about chances have, for example, sometimes been said never to be anything more than statements about relative frequencies. There are, however, difficulties about this in the case of unrestricted statements. This is one reason why it is safer to speak, less definitely, of chances.

wartime there is little hope of civil liberties being preserved'. Though we may regard some of these statements as only just falling short of being laws, we have to recognize that they differ only in degree from the more precise statements of more even chances such as 'There is a 51% chance that any baby born will be a boy'.

Our second distinction—that between restricted and unrestricted general statements—cuts across the first. By a restricted statement we mean one which concerns what always, or what usually, happens within certain limits of space and time, whereas in an unrestricted one no reference is made to any such limits. In England before 1830, an historian might say, political parties were never sharply defined. In saying this he would be making a statement which was universal, but restricted by the mention of place and dates. Since the word 'law' is commonly reserved for universal statements of the unrestricted kind, we have no shorter way of referring to these others than as restricted universal statements. Side by side with them we may put restricted rules of chance, such as 'The present-day inhabitants of Polynesia are, for the most part, splendid seamen', or 'In modern Europe, the chances of obtaining political power without popular support are very slight'.

The regions of space and periods of time referred to in such statements may vary from very small to very great. But so long as they are there, the particular things or events which have the characteristics we are speaking of will be finite in number, and could conceivably be enumerated; whereas in the case of unrestricted statements, there is no limit to the number of particular things or events which may have these characteristics. In other words, we are concerned in the one case with closed classes, in the other with open ones. Though it would be quite possible to regard statements concerned with closed classes as statements about particular *sets* of things—or about the particular periods and places named—and for that reason cease to classify them as general at all, they nevertheless resemble other general statements in making no mention of any individual member of the spatio-temporally restricted class with which they are concerned.[1]

One reason for making these distinctions is that the different types of general statement vary in the extent to which they fulfil the purpose of

---

[1] A comprehensive classification of types of general statement is not intended here. In particular there are certain types of general statement which we have not mentioned and which even the most severe critic of generality would not wish to exclude. These are:

   (1) Existential statements, e.g. 'There are such things as matriarchal societies'.

   (2) Restricted general statements established by complete enumeration, e.g. 'All British Prime Ministers in the nineteenth century were good

(Continued at foot of next page)

facilitating discoveries, providing explanations and guiding actions. Laws are superior to other types on all three counts—and best of all are the straightforward empirical laws. Once a straightforward law has been established, we can draw conclusions automatically about any particular case to which it applies. If we are really quite sure that *every* society is hierarchical in structure, we can conclude without further investigation that this is the case in present-day Russia, say, and will be so in the future. Whereas with tendency statements, however well established, we must allow for interfering conditions; with rules of chance we must allow for possible exceptions; and with restricted general statements we are unable to support conclusions about anything outside the period and region specified.

Similarly with explanation. If we want to explain a particular decline in productive efficiency, we may start by saying: 'This is what usually happens when a tariff is imposed.' But this, we feel, is not enough. To strengthen the explanation we try to replace this approximate generalization by a law or a set of laws relating to the causes of productive efficiency. Again, if we want to explain some shift in party alignment in Britain in the 18th century, we may start by saying that this sort of thing was always happening in the British politics of that period. But for a more satisfactory explanation, we will try to replace such a restricted universal statement by laws concerned with the conditions of party stability.

And once again, where we are concerned with means to practical ends, we are on safest ground if we can establish what are the invariable results of a given kind of action. It is true that in this case there is no objection to the universal statements being restricted ones; all that is needed is that the spatio-temporal limits referred to in such statements lie beyond the time and the place in which we propose to act. But the objection to allowing for interfering conditions and for exceptions remains. Where such allowances have to be made, the risk of failure is increased.

Thus it is that a 'science' is often so defined that it must include laws, and criticisms of generality in social enquiries are often identified with criticisms of the attempt to establish laws. This, however, would be to make the definition of 'science' narrower than we have done. In view of the superior effectiveness of laws, we should not ignore criticisms of the attempt to establish them in social enquiry. But even if such criticisms were sound, there would remain the possibility of an enquiry which was

public speakers' (this being already known to be true of each of the individuals concerned).

In both these cases, the general statement follows directly from statements about particulars ('This is a matriarchal society', 'Disraeli was a good public speaker', 'Gladstone was a good public speaker', etc.) and hence could not be excluded by anyone who admits such statements.

scientific in the broader sense, making use of rules of chance and restricted universal statements.

We now turn to a consideration of the features of social life which are alleged to prevent us from establishing general statements about it, and the features which are alleged to enable us to discover and explain social facts and guide social action in another way.

Since we are concerned only with social enquiries, we will not discuss the general problem about the possibility of establishing general statements by inductive reasoning. Philosophers have often asked: how can we justify an inference which takes us from what we have observed to what we have not observed? Some have claimed to provide such a justification; some have denied that any justification is called for. If it were called for and could not be given, there would undoubtedly be ground for a general challenge to all scientific procedure, in social enquiries as well as others. But such a general challenge could only be met by general considerations, and raises no special problem about the application of scientific procedure in the social field. We will presuppose, therefore, the general possibility of establishing general statements inductively, and ask what special reasons there might be for doubting whether it can be done in this field.

Freedom

The first is the fact of human freedom. It is this which has very often led people to fix a clear gulf between social enquiries on the one hand and the natural sciences on the other. Men, it is said, having the power to choose for themselves, are the makers of their own destiny. However regular their actions may appear to be at certain times, it is always possible that they could have decided to act otherwise. Hence the impossibility of accounting for their social activities in terms of general principles, or of discovering by means of such principles what they have done in the past or what they will do in the future.

In considering this argument we see at once the importance of distinguishing between different types of general statements. For the argument is often brought forward as though it were an argument against the use of *any* type of general statement, whereas, in fact, it is only an argument against the admitting of universal laws. Even if it were the case that the fact of human beings being free agents made it impossible to give an account of their actions in terms of laws, it would still remain possible to argue from the *chances* of their acting in one way rather than another. This is in fact regularly, and quite legitimately, done by people, whatever their views about freedom. For example, the rule that there is a very good chance that a man will buy in the cheapest market and sell in the dearest, whatever any particular freely-acting individual may decide to do, is persistently used in economic argument

21

and is what gives its significance to the whole system of classical economic theory.

We must beware then of falling into the trap of supposing that an argument directed against generality of a special kind is effective against generality of every kind. Even if the argument were sound, it would leave us with the possibility of working with general statements of a sort —and ones which in fact are very freely used in all social enquiries.

Since, however, it is most desirable to be in a position to establish laws, it is as well that we should consider whether the argument, taken in itself, *is* sound. When people exercise freedom of choice, as this is ordinarily understood, does it become impossible in principle for social enquirers to explain their conduct in terms of laws which relate that conduct to their character and circumstances?

The obvious answer seems to be that there is no such impossibility. To see this, let us consider what it is that people normally claim for themselves when they regard themselves as free. They undoubtedly claim that what they do is not entirely determined by the circumstances in which they are placed. They often claim further that when they act freely, what they do is not determined merely by habit, nor by isolated and intractable impulses which have their effects in relative independence of the rest of their character. But would they also claim that what they do is not determined even by the sort of people they are, considered as whole individuals possessing a certain disposition, a certain character, certain motives, and so on? And would they therefore be prepared to say that the exercise of freedom of choice implies that the choice might have been different even if there were no change in their make-up of any kind?

Once the issue is put clearly, it seems very doubtful whether anyone would wish to insist that he was free in such a sense. For it would certainly be curious to insist on a freedom which made one's actions, or one's choices, independent of *oneself*. And if people are prepared to waive their claim to such freedom, this at once removes any reason there might be for asserting that they possess it. The trouble appears to be that a confusion easily develops between acting as we choose, that is, in ways not determined by external circumstances or by habits or by isolated impulses, and acting in ways which are not determined at all. Once this confusion is removed we may admit that men are to some extent makers of their own destiny without in any way precluding the possibility of framing universal laws about their actions and their motives.[1]

Thus if we find someone freely deciding to give up his job in order to take on another at a lower salary, this surely does not prevent us from speculating about why he came to this decision. Even if an economist

---

[1] The conclusion drawn here, and the main lines of the argument for it, are of course not new. Cf., for example, J. S. Mill—*System of Logic*, Book 6, Ch. 2, or G. E. Moore—*Ethics*, Ch. 6. There are also many who oppose the conclusion, but it is impossible to enter into the subtleties of this controversy here.

thought it not worth his while to trouble about such a case, a social psychologist might well do so. His speculation might lead him into an attempt to apply to this case not only rules of chance but universal laws of human behaviour. This would undoubtedly be a difficult thing to do, not only because of the difficulty of establishing such laws, but also because their application would involve a very detailed knowledge of the man's character and circumstances. But there is nothing to suggest that the fact of the man's freedom would preclude the attempt.

Change

A second feature which is sometimes taken as preventing us from establishing general statements about social life is the quite exceptional swiftness of social change. In discussing uniqueness, we have already noted that the sequence of social events appears to be comparatively non-repetitive in character. There are great differences between socia conditions and the ways people react to them in different times and places.

This, as we saw, provided no argument against abstraction. But it may be brought forward again to provide an argument against generality. Though it may be perfectly possible to describe, in an historical enquiry, what men have done at different times and places, it may yet be that the great differences between social situations make it impossible to generalize from what they do at one time or place to what they do at another.

Here again, as in the discussion of freedom, we see the need for distinguishing between different types of general statement—this time between restricted and unrestricted ones. For the argument clearly holds only against statements of unrestricted generality. What is objected to is the attempt to say something about social life as such—something which holds good for Ancient Egypt, for example, as much as for Modern Europe. There will always be *periods* of time, longer or shorter as the case may be, during which conditions will remain sufficiently the same to make possible general statements which are restricted to the period. And the longer the periods, the less force in the objection.

Unrestricted generality, however, remains the ideal of science, and it is as well that we should consider what point there is in the criticism considered as a criticism of the attempt to make unrestricted genera statements.

When we speak of a dissimilarity between one period and others we may have two different sorts of case in mind. The first is where a given feature is present in one period and, as far as we know, is not present in any other. We might take as an example the relatively free-market economy of Britain in the 19th century. The other case is where a given feature is common to various periods, but other differences are such that statements about it hold for one of the periods but not for the others. Democratic institutions, for example, have recurred in different periods of history, but while it might be said, in speaking of Modern Europe, that they protect religious freedom, this does not hold if applied to other periods.

The first type of case is sometimes made the basis for a criticism of unrestricted generality which is quite unmerited. It is sometimes said, for example, that the laws of classical economics should be regarded as restricted general statements holding only for the period in which a free market was predominant. But all that can be shown is that they only *apply* in such a period. This is perfectly compatible with their being unrestricted statements about what happens *whenever* free-market conditions are present. It so happens that the conditions mentioned only exist in the one period—but that restricts the application of the laws and not the laws themselves.

One source of this criticism lies in a tendency to confuse unrestricted general statements with ones which have instances at all times and places. It is assumed that while unrestricted statements can be made about atoms and molecules, they cannot be made about free markets, since these are only to be found at a certain period of human history. This clearly is not so, and to suppose it so would have the absurd consequence that there could never be any unrestricted statements in social enquiries at all, since these statements concern beings who, for all we know, have existed only for a limited period on the surface of one planet.

It is true, of course, that we have to be cautious about making unrestricted general statements when the feature under discussion is confined, as far as we know, to one period. Under conditions very different from those of the 19th century, it might be that the presence of a free market would not have the same effects, and we have no positive evidence to dispel this possibility. The question therefore does genuinely arise whether, in view of the swiftness of social change, we ever have sufficient evidence to establish statements of unrestricted generality. But this question arises more forcefully in connection with the second type of case.

This second type of case appears more serious, since the statements concerned have to be regarded as restricted in themselves and not merely in their application. We could not without contradiction generalize from the experience of Modern Europe and say that democracy always ensures religious freedom. If it could be shown that all statements about social life were of this kind, the case against unrestricted generality would be proved.

It is clear, however, that this can never be shown conclusively. It may be admitted that because of great differences between periods, restricted general statements play a specially important part in social enquiries. But the scientific enquirer will always try to go beyond them and find others which are unrestricted and applicable at all times and places. There is nothing in the swiftness of social change which will show that this is impossible in principle. The issue, as in the previous type of case, is rather whether it is ever possible in practice to find sufficient evidence for a significant number of such statements.

When put in this way, the issue clearly allows for no cut-and-dried decision. This is because the criteria are fluid. Produce a few statements and they may always be dismissed as insignificant. Produce some evidence and it may be dismissed as insufficient. Even if the criteria of significance and sufficiency are fixed, a scientific genius or large sums for research might make practically possible some things which were not possible before. In these circumstances all that is really worth saying is that swiftness of change makes unrestricted generalization difficult and that this is a handicap with which any social enquirer has to start.

There is, however, one consideration which should trouble the critic who regards these difficulties as largely insuperable. This is that without general statements known to hold beyond the limits of the period in which we live, it would not be possible for us to find out anything about other periods at all. We have been speaking as if we could describe what happened in other periods, even if we could frame no general statements to cover them all. We have assumed, for example, that we know of periods in which there was no free market, and periods in which democracy did not ensure religious freedom. But remembering what we said at the beginning of the chapter, how could we know these things if there were no general statements to bridge the gap?

This point can of course be made equally against our ability to predict what is going to happen in the future. But this does not trouble the critic in the same way. He is prepared to admit that we cannot predict in social enquiries. What he tends to neglect is the parallel conclusion that we cannot discover what has happened in the past. There is a tendency to assume that the rejection of unrestricted general statements permits one form of social enquiry still to remain, and that is the study of the *history* of social activities in various periods up to the present time.

It is true that the study of history does differ from other social enquiries in an obvious way.[1] Historians are primarily interested in the discovery and explanation of particular facts in their temporal sequence; economists, political scientists and so on, are primarily interested in arriving at general statements which they can apply in various contexts. From this, however, it does not follow that historians need make no reference to general statements. Even though they do not normally include general statements among the results of their enquiry, they may still need to use them in order to discover and explain particular facts.

It appears then that if this criticism is pressed, we must conclude that

[1] For fuller discussion of the study of history, see Ch. XV.

there can be no social enquiry at all—at any rate none which extends beyond the period in which we live. If the critic is not prepared to accept such a sceptical conclusion, he must show that there is some alternative procedure for discovering and explaining what has happened in the past. Here is the point at which we must turn from considering whether scientific procedure should be abandoned to considering whether it can be replaced—at least for the study of history.

How then can historical enquiries be exempted from the criticism of generality? One possibility is to take up the appeal to sympathetic understanding left over from the previous chapter, and say that historical descriptions are to be regarded not as inferences from general statements about social life, but rather as extracts from that deeper non-descriptive knowledge which an historian gains by entering into the life of a period or identifying himself with an individual.

Before discussing this far-reaching appeal, we will consider other possibilities for discovering—or at any rate explaining—in a non-generalizing way the facts of social life.

IV

THE CRITICISM OF GENERALITY: PURPOSES AND REASONS

HUMAN beings usually act with some purpose in view. And again, for much of what they do they may be said to have reasons. These are undoubtedly important features of social life, and their presence invites the assumption that in a large field of social enquiry no reference to general statements is required.

These two features are not often clearly distinguished, and there is one use of 'reason' in which to have a reason for acting is the same thing as to have a purpose in view. But to speak of reasons is to introduce a complication, and to suggest a further ground for denying the need for general statements, not present in the simple reference to purposes. It will be better, therefore, to insist on a distinction, and to discuss purposes first.

PURPOSES

To explain an action, it is said, is to say *why* it is done; and to say why a person does something, no more is needed than to point to the purpose the person has in mind. The Prime Minister spoke as he did because he wanted to influence the electorate in his favour. Hitler's armies invaded Russia in 1941, let us say, because Hitler's aim was to make Germany the dominant power in Europe. In these explanations, we only mention the wants and the aims of the individuals concerned. And yet the explanations give the appearance of being logically complete as they stand, without having to be filled out by reference to laws or other general statements about the behaviour of Prime Ministers or dictators.

To bring out this point a contrast may be drawn between these cases and those in which the special feature of purposiveness is absent. If we are asked why there was an earthquake in Japan in 1923, we have to refer not only to the particular state of the earth's crust at the time, but also to the relevant geological laws. If we are asked why someone's hand is shaking, we have to refer not only to the fact that he is afraid but also

27

to some accepted psychological generalizations about the physical effects of fear. But, it is said, purposive activities are different. We can explain them without using general statements at all.

Though this view is commonly expressed as one about the explanation of actions, it could also be applied to the making of discoveries about them. Not only do we explain the actions of people in terms of their aims; we also infer their actions from their aims. And if general statements are not required in the one case, there is no reason to suppose that they would be required in the other. For simplicity, however, let us exclude from our discussion the application of the view to discovery.

Furthermore, let us also exclude for simplicity the case where the enquiry is put to a practical use. If we chose, our discussion could be extended to this. For if general statements are not required either for explaining people's actions or for discovering what they are, they will also not be required for establishing those conditional statements about means to ends on which action is based.[1]

Generality in Purposive Explanations

Let it be admitted straightaway that there is a definite difference in kind between, say, the explanation of the Japanese earthquake and the explanation of Hitler's invasion of Russia. No one doubts that a reference to the aims of human beings is very different from a reference to rocks and strata; so different, in fact, that it is often apt to put a request for explanation in the form of the question 'Why?' in the one case and the question 'How?' in the other. The question we must consider is whether this factual difference between the terms of the explanations implies a corresponding logical difference between explanations which involve generality and those which do not.

The answer to this question is that the belief in such a logical difference is a mistake, and that purposive explanations are like any other explanations in presupposing general statements. The general statements, admittedly, may be of different kinds. They may be laws or incomplete statements of laws or restricted general statements of a special type. But in each case we may call them 'causal' if we mean by this no more than that they relate the action to some feature or features of the state of affairs which is already in existence when the action takes place. They are not usually mentioned when the explanation is given, and this is no doubt one reason why they are thought not to be required for the

[1] Questions about the practical application of the results of social enquiry will be considered in Ch. XVI. In the meantime we will make, in general, the simplifying assumption that social enquirers have in view only the theoretical ends of discovering social facts and explaining them. The application in practice of the beliefs of the human beings who form the subject-matter of a social enquiry will of course be brought into the discussion; we could not, for example, discuss explanation of actions in terms of reasons later in this chapter without doing this. It is the practical application by social enquirers of the results of their enquiry about these human beings that we reserve for separate discussion.

explanation. But there is no more reason for denying that they are presupposed than there is in the case where we explain a broken window by saying it was hit by a stone, or the shaking of a man's hand by saying he was afraid.

To support this answer, what we need to do is to bring into the open the general statements which purposive explanations presuppose.

Intention-Explanations

Let us start with a very simple principle which, at first sight at least, seems to be presupposed by every purposive explanation. This is the principle that whenever anyone intends to do something, he will do it. We will assume that the word 'intend' is here used to indicate a mental act or mental occurrence which immediately precedes the performance of the action.[1] Given that the general statement involved is always some specification of this principle, a purposive explanation appears as a simple case of causal explanation, in which an intention is given as the cause of the action. In saying that the Prime Minister spoke because he intended to speak, we are doing the same sort of thing as when we say the window broke because it was hit by a stone. In the one case we presuppose that whenever a window is hit by a stone it breaks; in the other, that whenever a person intends to speak, he speaks.[2]

One thing that is wrong with this account as it stands is that it makes a purposive explanation appear extremely unilluminating. This is because it fails to take account of the distinction between means and ends. When we ask why the Prime Minister spoke as he did, it is not enough to be told that he did it because he intended to do it. We want to know what he did it *for*. It is only very rarely that people perform actions simply for the action's sake. In general they act *in order to* bring about ends which they *believe* will result from their actions. The Prime Minister, we say, spoke as he did because he intended to influence the electorate, and believed that his speech would have this effect.

A full purposive explanation, therefore, must include a reference not only to a person's intentions, but also to his beliefs about the suitability of his action as a means to what he intends.[3]

Furthermore, there are various negative conditions which we recognize must be present if intentions are to lead to actions. There must

---

[1] It is by no means always so used. It is often used as we will use 'desire' and 'want' hereafter to indicate an enduring state of mind or 'disposition'. People are after all said to harbour intentions over long periods. We are here deliberately specifying a use of the word for our own convenience. We are not specifying that the mental occurrence is a conscious one since psychologists sometimes maintain that there are 'unconscious intentions', and if there are such they would fit the principle equally well.

[2] See Braithwaite—*Scientific Explanation* (Cambridge 1953) Ch. 10. pp. 324–5, for a simple statement of a view of this kind.

[3] For discussion of further issues raised when we take beliefs into account in explaining actions, see below on 'reasons', pp. 39. et. seq.

be no unforeseen bodily or mental condition to prevent performance, such as paralysis or loss of memory. And if the intention is to act at some future time, there must be no forgetfulness or change of mind. In explaining an action in terms of an intention, in fact, we are commonly doing no more than point to an important causal factor. But we rarely do more in any explanation, and this in no way detracts from its generality. It merely means that we are using tendency statements rather than straightforward laws.[1]

When all this is said, however, it remains true that to speak of intentions is not to give an adequate account of purposive explanations. For there are cases of purposive explanation where the existence of an intention, in the sense of a mental occurrence preceding the action, is to say the least doubtful; our purposes may be manifested in our actions without our consciously setting ourselves to achieve ends.[2] And even where such intentions are present, a mere mention of them does not take the explanation very far. We want to know further how people come to have them. An intention, in our sense, is as it were a culminating point, given which in appropriate conditions the action follows. As well as this single intention of the moment, each one of us always has a variety of co-existing wants, desires, inclinations or tendencies, which for short we will speak of as 'motives'. It is only when such motives are, on given occasions, 'called into play' that we form intentions and perform actions. And the request for the explanation of an action is usually an enquiry about motives rather than about intentions. Furthermore it remains as an enquiry about motives even in those cases in which the presence of an intention is in doubt.

Motive-Explanations

The distinction between motives and intentions, as we are here using these terms, is an important one and should be made clear. Motives could not be called mental occurrences, conscious or unconscious. They are enduring states of mind which may last for longer or for shorter periods, surviving, for example, through periods of deep sleep from one day to the next, or through periods of absorption in other things from one year to the next. The Prime Minister's desire to influence the elec-

[1] For further discussion of factors and the use of tendency statements, see Ch. XIII.

[2] There are some who would deny altogether the existence of 'intentions' in our sense, saying that when we intend to do something, there are not two happenings, the intending and the acting, causally related to each other, but only one—the intentional action. On this view our simple principle would not be a truism, but a tautology, and would never serve an explanatory function at all. See Gilbert Ryle on Volitions in *The Concept of Mind* Ch. III, pp. 62–8. Also Jonathan Cohen's *Teleological Explanation* in Proceedings of the Aristotelian Society, 1951, pp. 262–266. This view seems to me difficult to maintain, but there is no point in discussing it here, since acceptance of it would merely mean eliminating the first part of our account of purposive explanation and relying entirely on the second.

torate, unlike the intention he had during the debate, was undoubtedly an affair of long standing. It had undoubtedly had an influence on his actions many times in the past. And at the time of the debate, it co-existed with many other desires, such as the desire to shine in repartee, the desire to get on with ministerial business outside the House, the desire to take a holiday, and so on. Such enduring states of mind have been called 'dispositions'; hence we will speak of motives as a kind of disposition. They are not the only kind—beliefs, for example, are another—but they are the kind which we are concerned with at the moment.[1]

We must ask, then, whether motive-explanations are like intention-explanations in presupposing general statements. The answer is that they are, but the general statements involved are more complex, and may be of different kinds. In particular they may be laws—inevitably incomplete in their statement because of their complexity—or they may be restricted statements of a special kind. Let us first consider motive-explanations as depending on statements of the law type.

Clearly it will not do to suggest as a principle, parallel to that about intentions, that whenever anyone has a desire to bring something about, he will do what he believes will bring it about. For this, as it stands, can be seen to be false. If anyone, in giving a motive-explanation, appears to use it, he will admit if pressed that it needs to be filled out in two ways.

In the first place, since a motive is an enduring state of mind, there must be something to explain why it is called into play at one time rather than another. Given that the Prime Minister wanted to influence the electorate, we may still be asked why he spoke when he did, and the answer will obviously be that it was the parliamentary debate which provided the occasion. We must mention the occasioning circumstances as well as the motive if we are to explain why the intention was formed or the action done.

In the second place, at any given time people want to do many things, and they can in fact only do one of them. A mere reference to what a man wants will therefore not explain why he does one rather than another. For this we have to take account of the relative 'strengths' of different motives. Such strengths may be more or less permanent features of a person's character; the Prime Minister, we might say, put his speech before other things because he was always very dependent on popularity. Or they may themselves depend on occasioning circumstances; he put his speech first because there was an election coming. But however it is itself accounted for, some statement of order among a person's motives is required.

Hence, if we are to present a model for the laws presupposed by

[1] Words like 'want', 'desire', 'intend', are, it must be admitted, frequently used almost interchangeably, sometimes to indicate mental occurrences, sometimes dispositions. But we are here concerned not so much with normal usage as with the need to emphasize a distinction.

motive-explanations, it would have to be : given certain occasioning circumstances, anyone will do what he thinks will bring about the end which he desires most.

The need to introduce these two considerations will inevitably make a *complete* explanation very much more complex than one which refers only to intentions. In any actual case we will take certain of the elements in it for granted and only mention the others. But even if pressed we are not likely to be able to state them fully. In other words, while we are able to point to the main factors which enter into the explanation, we can only approach in a greater or a lesser degree to a statement of the sufficient conditions for the action taking place.

This, however, need not surprise us, since we have already been prepared to accept that the material of human life *is* complex. It certainly gives no ground for an objection in principle to the view that motive-explanations presuppose general statements. Furthermore, when this point is made we can see why it is that it is much easier to explain a person's actions by referring to his motives, than to discover what his actions will be by a consideration of his motives. It is possible to give a reasonably satisfactory explanation without taking all the relevant features into account, whereas in estimating what a man will do, we cannot afford to stop short in this way.

Despite its complexity, this type of motive-explanation is, in its general structure, a familiar and a natural one. It is the one we have in mind whenever we seek to account for an action in terms of the effect of circumstances on character. If we knew enough of the circumstances and the system of motives which constitute people's characters, and had also established the laws which specified the effects of these on actions, we would have achieved the ideal of complete explanation. In principle such an explanation is like the explanation which we give of the igniting of a match when we say it is due to the striking of the match on a matchbox. Just as a matchbox is an enduring material object, so a motive is an enduring state of mind. When it is struck by the appropriate circumstances it flares up into an intention or an action.[1]

---

[1] In presenting this account, we are assuming that a motive *is* an enduring state of mind. It has been argued that to speak in this way is misleading, since to say that someone has a motive is only to say that in certain types of circumstance he always does what he thinks will achieve a certain type of end, just as to say a piece of glass is brittle is to say that it will break when hit. This is the 'phenomenalist' analysis of disposition-statements. It runs parallel to the phenomenalist analysis of statements about material objects like matchboxes. It is not to our purpose to discuss it here. It has been defended by Gilbert Ryle, op. cit., esp. pp. 43–5, 85–90, 117–125. For criticism of it, see R. J. Spilsbury—*Dispositions and Phenomenalism* in Mind Vol. LXII, pp. 339–354. If it were accepted, it would make the full statement of any law presupposed by a motive-explanation enormously complicated. Our simple way of speaking of motives as if they were enduring features of minds is, if nothing else, a great simplifying device. It is not surprising therefore, that the sponsors of the phenomenalist view regard it as precluding the law type of explanation, leaving only motive-explanations of the restricted type which we are about to discuss.

Restricted Motive-Explanations

We must not suppose, however, that all motive-explanations are of this kind. We frequently offer a more limited type of explanation in which we make no reference, however implicit, to anything beyond the particular motives of the individual concerned. When we do this, we clearly do not presuppose laws of any kind about the effect of circumstances on character. All that we presuppose are statements about how a particular individual can be relied on, in general, to react to circumstances of a given kind. It is these which we have referred to as a special kind of restricted general statement.

Let us consider the explanation of Hitler's invasion of Russia in terms of his desire to dominate Europe. In the account we have given this presupposes a general statement something like the following: whenever *anyone* who is in the position of a military leader has a desire to dominate neighbouring countries, and is confronted with the growing strength of a powerful neighbour, and further, believes that launching an invasion against that neighbour is necessary to secure domination, then he will take steps to launch such an invasion. But instead of referring in this way to what *anyone* would do in certain circumstances, we might instead refer only to what *Hitler* would do in certain circumstances. Hitler's desire to dominate Europe had manifested itself in various ways in the past. Whenever the opportunity arose he took steps which he believed would further that end. We can therefore explain his present action in terms of this general tendency combined with present opportunity.

There is no doubt that this is the type of explanation which critics of generality have in mind when they say that for a purposive explanation no general statement is required. They see that in this case no laws are involved, and that no reference is made to motives other than those of the person concerned. What they fail to see is that the explanation depends on another type of general statement—a restricted one about what would always happen in given circumstances throughout a period of that person's history.[1] Hitler's desire to dominate Europe undoubtedly lasted throughout many years. To say this is to imply that throughout that period, given appropriate circumstances, and given that other motives did not have priority, he would always have acted in the way he believed would further his end. This is a general statement concerning events occurring within a restricted period of time and a restricted, though shifting, region of space—namely that occupied by Hitler. And it is this, taken together with the fact that at a given point

---

[1] Ryle, loc. cit., refers to these as 'law-like' statements. As we have seen (note p. 32) he regards statements about motives and other dispositions as equivalent to these. The use of such law-like statements where actions are explained in terms of motives is brought out by him on pp. 113–114.

within that time—October, 1941—the appropriate circumstances arose, which constitutes the explanation.

The possibility of this type of explanation, it should be noted, depends not on the fact that we are concerned with a purpose, but on the fact that we are referring to an *enduring* feature of the situation. Wherever we are concerned with events which form part of the history of enduring objects, both types of explanation are possible. To make this clear, let us return from motives to matchboxes. In explaining the igniting of a match, we can say that whenever *any* matchbox is struck with a match, the match ignites. But we can also say—whenever *this* matchbox is struck with a match, the match ignites. In this case it is easy to pass over from the latter type of explanation to the former since matchboxes are alike, and it is easy to detect the crucial common feature which they all possess. Human motives are like matchboxes in that they have a history, and hence permit both types of explanation. But they differ in being more various and more complicated, and it is this which gives the restricted type of motive-explanation its special importance. It has to be recognized that it is often impossible in practice to give even a moderately complete explanation in terms of laws.

It is true of course, as we have already pointed out, that restricted general statements are less satisfactory than laws for the purposes both of explanation and discovery. But there are occasions when nothing more may be required, as well as occasions when nothing more is possible. The important thing is that an explanation which makes use of restricted general statements of the 'motive' sort should not be mistakenly assumed to be an explanation which makes no use of general statements at all.

Sources of confusion about purposes

So far it has been our aim to show that to deny generality to purposive explanations is a mistake. How then is it that people have come to make this mistake?

(a) Action

One of the courses of confusion undoubtedly lies in the apparent implications of the term 'action'. When human beings act, it is admitted, they may be said to be causing changes in their environment. But in this case, it is felt, the relation between the cause and the effect is one which can be immediately recognized without presupposing any *general* causal statement at all.

It is true that the ideas of causing and acting are very closely associated in our minds. But from this it does not follow at all that when people act, the causal relationship is somehow immediately discoverable in the particular case. This point may be developed in the following way. The interests of human beings have always been primarily practical.

They have sought food and shelter and have produced changes in their environment in order to obtain it. Hence, when they have turned their interest to changes which they have not produced themselves they have still thought of them as *produced*, at first perhaps by purposefully acting non-human agents but finally by inanimate things *acting* on each other. Such action may be belittled as blind and purposeless, but it is still thought of as action. This is why reference to production, to the operation of forces and to the exerting of pressures is almost inseparable from talk about causation.

In the case of inanimate things, it is soon seen that to speak simply of one particular thing producing changes in another is not enough. For how is anyone to say what produces changes in what? If one billiard ball hits another, and at the same moment the light is switched on, how is anyone to say whether it was the first ball or the light rays that produced the movement of the second ball? Clearly the notion of action must here be taken to be one of *regular* action, and no effect would be said to be produced at all unless it came about in accordance with causal *law*. Since it is the regularity of the changes which must be known if people are to accommodate themselves in advance to what goes on in the world, they easily come to admit that talk of action, production and so on is in the case of inanimate things mere pictorial colour, and no more.

But they are not so easily convinced when purposive human action is involved. For in this case the reference to action cannot be dismissed as mere pictorial colour. We do exert ourselves and push things around so as to achieve changes which we desire. We are here brought back to the genuine case of action, and because of this it is thought that any reference to the regularity of changes becomes unnecessary. If a man strikes a billiard ball with a cue, it is argued, he knows very well that it is he who has produced the movement of the ball, and there is no need to investigate regular sequences in order to show that light rays had nothing to do with it.

The defect in this argument is that it is not asked *how* the man knows that he produced the movement of the cue. It is true that he does not have to investigate regular sequences in order to show that the light rays are irrelevant. But the same may be said in the case in which one billiard ball hits another. In the latter case he already has general knowledge about the movements of balls which dates from early childhood. May we not say also that in the former case he has a general knowledge about the movements of muscles which dates from early childhood? In the one case he knows that under certain standard conditions which could be specified, whenever one billiard ball hits another, it will move. In the other case he knows that under certain standard conditions, whenever he intends, or desires, to swing his arm, it will move. If in this second case the general statement were not true, he would not say that he had produced the movement, but would look around for other causes, just as he would if the general statement in the first case were not true.

We conclude, therefore, that to think of causation in terms of action does nothing to show that a reference to general statements can be kept out of the account of a causal relationship, and that this applies equally in the special and important case of human action itself.

(b) Agent and Enquirer

It is true, of course, that while we are acting we do not look on the matter in this way. It is this which brings us to a second reason for the failure to notice the generality implied in the explanation of human action.

As human beings we are agents as well as enquirers. If I perform an action—for example, hit someone—and am asked why I did it, I will simply state the purpose I had in mind—say, that I wanted to stop him hitting me. This may be described—and in a sense quite properly described—as 'explaining why I did it'. I accept the question 'why?' as a request for information about my intentions. As an agent I do not feel called upon to take the matter further.

But suppose someone wishes to enquire into the situation and asks why I hit the man at that time in those circumstances. He will undoubtedly start by finding out what purpose I had in mind, and he may say that this explains my action. But in this case, it would be recognized that, if he were pressed, he would have to complete the explanation by adding something further. It would be relevant, even if obtuse, for someone to ask what my wanting to stop the man from hitting me had to do with my hitting him. The answer would have to take the form of a general statement about defensive actions. In its simplest form it would be that whenever anyone, in certain specifiable circumstances, wants to defend himself against being hit by another, he will hit first. It is only when some such statement is introduced that the explanation, in the enquirer's sense of explanation, is completed.

It is easy to see how the one word 'explanation' comes to have these different uses, and it is also easy to see how features of the agent's use come to be wrongly supposed to belong to the enquirer's use. In particular, it must be remembered that anyone may take up the attitude of an enquirer in regard to his own actions as well as other people's, so that a first-person answer to the question 'why?' may be of either type, or an uncertain mixture of both. It may be that in order to decide whether we mean simply to state what our intentions were, or whether we mean to say how it came about that we acted as we did, we have to test how we react if pressed to complete the explanation in the manner that has been described.

The fact, however, that we sometimes do not know which of these two things we are doing is no reason for failing to draw a sharp distinction between them, or for failing to recognize that, from an enquirer's point of view, a mere statement of the purposes we have in mind is an insufficient explanation of our actions.

(c) Ends

A third source of confusion about purposive actions lies in the use of the word 'end'. Purposive actions may be described as actions directed towards ends, and an explanation of them requires a reference to the ends for which they are performed. This is why explanations in terms of purposes are sometimes referred to as teleological ones. The trouble comes when this gives rise to the idea that the time-order of an ordinary causal explanation is being upset; that the action is being explained in terms of something which succeeds it in time, not in terms of anything in the existing condition of the person who performs it.

About this there are two things to be said.

In the first place, the suggestion that a purposive explanation involves a reversal of time-order is a mistake which arises from a failure to notice a simple ambiguity in the use of the word 'end'. On the one hand 'the end' may be used for what a person *does* bring about—the result of his action; on the other, it may be used for what he *intends* to bring about,[1] and *believes* that by his actions he will bring about. We know very well that what a man intends to bring about—the end he has in mind when he acts—may in fact never come about at all. But even if it does not, we can still give a perfectly good purposive explanation of his action. For such an explanation refers only to his intentions and beliefs—that is, to what he has in mind *at the time*.

In the second place, this confusion is made easier by the fact that there *is* a type of explanation in which things are explained by pointing to their results. Furthermore, these explanations are generally referred to as teleological ones, and the results referred to as ends. They are sometimes called functional explanations, and for clarity we will refer to them as such. We must say sufficient about them here to distinguish them from purposive explanations.

Suppose that exogamy in primitive societies is explained by saying it is a means whereby smooth co-operation is ensured in the group.[2] Or that parliamentary government is explained by saying that it is a means for ensuring the maintenance of the capitalist economic system. In such cases certain states of affairs are explained by pointing out that certain other states of affairs, called 'ends', could not be achieved or maintained without them. In other words, they are explained by pointing to the function they perform.

Such explanations are common in biology, and there is no doubt that

---

[1] It might of course be used for what he desires to bring about. For simplicity we speak here only of intentions, and not motives.

[2] See B. Malinowski—Article on Culture in *Encyclopaedia of Social Sciences*.

they are frequently used to effect by social enquirers. When they are given, it is a matter of interest why certain states of affairs and not others should be singled out and spoken of as ends, and what justification there is for explaining their contributing conditions in terms of them. For the present, however, what we need to point out is that they make no reference at all to the intentions, motives or beliefs of human beings, and hence that they are not to be classed as purposive explanations.[1]

Confusion on this point is easy because it is sometimes uncertain which type of explanation is being given. Exogamy could be regarded as having been set up by the ancestors of the group in order to ensure co-operation. Parliamentary government could be regarded as a device arranged by capitalists in order to preserve their basic economic interests. This in fact is how the matter is often presented in popularizations of the Marxist theory of politics from which the second illustration is taken. On a different level, the conditions which ensure the survival of a species are often popularly referred to as contrived by a provident being called 'Nature'. There is thus a tendency for functional explanations to be treated as purposive ones, and we have to consider carefully which is meant in each case.

Finally, we must point out that even if this confusion is fallen into, and purposive explanations interpreted as if they were functional ones, general statements would still be presupposed. For to explain an action as contributing to an end, we need some causal statements about the connection between actions and ends of the sorts in question. And these will be general statements just as much as will be the statements we make about the connection between actions and motives. Thus the fact that reference is made to ends will under no circumstances support the critic of generality.

If then a purposive explanation is like all others in this fundamental respect of generality, why should it seem to be so peculiarly satisfying? Why should the question 'Why?' be set above the question 'How?'

In answer to this, we need only refer to what has been said about action. As human beings we are primarily concerned with bringing about states of affairs which we desire. Hence to account for something by showing that someone has desired it seems to settle the matter in a peculiarly conclusive way. But we should not let this effect of our practical interests mislead us as to the logical character of our explanations.

[1] For a clear distinction between purposive explanation and functional explanation, see R. B. Braithwaite—*Scientific Explanation*, Ch. 8, (Cambridge, 1954) and Jonathan Cohen—*Teleological Explanation* in the Proceedings of the Aristotelian Society, 1951.

REASONS

We must now consider the suggestion that in the case of at least some human actions, to explain them is to give the reasons for them, and that this is different from giving their causes and thereby having to appeal to general laws.

The word 'reason', even when restricted to this type of context, appears to have various uses. It is not difficult to see the close connection between these uses. But if we are to avoid confusion about the logical character of social explanations, it is as well that we should emphasize the differences.

In the first place, 'giving a reason' for something happening is often used quite generally as a synonym for 'giving an explanation'. Thus we may speak of trying to find out the reason for the Japanese earthquake or for a man's hand shaking or for a car breaking down. In such cases it is evident that in looking for reasons we are looking for causes and expecting to use general statements in our explanations. Hence if, using 'reason' in this way, we were to ask about the reason for Hitler's invasion of Russia, we would not expect anything different in kind for an answer.

Secondly, to say that someone 'has a reason' for acting in a certain way may be to say that he has some purpose in view. Thus, asked for Hitler's reason for ordering the invasion of Russia, we might reply that he was aiming at general domination of Europe. Since we have already discussed explanation in terms of purposes, we need say no more about 'reasons' in this sense.[1]

Reasons as Beliefs

When we speak of a person's reasons for acting, however, we commonly mean to refer not to what he intends to do, but to what he believes about the means for achieving it. Hitler's *reason* for invading Russia was not so much that he had a certain aim as that he thought the invasion would help to achieve the aim. It is especially apt to refer to this as his reason, since it is this belief in a causal relationship between two possible things—the action and the end—which enables a person to conclude from his desire for the one that he must do the other. In other words, 'having reasons' (in this sense) implies 'using one's reason' about the suitability of means to ends, and this becomes more obvious the more elaborate is one's plan of action.

There is a complication about reasons taken in this sense. Among the beliefs which constitute such reasons, we may have to take account not only of beliefs about the suitability of means to ends, but also of beliefs

---

[1] This for example is the way 'reason' is used by Gilbert Ryle—*The Concept of Mind*, pp. 113–114, where, in distinguishing the reasons from the causes of actions, he identifies the former with motives, and explanation in terms of reasons with the motive-explanations we discussed at the end of the last section.

about the desirability of the ends themselves. When asked for the reason why he does something, a man may be concerned not only to state what he thinks he will achieve by it; he may also be concerned to *justify* it. Asked why he hit somebody, he may say not merely 'Because I thought it would teach him a lesson', but rather 'Because I thought he *should* be taught a lesson'. Such beliefs about what we *should* do—beliefs about the goodness of ends or the rightness of actions—may be called 'moral' or 'ethical' beliefs.[1] They differ in many ways from 'factual' beliefs about the relation of means to ends—so much so that some would not wish to classify them as beliefs at all.[2] But however they are to be interpreted there is no reason to suppose that they are not sometimes among the features of a person's state of mind when he acts or that they do not constitute a reason (in our present sense) for his acting as he does. To say that Hitler was an idealist, for example, is to say that he acted as he did not only in order to achieve his ends, but also because he believed these ends were right. People are of course always anxious to claim that they did what they did because they thought it was right, but we must not assume that such claims are always bogus.

Where pointing to a person's reasons for acting is pointing to his beliefs, factual or moral, it might appear that generality must at once be admitted into the explanation in a way for which there is no parallel in the case of purposes. For even if mentioning the belief were to suffice as an explanation without there being any presupposed general statement about the relation between belief and action, it could still be argued that the belief itself might be a belief in the truth of a general statement. Thus Hitler might have drawn on his *general* knowledge about the consequences of invasion, and this might be considered his 'reason' for action just as much as his belief about the particular invasion he had in mind would be considered as a reason. The generality of the *agent's* belief would thus involve the enquirer in introducing generality into his explanation in at least a secondary way.

To argue in this way, however, would be to prejudge the issue. Anyone who challenges the generality of the enquirer's explanation of the agent's action would likewise challenge the generality of the agent's belief about means to ends. If we could explain Hitler's action simply by pointing to his beliefs, there is no reason why Hitler could not infer in the same non-generalizing way how other people would react to his proposed action. We must therefore consider directly what is involved in explaining actions in terms of beliefs, without making any premature assumptions about the generality of what is believed.

---

[1] The word 'moral' is used in various ways, and is commonly given a narrower meaning than this; but a suitable alternative is lacking.

[2] For further discussion of ethical statements and their relation to factual ones, see Ch. VI.

Now if we concentrate on this question, it will be clear that the same considerations which hold for purposes hold also for 'reasons' taken in this sense. To state the reasons is in no way inconsistent with giving an explanation of the action which relies on general statements; on the contrary it is a contribution to that explanation. The explanation to which it contributes may be of the law type or of the restricted type. Where the appeal is to laws, beliefs, both factual and moral, have to be taken along with motives as conditions relevant for the full explanation of an action. Whether we mention the beliefs or the motives depends on which we already take for granted. As we have seen, the full causal explanation is always complex, and the general statement which it involves has to mention various conditions. When we explain in terms of a person's reasons, what we do, in this case, is to mention certain beliefs as conditions which, in the context, are especially significant, and point out that these beliefs were held by the person in question.[1]

All belief-explanations, however, are not of this kind. Like motive-explanations they may imply no reference beyond the particular beliefs of the individual concerned. For beliefs, like motives, are not mental occurrences but enduring features of a person's state of mind. Hence a belief-explanation may rely on a restricted general statement about the sorts of means to his end an individual will judge[2] suitable, and will adopt (or the sorts of end he will judge desirable and will pursue), in various circumstances throughout a given period—the period, that is, in which he holds the belief.

Hitler, for example, may have believed for months that the invasion of Russia would further his aim. During this period the belief may have manifested itself in various ways—in what he said to his advisers, in his calling for reports on Russian military strength, and so on. To accept that he had the belief is to imply that at *any* time during the period, when appropriate circumstances arose, he would launch the invasion of Russia as a means to his end, rather than, say, concentrate on the war in the West. When we are asked why he launched the invasion, and give his reason for doing it, we may be referring to this general statement, taking it together with the fact that the appropriate circumstances arose in October 1941. We thus have, as in the case of motives, a type of explanation in which we restrict ourselves to the individual's reasons, without forgoing the general element in the explanation. And the same

---

[1] When we mention a moral belief (He did it because he thought it right), we might raise the question whether a complete explanation would require the mention of a corresponding moral motive (He wanted to do what was right). We commonly speak as if it would, but we must keep in mind that such a belief might be thought of as itself fulfilling the function of a motive. Thus it might be suggested that to think an end desirable itself inclines a person to promote that end.

[2] The old-fashioned word 'judge' here is introduced to indicate a mental occurrence which stands to a belief as an intention stands to a motive. Whether, for a 'reason' explanation, there must be a judgment preceding the action, is not the main issue, any more than in the parallel case of intentions.

41

could be said if the reference was to Hitler's moral belief about the rightness of his end of dominating Europe.

The parallel between reason-explanations and purpose-explanations is brought out again when we consider one main source of the confusion which has led to the false opposition of reasons to causes. For here again there is the failure to notice the difference between the answer to the question 'Why?' expected from the agent and that expected from the enquirer. When someone is asked why he did something, all that he feels called upon to do is to state what *his* reasons were—that is to state his relevant beliefs. But when the enquirer asks why he did it, it is not enough for him to mention these beliefs or reasons. If pressed, he would have to show what the agent's having those reasons had to do with his performing the action. In order to do this, he would have to formulate the general statements required to complete the explanation.

In this case, the confusion is made peculiarly easy by the free use of the word 'reason'. To ask for *the* reason for an action may be, as we have seen, to ask for the explanation. Whereas to ask someone about *his* reason for acting is to ask about his beliefs. It sounds plausible to say that to state the reason for an action all that is needed is to state what the agent's reasons were, and hence that no mediating general statement is required. But this only sounds plausible because we fail to notice the shift in the use of the word 'reason'. To explain an action we must do more than state the agent's beliefs, we must show the causal relevance of the beliefs to the action.

Reasons as Rational Beliefs

So far the issue about reasons has been shown to run parallel to the one about purposes. We must now notice a very important difference—one which suggests a further ground for denying the generality of explanations in terms of reasons, not present when the reference is simply to purposes.

Beliefs about means to ends may, as we have pointed out, be *mistaken*, and it is natural to say the same about moral beliefs as well. A person's reasons for acting may be sufficient or insufficient; they may be good reasons or they may be bad reasons. And in fact we do find a fourth use of 'reason' in which nothing counts as a reason unless it is a *good* reason.

We may say of someone who was mistaken in believing that he would achieve something by his action that he had no reason for acting as he did. Thus it may be argued that Hitler had no reason for invading Russia, since he should have seen that by engaging all his enemies at once he lessened his chance of winning. It might be added that he had no reason for subordinating everything to the aim of German domination, since, though he took this as his ideal, he was misguided in doing so. Here we have a use of 'reason' in which only certain beliefs are counted as reasons—those which involve a correct estimate of means, or (we might add) a correct view about the worthwhileness of ends.

To have a reason for acting—i.e. to have a good reason, it is not necessary that one's belief should be a true one. All that is needed is that it should be a reasonable one to hold, given the evidence at one's disposal. Hitler may have had a very good reason for acting as he did, even if he in fact failed in his object because of circumstances that he could not have foreseen. When we speak of mistaken beliefs, we must be understood to refer to those based on insufficient evidence, and not to those which are actually false.

We can see now why we need to be cautious about making the distinction between good and bad reasons when we are considering moral beliefs. We certainly speak of people having correct or mistaken ideas about what they should do. But in this case it is not at all clear what is to be counted as evidence for or against these ideas. Hence it will be simplest to restrict ourselves here to the consideration of factual beliefs, and to leave till later the special problem raised by the suggestion that we can have good or bad reasons of the moral sort.[1]

It is only when someone has a *good* reason for acting that we speak of him as acting *rationally*. Sometimes, it is true, we think of irrational actions as those which are done on mere blind impulse, without any consideration of means at all. But this is by no means always so. If someone were, carefully and deliberately, to walk round a ladder because he believed, without evidence, that walking under it would bring him bad luck, we would not hesitate to say that he acted irrationally. It is the consequences of recognizing that people sometimes act rationally —in the sense of having good reasons for their actions—that we have now to consider.

It will seem at first sight that the distinction between good and bad reasons is quite irrelevant for giving explanations of people's actions— and for making discoveries about them. If we are considering the truth of a belief, it is, of course, necessary to see whether there is sufficient evidence for it. But if we are considering the effects of a belief on a person's actions, it is evident that it will have precisely the same effects, whether it is soundly based or not. We may take the view that Hitler made a mistake in thinking the invasion of Russia would further his aims, but to explain his action all we need to know is that this is what he thought. The question about the evidence for beliefs must not be confused with the question about the part they play in a causal explanation.

This is true enough, as far as it goes. But if we look further into the causal explanation, we will see that there comes a point when the two questions cannot be so neatly separated. We reach this point when we consider how a person *arrives* at the belief which affects his action.

To have a good reason for acting, three things are necessary. There

[1] See Ch. VI, pp. 63–66.

must be a belief that the action will further one's ends. There must be sufficient evidence available to one to make this belief a reasonable one to hold. And finally one must *take account* of this evidence and appreciate that it is sufficient to justify the belief. This last feature is clearly essential for a rational action. If someone bought shares on the stock exchange because the stars told him share prices would rise, the fact that there happened at the same time to be good economic evidence available to him that they would rise would not be sufficient to clear him of the charge of acting irrationally. He must also have taken account of this evidence and drawn the correct conclusion from it.

If we keep this point firmly in mind we will see that the evidence which there is for a belief is very relevant when we are explaining rational action. For as soon as anyone takes account of the evidence, the evidence will make a difference to what he believes, and hence to what he does. If we say of someone that he bought shares because he believed their prices would rise, we may say also that he believed their prices would rise because he noticed certain facts (e.g. increased rate of company profits) and that he noticed these facts because, among other things, they were there to be noticed. If these facts had not been what they were, he might never have bought the shares at all.

What we call evidence, then, appears to have two roles. On the one hand it is that by which we judge whether what someone believes is true. On the other hand, through its being taken account of by that person, it helps to explain why he had the belief. It is because it has this second role that people sometimes say that rational actions have to be explained in terms of reasons, while irrational actions can be explained in terms of psychological or social causes.

However it is expressed, it is clear that there is an important difference here, and that explanations of rational actions are of a somewhat special kind. This is something which social enquirers have often been loath to admit. They have felt that the explanation of any action must always be in terms of the prior states of the person who performs it and of the social conditions which give rise to those states. This has seemed necessary in order to keep it in line with the scientific explanations given in other fields. Given the laws of mechanics, we explain the movement of a billiard ball in terms of its internal structure and the forces to which it is subjected. Similarly, it is assumed that given the laws of psychology and sociology, we should be able to explain a person's action in terms of his inherited constitution and environmental influences. So deeply ingrained is this assumption, and so difficult is it to reconcile with the fact of rational action, that social theorists have sometimes been led to treat all human action as if it were irrational.[1]

[1] It is not suggested that this is done explicitly, but a tendency towards it is often found in the psychological explanations given by Freudians and in the social explanations given by Marxists, and by the upholders of Karl Mannheim's programme for a 'sociology of knowledge'.

This, however, will not do. Rational action may, in some circumstances, be rare, but no one doubts that it is regularly found in the ordinary conduct of life. If it is asked why a garage mechanic adjusts one screw rather than another, the answer will clearly be that it is because he has seen what is wrong with the car. To explain his action we need a knowledge not of psychology but of motor-mechanics, since we want to know what evidence he has for his diagnosis.

If anyone wished to mark the peculiarity of this kind of explanation by saying it is explanation in terms of reasons rather than of causes, he may of course do so. But in an important respect this is misleading. For it suggests that it differs from explanation of the causal kind in not requiring the mediation of general statements. And this, we must point out, is precisely what it does not do.

Even if we do not consider the evidence in the light of which a person acts as part of the cause of his action, it has at any rate to be admitted that its presence is a feature of the situation which, taken along with other features which we would count as causes, contributes to the explanation of the action. We can therefore hardly avoid speaking of it as a relevant condition, which is present when the action takes place. And as with the other conditions of the occurrence of an action, we could not speak of it as relevant unless some general principle were presupposed.

Thus if we say of Mr. Smith that he bought shares because prices were rising, we could always go on to ask what the fact of rising prices had to do with Mr. Smith's buying shares. The answer (assuming it to be of the unrestricted-law type) would have to take the form: whenever prices are rising and certain other conditions are present, a person will buy shares. This would not in itself be very illuminating, because in this case, certain of the other conditions are of crucial importance. We might list the more important ones as follows. The person in question must want to make a profit, and this want must have priority over other wants. He must be interested in stock-exchange transactions and have funds at his disposal. And finally he must take account of the condition of rising prices and recognize that it is good evidence in favour of the view that buying shares at that particular stage would be profitable. Assuming such conditions, we are able to show *in general* the connection between rising prices and the activity of buying shares, and it is this which makes possible the explanation of Mr. Smith's action.[1]

When therefore we say of someone that he acted because he had good reasons, it does not appear that we are using 'because' in any sense other than that in which it is used in a causal explanation. The fact that people do sometimes act rationally is, as we shall see, not only an important fact about them in itself, but one which makes the conduct of

[1] A parallel illustration could be given, making use only of a *restricted* general statement about what Mr. Smith would always do under given circumstances.

certain types of social enquiries much easier than it would otherwise be. If we know that someone is guided by evidence, we may, given certain conditions, explain or predict his actions by considering the evidence for ourselves. For this reason, it is most important not to ignore the distinctive character of rational action.[1] What concerns us at this point is simply that this distinctive character should be understood for what it is, and not made the basis for a criticism of generality.

[1] For a fuller discussion of it, see Ch. XIV.

V

EMPIRICAL EVIDENCE AND SYMPATHETIC UNDERSTANDING

WITHOUT abstraction and without generality of statement, there could be no inductive reasoning. Hence the defence of abstraction and of generality is an important part of the defence of inductive procedure in social enquiries.

When we speak of induction, however, we have in mind something more. This is that the evidence in support of any statements we make must be of the empirical kind. In the last resort, that is to say, it must be obtained from our sensory observations of the world around us or from our awareness of our own mental processes.[1] This, it will be remembered, is the third of our basic requirements of a scientific procedure.

Thus there might be no reason why we could not describe social events or make general statements about them, and yet we might not in fact be able to support our statements because of the lack of the necessary empirical evidence. If this were so, and there were no other kind of evidence to which we could appeal, we would be driven to a surprisingly sceptical conclusion. Hence doubts about the sufficiency of empirical evidence are commonly associated with the belief that there is evidence of another kind. This is the evidence which is alleged to come from what we have referred to as sympathetic understanding.

Once we were to admit that there was such evidence, the consequences would, as we have seen, be far-reaching. For the insight into social processes which we would gain in this way might be held not merely to provide a different kind of support for general statements and,

[1] The word 'empirical' has various uses, and the one we adopt is to some extent arbitrary. In particular, the word may be used more broadly to indicate any evidence for the existence of particular things and occurrences, as distinct from the 'self-evidence' of logical, mathematical, and (some would add) ethical, principles, and what can be deduced from these. If used in this way it would include the evidence alleged to be obtained from sympathetic understanding. But in the absence of accepted terminology it is impossible to find a term which does not mislead in some respects.

47

by means of these, for particular conclusions about the abstract features of various social situations. It might be held also to give us a knowledge of social events which would make abstracting and generalizing unnecessary. Thus the discussion of it is necessary not only for our present purpose but also in order to complete the argument of the preceding chapters.

In this chapter, therefore, we will be concerned to do two things—to defend the sufficiency of empirical evidence in social enquiries, and to deny that sympathetic understanding provides us with any evidence of an alternative kind.

EMPIRICAL EVIDENCE IN SOCIAL ENQUIRIES

We will not spend much time on the first part of this thesis. This is because doubts about the sufficiency of empirical evidence are commonly not of the absolute kind. They depend on our setting high standards for sufficiency, standards which we would have no reason to set unless we had an eye on an alternative and superior sort of evidence to which to appeal.

Thus the possibility of effective use of empirical evidence in social enquiries has often been challenged on the ground of the limited scope that exists for experiment and for exact measurement. The observations required for supporting social theories cannot usually be made under controlled conditions, nor can they usually be made with quantitative precision. Our observer of the parliamentary debate, for example, can do no more than watch what happens, and he can use no measuring instruments.

There is no doubt that these are two serious disadvantages which the social enquirer has to face. But just as with the case of the multiplicity and variety of observable features, the extent of the disability is a matter of degree. There are some occasions in which experiment and measurement are possible. And even where they are not, we still have evidence, though of the uncontrolled and qualitative kind. Whether the disability is regarded as sufficient to vitiate the enquiry depends therefore on the standards we choose to set for ourselves.

Again, in so far as social enquiry requires that we gain information about the states of mind of people other than ourselves, it must be admitted at once that the empirical evidence available to us cannot in principle be anything but indirect.[1] We observe bodily movements, our own and those of others, and we are aware of our own experiences. But statements about other people's experiences, and *a fortiori* state-

[1] We are ignoring the behaviouristic way of avoiding this objection. Cf. note 1 p. 12. We are also ignoring the more subtle way of avoiding it (as expounded for example by Gilbert Ryle—*The Concept of Mind, passim*) which consists in denying not the relevance of states of mind but their privacy.

ments about their dispositional states of mind such as motives and beliefs, can only be empirically supported by inference from these. The empirical knowledge we have of the thoughts and feelings of others depends, in short, on generalization from our own experience. And such generalization is often not very reliable. If a man shakes his fist, we may be mistaken in inferring that he feels what he calls anger. And in more complex cases the difficulty in knowing what others feel may be extreme.[1]

It may be enough to point out here that the position of the social enquirer in this respect is similar to that of other enquirers. We cannot, for example, observe *any* past events of whatever description, yet we make statements about them which we support by reference to what we do observe. Again we cannot observe light-waves, electrons or genes, yet this does not stop physicists and biologists from formulating and producing evidence for theories about such entities.[2] In all such cases, the indirectness of the evidence may be considered a defect. The only reason for concentrating attention on it in the case of social enquiry lies in the suggestion that we have evidence of a more direct kind about our fellow human beings. Hence once again we are led on to the consideration of the constructive side of the criticism of empirical evidence.

SYMPATHETIC UNDERSTANDING

Is it the case that social enquirers are in the peculiarly fortunate position of being able to support their conclusions in a special kind of way not available to natural scientists?

The view that they have has some apparent support from common sense. We speak of having a sympathetic understanding of our fellow-men, of finding a meaning in their activities, of grasping intuitively how they feel, what their plans are, what they are driving at; and we do not speak in the same way of inanimate objects. The German word 'Verstehen', of which 'understanding' is a partial translation, has been adopted by certain German writers to indicate this peculiarity, and the possibility of such understanding came to be regarded by them as the distinguishing mark of the human or cultural enquiries.

[1] This objection may take a more radical form through it being denied that the argument from the analogy of our own case provides *any support at all* for statements about the thoughts and feelings of other people. This denial appears quite unmerited, but detailed argument concerning it cannot be entered into here. If it were upheld, it would, of course, mean that scepticism could only be avoided either by resorting to behaviourism or asserting the possibility of a special kind of social awareness.

[2] In each case there is admittedly a difficult further problem about the status of such statements and theories. But physicists and biologists commonly leave this to the philosophers, and there is no reason why social scientists should not do the same.

Acceptance of this common-sense distinction, we will maintain, does not in itself commit anyone to any special view about *procedure* in social enquiries. Once it is made, however, it is very easy to take the step of regarding such understanding as a distinctive procedure—one which goes beyond the use of empirical evidence. This step seems to have been taken by some (though not all) of the writers who have spoken of 'Verstehen'. But the tendency is much more widespread than this. It has in fact survived best where it has been least explicitly formulated, and part of our task is to make it explicit.[1]

The central notion, as we have seen,[2] is that we understand what is going on simply by participating in it. This is easily recognized in the case of ourselves; we live through our own experiences, and in doing so become aware of them. But we also participate, along with others, in social processes, and in doing this are able to grasp the situation not only from our own point of view, but from theirs. By identifying ourselves with them, we come to feel what they feel, or at any rate to think their thoughts. And this applies not only for present social situations in which we are actually participating, but also for the past which we can, as historians, relive or re-enact for ourselves, thereby achieving a vicarious participation. Since it is by participation in the social process that we are said to gain this knowledge, it may be quite properly spoken of as internal knowledge, and contrasted with the knowledge that could be gained by a spectator looking on it from outside.

Closely connected with this thesis is another. This is that social consciousness is primitive. We do not, it is said, first become aware of our own private stream of consciousness, and then have to argue our way beyond it to the parallel private worlds of others. On the contrary, being involved in social life from birth, we only become aware of ourselves through our awareness of others.

Those who put forward or imply these views do not of course mean to suggest that the observation of the bodies and movements of others plays no part. Such observation is clearly presupposed. The function of the special social awareness which they have in mind is to enable the

---

[1] It is difficult to illustrate this tendency from the work of any well-known writer without the fear of being charged with having misunderstood him. Among those who have spoken of 'Verstehen', Wilhelm Dilthey is perhaps the clearest case (See *Gesammelte Schriften* Vol. VII, or, for an exposition in English, Hodges— *The Philosophy of Wilhelm Dilthey*, Ch. 5). Among others, we might mention Henri Bergson (cf. note 1 to p. 12), Samuel Alexander (see *Space, Time and Deity*, Vol. II, Book 3, Ch. 1B), F. Znaniecki (see *The Method of Sociology* Ch. 2, Scts. 2–5, Ch. 4, Sect. 3). R. G. Collingwood has commonly been interpreted as adopting this type of view (see *The Idea of History* Part 5, Sects. 1 & 4). This interpretation has, however, been disputed (see A. Donagan in the *Philosophical Quarterly* Vol. 6, No. 24 (1956) pp. 193 et. seq.). The purpose in this section as elsewhere is to criticize a common anti-scientific tendency of thought, rather than to do full justice to any individual writer.

[2] Ch. II, p. 14.

immediate recognition of already known bodily movements as the actions of conscious human beings. The question which concerns us is whether anyone ever has an awareness of this kind.

If someone were to make a personal claim to have it, it must be admitted it would be impossible to disprove him. All that could be done would be to point out that he appeared to gain by it no great advantage in the prosecution of his social enquiries over those who make no such claim. But in fact those who maintain or imply that there is such an awareness make no claim to a unique capacity; what they assert is rather that there is a capacity common to all. And they support this assertion by reference to common experiences and common achievements such as are indicated by phrases about sympathetic understanding, gaining an inner knowledge by participating in social processes, finding meaning in people's actions, identifying ourselves with others and re-enacting their experiences, having an intuitive grasp of social situations. What we need to show, therefore, is that these common experiences and achievements are being misinterpreted when they are said to indicate or to be based upon a special and independent source of evidence.

Knowledge through Participation

Let us start with the simple idea that we gain knowledge of things by participating in them. The anthropologist, for example, who goes to live with a primitive tribe is said to understand its customs in a way that would be impossible if he merely paid a visit and took notes. Someone who lives in a country is said to understand its political institutions in a way which is closed to the foreigner.

There is no doubt that in many cases it makes perfectly good sense to say things like this. The man to ask is the man who has the inside knowledge. But when we say it, we do not mean to suggest that the man with the inside knowledge has evidence for his conclusions which is different in kind from that of others. What we mean is that he is in a peculiarly favourable position to accumulate evidence. Unless the anthropologist becomes accepted by the members of the tribe, there are many things he will not hear about. Unless he is in a position to observe the daily round of inconspicuous activities, he will not have the material from which to infer beliefs and attitudes. In this respect he is like the pilot, who has an understanding of the shoals and channels in an estuary which is not possessed by the visiting ship's captain. The pilot would not be said to be participating in the currents and the tides, simply because we do not speak of participation unless the contact is a social one. But while we recognize that there is a difference between social contact and contact with inanimate objects, it does not follow from this that knowledge gained through making social contacts is knowledge gained in a peculiar way.

51

We may bring this out further by pointing to the fact that closeness of social contact is sometimes considered a disadvantage for a social enquirer. It puts him in a peculiarly favourable position to accumulate evidence, but it also puts him into a position in which his conclusions are more likely to be affected by his interests and emotions. Again it may prevent him from taking the broader view—that is, from making use of evidence derived from various other sources. This weighing of advantages and disadvantages would seem quite unreasonable if the man on the inside had a separate and special kind of evidence available to him which was inaccessible to others.

The Meaningfulness of Actions

What is said about 'participation' may be said also about the idea of people's observed movements having meaning. In all kinds of diagnosis, we speak of an observed condition having meaning if it indicates the presence (or the earlier or later existence) of something else. Spots on the skin have a meaning—they mean measles. Shells dug up in an inland desert have a meaning—they mean the earlier existence of an inland sea. Similarly, your smile has a meaning—it means that you are feeling pleased. In this last case the something else is a state of mind, and that is the difference. Talking about the meaning of people's movements does not suggest that the way of ascertaining its presence is not the same as the way of ascertaining the meaning of anything else.

Imaginative Identification

We come now to the idea of identifying oneself with other people, and gaining an inner understanding in that way. It has to be emphasized that identification, as it is spoken of in this context, is a metaphor. No one supposes that he can literally put himself into another's place, let alone *be* that person. What is meant is that anyone can *imagine* himself being in the same situation as another, and he can then proceed to imagine how he would feel and what he would do in that situation. If any person *were* to be in another's place, he would undoubtedly be in a position to know various things about the other's experiences which he does not know. But in fact he never is in that position. Re-enactment of other people's experiences is essentially the work of one's own imagination, and we should not be deceived by its metaphorical flavour into supposing that it is anything more.

When we use our imagination in this way, we are clearly not free to imagine anything we like. When I see someone being pricked with a pin and imagine myself in his situation, I can perfectly well imagine myself experiencing, let us say, what counts for me as the taste of strawberries. But doing this would tell me nothing about what *he* experiences in that situation. If, instead, I imagine myself experiencing pain, this is because I know that I do in fact experience pain in such situations and have good reason to suppose that he is like me in this respect. In other words, if what I imagine is any guide to what he feels, it is because it is subject to the control of the empirical evidence.

It turns out then that finding out about others by putting ourselves in their place presupposes a reference to ordinary empirical evidence. It is often unreliable because it encourages us to make a use of this evidence which is excessively naïve. It encourages us, in fact, to ignore the differences between ourselves and others, and simply to assume that other people will react to a given situation in the same way as we would. If I were simply to put myself into Napoleon's place, I would imagine myself reacting in ways very different from those in which I know he did. In order to correct this I would have to draw on my already acquired knowledge of Napoleon's character. This is why the metaphor of identifying myself with another person is more adequate than that of putting myself into another's place. The thing is not merely to imagine myself in another *situation*, but to imagine myself being another *person*. This requires as evidence not merely information about how I feel and act in situations of that type, but also information about how he has acted in a great variety of other circumstances. Identification, therefore, is an ideal which it will be difficult to achieve. In attempting it we will certainly not gain that complete and immediate knowledge which was demanded by the critic of abstraction.

There is one assumption, admittedly, the acceptance of which makes this identification very much easier. This is the assumption that the people with whom we are concerned are acting rationally. A person who is acting in a perfectly rational way is one who, given the available evidence, will make the best choice of means to his ends which is possible in the circumstances. If an enquirer knows such a person's circumstances, knows what evidence is available to him, and knows what end he has in view, all he need do is to consider the evidence for himself and decide what he would do in those circumstances if he had that end in view. Thus, by putting himself in the other's place, he can 're-think his thoughts' and understand his action. He can do this without having to cope with the more difficult task of diagnosing the other's feelings or interpreting his character.

It must not be forgotten that this depends on the assumption that the other person is acting rationally, and the particular degree of rationality is something which has to be established in each case. In so far as a substantial degree of rationality can be taken for granted, the consequence that any two people, given the same evidence, will come to substantially the same conclusion, is of very great value for social enquirers.[1] But this clearly does not provide us with a special way of making contact

[1] For further discussion of this question, see Ch. XIV, *passim.*

with the thoughts of others. Rather it involves a double use of empirical evidence. Let us take the case of understanding the actions of the man who buys shares when their prices are rising. We must first use empirical evidence to establish that this is the best way in the circumstances to make a profit. We must then use empirical evidence to establish that the man bought the shares because he recognized this, and not merely from ignorance or prejudice. We do this by observing that he talks intelligently about the stock market, that he has made similarly effective moves on other occasions and so on. It is only when we have evidence of these two kinds that we can understand him by re-thinking his thoughts.

To say, as we have done, that imaginative identification has to be under the control of the empirical evidence is not to belittle it. It has importance in two different contexts. In the first place, it is useful in the early stages of an enquiry in helping us to frame hypotheses to be tested. When we have not got much evidence at our disposal, we may think of ourselves as being in a situation and imagine what we *might* do in that situation. The possibilities so envisaged then serve as a guide to the enquiry which consists in looking for the evidence which will confirm or disprove them. It has often been said that a fruitful imagination which enables one to take a leap ahead of the evidence is one of the first essentials of constructive scientific work. This should certainly not be forgotten in the case of social enquiry. In this case in fact the similarity between the enquirer and his subject-matter makes the use of the imagination especially apt. But we should be careful not to confuse what is essentially a useful move with an independent source of evidence.

In the second place, when the evidence has been brought to bear and the conclusions established we may feel the need to clothe them in flesh and blood. This does not apply so much to those who are concerned with establishing general statements or making predictions about the future. But it does apply to the historian. We may *know* what happened, but it takes in addition some imagination to *feel* what happened. It is at this point, it might be said, that the re-enactment of the experiences, or the thoughts, of others really comes in. It is not a method by which we arrive at our conclusions or a source of evidence with which to support them; it is rather a final stage to be reached after the conclusions have been arrived at, one without which the historian feels his job has not been properly done. The trouble comes here when we confuse the method of enquiry with the achievement of that historical intimacy which, for some, is a consequence of its success.[1]

---

[1] It might be suggested that this is the trouble with what is said by R. G. Collingwood about the re-enactment of the past in *The Idea of History* Part V.

Intuitive Grasp

Let us now consider the idea that, by identifying ourselves with others or in some other way, we achieve an intuitive grasp of social situations. Here again there is no doubt that we frequently do this sort of thing. When attending a parliamentary debate I may be said to be intuitively aware of the tension created by the interjections of the opposition. When someone comes into the room I may know intuitively that he is angry. His historical intuition may tell an historian what Napoleon would do when he escaped from Elba.

What is common to these cases is that the conclusions are not arrived at as a result of considering the evidence. Moreover, if asked for the evidence the person who draws the conclusion might quite well not be able to say what it is. Just as a skilled craftsman, from long experience, is able to make things without being able to tell you how it is done, so also all of us, from long experience, are able to size up social situations without being able to say how it is done. It is because historians, in particular, tend to rely on this capacity that the study of history is sometimes said to be a craft and not a science.[1]

Since in these cases the evidence cannot be pointed to by the person concerned, it is easy to take the step of saying that no inductive inference is involved, and that we establish our conclusions in another way—a special intuitive way. It should be clear, however, that this step is quite unwarranted. Our capacity to make intuitive estimates always depends on long experience. And if it is asked what this long experience consists in, it would be arguing in a circle to suggest that it consisted of earlier intuitions. What is meant is clearly experience of how people behave in various special sorts of circumstances. Given such observations, combined with continual comparisons with ourselves, we have gradually built up a very complex set of habitual interpretations. When a new case comes up, we do not go over all the evidence again. Moreover, if challenged to produce it, we often could not do so, because it is so varied and so subtle and we have never bothered to formulate it in words. If an intuitive estimate is wrong, as it may well be, this is unfortunate, because we are unable to provide any way of checking it. But we recognize that it may be wrong and that the way to check it, if we wish to do so, is not to make a further resort to intuition but to try to formulate the inductive evidence or produce more.

Sympathy

Finally, we must consider the reference to sympathy involved in the use of the phrase 'sympathetic understanding'. Human sympathy is an

---

[1] See D. A. T. Gasking—*The Historian's Craft and Scientific History* in Historical Studies, Australia and New Zealand, Vol. 4, No. 14, May 1950, pp. 112–116.

important social fact. Feelings are contagious, and when we become aware that others feel tense, for example, or friendly, or distrustful, a corresponding feeling is aroused in us. This is sympathy in the broad sense. A special case of it is where we sympathize *with* other people. This is the case where the others are feeling unhappy or dissatisfied in some way, and our awareness of this makes us also feel unhappy. In such a case we say 'I know how you feel', but we imply also that we are emotionally affected by this knowledge.

It seems clear then that sympathy is a matter of feeling, and we may well ask what it has to do with understanding. It is at this point that the suggestion creeps in that it is the sympathetic feeling which gives us the understanding, providing us with its own unique source of evidence about the states of mind of other people. On the face of it this is a curious suggestion since we commonly suppose that we must already have beliefs about the feelings of others before any sympathetic feeling can be aroused. And in so far as these beliefs are based on evidence, this evidence could hardly be derived from the sympathetic feeling itself. It is not our sympathy which tells us that a friend is in pain, for unless we already accepted that he was in pain, we would not sympathize.

We do, however, speak of sympathetic understanding, and what is required is that we bring out the real point of the phrase. What it refers to is the understanding of other people which we gain as a result of adopting towards them a general sympathetic attitude. It does not suggest that sympathy provides us with a new source of evidence; it suggests rather that a predisposition to be sympathetic is a condition without which we would not make proper use of the ordinary empirical evidence at our disposal. The impartial observer or the hostile critic are said to miss the relevant features in the behaviour of other people and to misinterpret what they do observe. In particular, it is said, they will not try to use their imaginations in the fruitful way we have suggested.

We may question whether these assertions are entirely true, but it is undoubtedly the acceptance of them which gives the connection between sympathy and understanding. So that here again, as in the case of imagination, we must beware of confusing what is held to be a useful aid to enquiry with a source of evidence.

We should perhaps add to this that, through its association with sympathy, understanding has come to include something more than merely finding out about people. Once we know the truth about someone, we tend to be more tolerant than we might otherwise be. We might say not only that sympathy is an aid to understanding but also that understanding is an aid to sympathy. Hence we come to mean by an understanding parent or an understanding judge one who, at the very least, does not judge too harshly. When this shade of meaning has crept in, understanding ceases to be the goal of enquiry and becomes rather a social attitude which is often the result of enquiry. As such, its existence does not raise the issue about evidence at all.

Social Awareness as Primitive

We conclude then that the belief in a special sort of social awareness gains no support from an appeal to any of the common phrases which we employ in speaking of our knowledge of others. There remains only to consider the more direct assertions that such social awareness is primitive, and that without it we would not acquire that awareness of ourselves which we in fact have.[1]

The first of these assertions is made plausible by pointing to the obvious fact that men are inherently social and the equally obvious corollary that the experiences and characters of each one of us would have been very different if, *per impossible*, we had grown up in isolation.

We have to recognize this universal social dependence, and we have to recognize that this dependence implies belief in the existence of others like ourselves. But it does not imply anything about the reasons we have for this belief. In our early years the belief may be instinctive, and its correctness may be guaranteed by the necessities of survival. But instinct is not a way of finding out about anything. And once we start supporting our belief, there is nothing in the fact of social dependence to make us suppose that the evidence on which we base it is of a special kind.

Again, it is admittedly plausible to say that our awareness of ourselves presupposes our awareness of others. But this is a point at which we must refer to the distinction between experiences and character. We may well admit that the knowledge we have of our own character is built up side by side with our knowledge of the characters of others. Without perpetual comparison with others we would in fact have very little idea about ourselves as persons. Their motives and other dispositional states, which we judge from a consideration of their behaviour, are often better known to us than our own. But it does not follow from this that the same could be said about our experiences. I might well not know that I was vain, for example, unless I was in some way aware of vanity, and its opposite, in others. But it is a very different thing and quite unplausible to suggest that I would not know what it was to feel angry unless I was aware of the feeling of anger in others. And yet it is on the elementary awareness of the experiences of others that the advocate of social awareness has to rely.

In general, then, there seems no reason to suppose that social

[1] See for example S. Alexander—*Space, Time and Deity* Vol. II, Book 3, Ch. 1B.

enquirers can ease their path with a special way of gaining access to their material denied to the ordinary scientific worker. The empirical evidence can be used and they must use it. This being so, we can now dismiss also the alternative procedure which emerged as providing the last stand for the critics of abstraction and of generality.

VI

FACTS AND VALUES

W E have been assuming so far that social enquiries are concerned with the facts of social life. The issue has been about the ways in which we can explain what has happened, and the ways in which we can find out what has happened, what will happen and what would happen under given conditions.

And yet those who have been interested in social problems have been concerned to a very large extent with something else. They have been concerned not so much with facts as with values, not so much with the actual ends people seek to achieve as with what ends are good and what bad, not so much with what people do as with what they ought to do. These questions we may call ethical questions. There is no doubt that they have played a very large part in traditional social enquiries.

A simple attitude to take towards these questions is to recognize their importance but to insist that they be distinguished sharply from questions of fact. On this view—sometimes accepted in an unqualified form as the scientific view—the social enquirer, when engaged in his task of examining the facts, must regard any ethical question as an additional and independent one, to be excluded automatically from his consideration. In this respect, it is claimed, his position is precisely the same as that of the natural scientists. Like these, he may recognize that it is his business as a human being to consider ethical questions. But just as the physicist who considers whether atomic bombs should be made is not held to be engaged in a physical enquiry, so also the economist, for example, who considers the virtues of state control of banking, should not be held to be engaged in a social enquiry. Factual enquiries, whether physical or social, may be useful for people considering ethical questions, since it is necessary to know what things are like and what their consequences are, before judgments of value can be passed upon them. But this does not alter the fact that the considering of ethical questions is a different activity which neither physical nor social enquirers *need* enter into. To the extent that it is carried on systematically and without prejudice, it might be given a separate name and called an ethical enquiry.

59

Put in this simple way, the case for the autonomy of factual social enquiry is, as we shall see, overstated. But there are some who would reject it out of hand. The analogy between physical and social enquiries, they point out, breaks down in an important respect. It is social facts and social facts alone which can be said in the last resort to have value. It is states of mind and ways of life which we speak of as good and bad. When we call other things good or bad, it is because of their effects on these. Again it is only human actions which we speak of as right or wrong. Hence it is true that the question whether atom bombs should be made is not a question of physics. But it *is* a social question, in the sense that it is concerned with what human beings should do, and with the desirable or undesirable effects of their actions on their ways of life. The question about state control of banking is a social question in the same sense.

Once this is pointed out it is easy to take a further step. Since ethical questions always have to do with social life, we may be led to deny that social life can be studied adequately when the ethical questions are ignored. The objects of social study are unique in that they can have ethical terms applied to them. Should we not then expect the ascription of these terms to have an effect on our understanding of the facts?[1]

THE AUTONOMY OF SOCIAL ENQUIRY

We cannot settle this question satisfactorily unless we recognize the complexity in the use of words like 'value', 'good', 'ideal', 'right', and 'obligation'. If certain features of their use are emphasized the scientific answer can be accepted in its simple form; if others are emphasized, it will need to be stated more carefully. In ordinary speech the uses often coalesce in various ways, and where they are inconsistent we are often hard put to it to decide which we have in mind. To consider the relations between them, and in particular to consider which is primary, are among the main tasks of the student of ethics, since until these things are done the whole subject-matter of an ethical enquiry remains unsettled. But we do not need to deal with these questions here. It will suit our purpose if we take certain principal uses of these words separately, and consider in each case whether the assertions made in terms of them are in any way relevant to a factual social enquiry.

The Expressive Use of Ethical Words

To say something is good[2] may be merely to express approval of it, to

---

[1] See, for example, Morris R. Cohen—*Reason and Nature* (Kegan Paul, Trench, Trubner and Co., 1931) Book 3, Ch. 1, Sect. 1, p. 343. 'We cannot disregard all questions of what is socially desirable without missing the significance of many social facts.'

[2] The distinctions made here apply with some modifications to other ethical words. It is for simplicity that we speak mostly of 'good', using 'value' as a

(*Continued at foot of next page*)

recommend it to others or to advocate it. In so far as this is what is being done, it will be quite clear that assertions of value are on an entirely different level from assertions of fact. When we express attitudes or make recommendations, we are not making statements about any-thing—we are using words for a quite different purpose. Others may disagree with us, but this does not mean that they think what we say is false—it means that they regard it as wrong—that is, they are expressing an opposed attitude.[1]

The fact that someone adopts an attitude is of course a fact like any other. If someone says that the Government has a good policy, his attitude of support can be recorded in opinion-poll statistics. But when he says the policy is good, he is expressing his attitude and certainly not stating the mere psychological fact that he has it. And from the expres-sion of an attitude nothing whatsoever can be inferred about the facts. Recommending and enquiring are two different sorts of activities. Enquiries may help us when we wish to make recommendations, and the need to make recommendations on a given subject may determine the sort of thing we make enquiries about. But no recommendation is ever relevant for explaining any social fact or for finding out anything new. Hence, when ethical words are used exclusively in this way, the simple distinction between social and ethical questions can be maintained.

The Naturalistic Use of Ethical Words

The expression of attitudes and the making of recommendations, however, by no means cover all that is normally implied in our use of ethical words. This is shown by the fact that we often do not seem merely to be repeating ourselves when we say we recommend some-thing because it is good. In saying this, we suggest that in calling some-thing good we have in mind some feature which it possesses or some criterion to which it conforms in some degree.

The feature in question may be of one or other of two kinds. In the first place it may be one which can be identified, directly or indirectly, by sensory observation or awareness of our own experiences. Thus the feature we have in mind may be the satisfying of wants, the production of happiness, conformity to an existing social code, or contribution towards evolutionary development. Where ethical words like 'good'

---

[1] See C. R. Stevenson—*Ethics and Language* (Yale University Press, 1945) for a standard exposition of a view of ethics which takes this as the primary use of ethical words.

synonym for the clumsy noun 'goodness'. The distinctions apply in a correspond-ing way to the contraries like 'bad' and 'wrong'. There are important differences between the use of words of the 'good'—'value'—'ideal' group and those of the 'right'—'ought'—'obligation' group, but these are not relevant for the distinc-tions we need to make.

are used to indicate any such feature, we will speak of them being used in a naturalistic way.[1]

Where they are so used, it will be clear that ethical enquiry simply becomes a part of social enquiry. For human wants, established codes and social trends are all empirically discoverable features of social life, and it is part of the business of social enquiry to investigate them. Thus when economists discuss welfare, they may be said to be raising ethical questions. But if welfare is identified with the satisfaction of wants, the discussion of these questions is at the same time rightly admitted as a natural part of a factual social study.[2]

It follows then that, if this is the use of ethical words which we have in mind, the simple distinction between social and ethical questions cannot be maintained. Ethical questions can no longer be regarded as something separate which social enquirers can ignore. It remains the case, however, that social enquiries remain completely unaffected by this absorption of the ethical. The fact—where it is a fact—that certain words like 'good' and 'right' are used to refer to certain empirically discoverable features of social life makes no difference at all to the course of the social enquiry itself. By speaking only of wants, social codes, and such-like, the use of these words could be avoided without loss. The tendency, therefore, to give this sort of factual meaning to ethical words is quite compatible with saying that it is the business of the social enquirer to examine the facts and that he can do this without taking any but factual considerations into account. This is all that defenders of scientific procedure really wish to maintain, and it is this which we have included as the fourth item in our list of the requirements of a scientific procedure.

The 'Irreducible Feature' Use of Ethical Words

We now come to the second kind of feature which we may have in mind when we use ethical words. There is a persistent feeling that when we use these words the expressing of attitudes and the stating of

---

[1] Correspondingly a view of ethics which takes any such use as primary may be spoken of as a naturalistic view. Naturalism in ethics takes various forms, but there will be no need for us to decide the issue between them, or even to discuss whether ethical words are ever really used to indicate any particular feature which may be proposed.

[2] Jeremy Bentham is a clear case of one who accepted these premisses and openly drew the conclusions. Others who have discussed the economics of welfare (e.g. Pigou—*The Economics of Welfare*) have identified welfare with satisfaction but claimed not to treat it as an ethical word. Others again (e.g. R. G. Hawtrey—*The Economic Problem*) have treated it as an ethical word but have refused to identify it with the satisfaction of wants or any other natural feature of social life. The difficulty of comparing satisfactions has admittedly led many economists to avoid discussion of them and to give a more limited factual definition of welfare in terms of quantities of goods produced and the character of their distribution. But this raises a different question, viz. that of our capacity to gain knowledge about the states of mind of others.

empirical facts of certain kinds does not exhaust our meaning. When people say, for example, that liberty is a good thing, or that men ought all to be treated equally, it seems that they usually claim to be saying something about liberty and equality, not merely approving of them or recommending them. Furthermore they are not happy about the suggestion that they are really making statements about wants or codes or trends. They appear, in other words, to be claiming to state facts, but facts of a peculiar kind. If asked for evidence, they may be puzzled, but they will not appeal to empirical evidence. Philosophers have come to their assistance by speaking of 'intuition' or 'the light of reason'.

It may be that all such claims are mistaken and that there are no such indefinable ethical features to be discovered. But supposing that there are and supposing that there is some non-empirical way in which they can be discovered, we must ask how this affects the scientific view that considerations of value do not affect the study of the facts.

It will be clear that in this case the answer is not as straightforward as it was in the previous ones. For on the one hand value-statements are not here absorbed as a species of factual statement, and on the other, since both kinds are accepted as genuine statements, it ceases to be logically impossible to deduce statements of the one kind from those of the other. It is true that where we have merely factual premises we will never be able to deduce a value-conclusion. But from two value-premises it is perfectly possible to deduce a factual conclusion, as long as the value term is the middle term common to the two premises. Thus from the statements that liberty is good and that the good will triumph, we may infer the statement that liberty will triumph. If the premises can be established independently of the conclusion, we would arrive in this way at what is clearly a very important assertion about human affairs.[1]

This illustration may seem unduly grandiose. But the same logical point may be illustrated more realistically if we consider the crucial case of the effect of moral beliefs on action.

We have seen that when a person believes that some state of affairs would be good or that something ought to be done, this may have to be taken account of, along with his factual beliefs, in giving an explanation of his action. In the case of factual beliefs, we have also seen that where a belief is formed as a result of taking into account the evidence in favour of it, the character of the evidence will in some degree determine the character of the action.[2] The time has now come to consider whether the same point may not be made for the case of moral beliefs.

[1] For a precise statement of these logical points, see C. D. Broad's discussion of the 'Ethical Arguments for Human Survival' in *The Mind and its Place in Nature*, Ch. 11, pp. 482–491. (Kegan Paul, French and Trubner, 1925).

[2] See pp. 39–40, 43–46.

In this case we would not normally speak of evidence. Nevertheless, if goodness is a feature of certain states of affairs, and there is some way of ascertaining whether it is present or not, it is clear that we must distinguish between those who recognize its presence and those who do not. If the recognition is regarded as the work of reason, we may speak, as with factual beliefs, of those whose moral beliefs, and consequent actions, are rational, and those whose moral beliefs and consequent actions are irrational. Where an action is in this sense rational—that is, where it results from the recognition that a state of affairs is good, it can be argued that it is not possible to explain it entirely in terms of the facts of the person's character and circumstances, or of the facts he takes account of in estimating means to ends. We will need also, it appears, to refer to what is good. Given that certain other conditions are present—in particular that the person in question desires to do what is good and that this desire is stronger than his other motives—it will be the value of the states of affairs he envisages which will determine his action.

It is in this way, it may be suggested, that ideals such as liberty have become operative in human history. There have been some people who have seen that liberty is good, and seeking to promote good, have fought for it. The possibility of giving this type of explanation of men's actions clearly presupposes an ability to infer factual conclusions from value premises. Stated schematically the value premises in this case would be, first, that liberty is good, and second, that the good is what certain types of men in certain situations seek to promote.

To have to admit the possibility of this type of explanation is extremely awkward for the social enquirer. For it faces him with the need to decide between those cases where people do really recognize what is good and those where they do not. As is well known, what people have thought to be good has varied greatly from age to age and place to place. Some have been impressed with the value of liberty, for example, others with the value of social harmony. Where such ideals are inconsistent someone must be misguided in his judgment, and the question is who? That there is difficulty in deciding such ethical questions is bad enough in itself. But the position becomes worse if we have to admit that the kind of explanation we give of a person's action depends on whether his judgment of value is correct or incorrect.

We could of course avoid this difficulty if we were to resort to one or other of two quite plausible alternatives. In the first place we could deny that there are any indefinable ethical features of actions or states of affairs. We would then have to say that in so far as people do really use ethical words to indicate such features, they are mistaken, and are assuming the existence of something which is not there. This would be drastic, and the more usual course is to deny that ethical words are ever in fact used in this way. But whichever course were adopted, we would be enabled to treat the expressive and the naturalistic uses of ethical words as the sole relevant ones, and to discuss the relation of value-statements to fact-statements in these terms.

In the second place, however, we might deny not the existence of the ethical features but their relevance for the explanation of human actions. We could do this if we asserted that people's actions are in fact, whatever they may say, always uninfluenced by their moral beliefs—that is, that they never perform any actions because they think them right but only in the pursuit of various ends which they happen to desire. Or we could do it if, without denying the efficacy of moral beliefs, we asserted that these beliefs are in fact never arrived at as a result of recognizing what is good, but can be explained entirely in terms of the psychological condition and social circumstances of the person who has them.

It would seem undesirable for a social enquirer to adopt either of these alternatives in a dogmatic way. If he adopts the first, he puts himself in the position of taking sides in an important issue about the nature of ethical enquiry. And it would be strange if the procedure of separating social enquiry from ethical enquiry had to depend on the reaching of a conclusion on this issue. If he adopts the second, he puts himself in the position of making sweeping statements of fact about the existence of moral motives and the origins of moral beliefs. These are, moreover, statements to which he is not likely to adhere consistently. When it comes to his own actions he is likely to assume that he sometimes recognizes what is the best thing to do and acts accordingly. If he assumes this for himself, he can hardly deny it in principle for those whose actions are the subject of his enquiry.

Here then is a point on which it is as well for social enquirers to keep an open mind. It may be that in certain special circumstances it will be impossible for them to achieve a full understanding of social events without entering into the non-factual consideration of the values which different sorts of states of affairs possess.

At the same time this can make little difference in practice, and it is on the ground of what is possible in practice that the scientific procedure can here be defended. In view of the diversity of beliefs about what is good or what is right, there is insuperable difficulty in deciding whether someone's belief arises from his recognition of what is good or in some other way which is susceptible of factual explanation. As a human being, the social enquirer will undoubtedly have his own views about what is worth while. He may, for example, maintain that liberty is something which should be fought for. But when he examines any historical struggle for liberty it will be impossible for him to tell whether the participants in that struggle acted as they did because they saw that liberty had that value, or whether their belief in its value could be explained in terms of other social facts. It will therefore be a reasonable policy for him to pursue his study of the facts as far as it will go, and not to cloak his inevitable ignorance on this particular feature of human motivation by the arbitrary attribution of moral insights to the people whose actions he is studying.

We conclude then that in whatever way ethical words are used the autonomy of factual social enquiry can be defended. It can be defended most easily and forcefully where they are used expressively. Those who insist on a sharp separation between factual and ethical questions do in fact generally do so on the ground that there is in the last resort no logical connection between stating facts and advocating policies. But it can also be defended where ethical words are used to make assertions, whether of the ordinary factual or peculiarly ethical kind. For in the one case the ethical questions are simply absorbed into the factual, and in the other it is always possible in practice, if not in principle, for the social enquirer to ignore them.

CONFUSION BETWEEN SOCIAL AND ETHICAL ENQUIRIES

Even though we have shown the separation of social from ethical enquiries to be less tidy than some have thought, there is nevertheless a very good reason for insisting on a clear-cut account of the possible relations between them. For there has been an inveterate tendency in the history of social thought to bridge the gap between ethical and factual questions in ways which could not be countenanced on any interpretation of ethical words. Those who insist on a social enquiry which is value-free are in fact mainly concerned to combat this tendency.

Shifts in the Use of Ethical and Factual Words

The tendency to confuse ethical with factual questions is to a large extent the outcome of a simple failure to make clear which sort of question is being discussed. The reason for this failure is not hard to discern. Questions of social fact and of social value have always been very closely associated in people's minds. As we have pointed out, it is primarily the facts of social life which have value words applied to them. And it is in questions of value that people have been primarily interested. Hence it is almost impossible, in our discussion of the facts, to avoid the intrusion of questions of the ethical kind. In itself there is, of course, no harm in this. But where the distinction is not clearly made, it is very easy to slide imperceptibly from statements of the one kind to statements of the other. A few illustrations must suffice.

(a) 'Good' and 'Welfare'

The very complexity which we have noticed in the use of ethical words itself invites confusion of this kind. Where the word 'good', for example, is used in a naturalistic way, it has a perfectly acceptable place within the context of a factual social enquiry. Thus, where political writers have spoken of the good of an individual and contrasted it with the common good, it has often seemed quite clear that they have been discussing interests. The issue has been what people want, or at any rate what they would want if they were sufficiently far-sighted and well-informed. And yet, once the word 'good' is used it is almost impossible to exclude the expressing of attitudes or the attribution to the state of affairs in which interests are satisfied of some irreducible ethical quality. There are thus introduced into what purports to be a factual enquiry ethical issues of a kind which have no place in it at all.

What applies to the word 'good' applies also to 'welfare'.

An economist who speaks of welfare may decide to identify it with the satisfaction of wants or with real income or with some other more precisely defined condition of the social system. In doing this, he may hope to exclude from his economic analysis all ethical considerations which cannot be interpreted in a factual way. But when he has found that something increases welfare, it is very likely that he will take this as meaning that it ought to be done, in some sense of 'ought to be done' which is not equivalent to 'increases satisfaction' or 'increases real income'. And yet this is not the sort of conclusion which can be established by a merely factual social enquiry.[1]

Confusion of this kind, however, is not due merely to uncertainty about whether or not ethical words are being used naturalistically. It is due also to uncertainty about whether certain words are being given a factual use or some kind of ethical one—an uncertainty which remains whether the ethical use is in its turn naturalistic or not.

(b) 'End' and 'Function'

In this category we may put, first, words like 'end' and 'function'. We have already noted a dangerous ambiguity in the use of the word 'end'.[2] It may be used either for what someone *does* bring about or for what he *intends* to bring about. We must now bring out the point that it may also be used for what someone *should* bring about. The end of social life, it has been said, is the promotion of the common good;[3] or again, the end of civil government is the preservation of the lives, liberties and estates of citizens.[4] Those who have said such things have not always made it clear whether they were giving purposive explanations of the facts of society and government, or stating what should be promoted by those concerned. These are clearly very different things, and constitute parts of a social and of an ethical enquiry respectively.

---

[1] See I. M. D. Little—*Welfare Economics* (Oxford, 1950) Ch. 5, for the view that the welfare terminology is a value terminology in the recommendatory sense.

[2] P. 37.

[3] See e.g. Thomas Aquinas—*De Regimine Principum*, Ch. 1.

[4] See John Locke—*Second Essay on Civil Government* Ch. 9, Sects. 123-4.

Some assistance is given towards recognizing the distinction when the end that should be promoted is referred to as the 'true' end, and hence opposed, at any rate by implication, to actual ends. But this has not helped greatly to remove the obscurity which confusions of this kind have brought about in writings on politics.

Similarly, when some social institution is said to have a certain function, this may mean either the function which it actually fulfils or the function which it should fulfil—its proper or 'true' function. To have a function, we have pointed out,[1] is to contribute towards the bringing about of a state of affairs which has already been singled out and called an end. If we take as the end what should be brought about, the corresponding use of the word 'function' will be ethical. If we take as the end a state of affairs which has certain factual characteristics, the corresponding use of 'function' will be factual. When it is said by economists, for example, that the function of speculation is to iron out movements in commodity prices, this may be taken as a statement about the results which on the whole follow from the actions of speculators. But it may also be taken to imply that these results are desirable in which case any speculation which has the reverse effect may be condemned as not fulfilling its proper function.[2]

(c) 'Ideal' and 'Value'

A crucial case of the same kind of confusion is to be found in the use of the words 'ideal' and 'value'. In this case the confusion is not, as in the case of 'end', between what is desirable and what is desired; it is rather between what is desirable and what is regarded as desirable.

It has already been made clear that the fact that someone holds a moral belief or adopts a moral attitude is itself a social fact like any other. The questions what people *regard* as good and what they *think* they ought to do are social questions and must be firmly distinguished from the ethical questions what *is* good and what they *ought* to do. If the latter are interpreted in a certain way, we have suggested, the answers to them may, at least in principle, be relevant for answering the former. But even to appreciate this point it is essential that we do not confuse the one with the other.

The trouble with the word 'ideal' is that it makes this confusion easy. When we speak of a person's ideals, we may be taken to be referring only to the fact that he holds certain states of affairs, as yet unrealized, to be good and worthy of realization. Whether they *are* good is, in this context, beside the point. The extent of the influence of ideals on people's actions may be discussed as a factual question in these

[1] Pp. 37–38.

[2] For this and other economic illustrations of this confusion, see Ronald H. Barback—*Economics and Moral Judgments* in the Australasian Journal of Philosophy, Vol. 32, pp. 40–41.

terms. But an ideal may also be taken to be an unrealized state of affairs which *is* good. And to discuss the influence of ideals, in this sense, on actions is to raise the different and much more puzzling question of the relation of ethical and factual statements which we considered earlier in this chapter. It is most important that the distinction between these sorts of question should be kept clear. There are some who in making statements about the former have given the impression that they were making statements about the latter.[1]

What is said here of 'ideals' applies also to 'values'. When we speak of a person's values, we commonly mean what he *regards* as having value, but may fail to notice that this is different from what *has* value. In this case, admittedly, what has value may be referred to as valuable, and this suggests a distinction between the valuable and the valued, parallel to that between the desirable and the desired. But the use of the noun 'value' remains as a source of confusion.[2]

(d) 'Norm' and 'Law'

Finally there is the confusion which arises when people speak about 'norms' and about 'law'. Ethical enquiries have sometimes been called normative, and distinguished thereby from factual enquiries which have been called positive. Norms have thus been identified with ideals, in the ethical sense, or with standards of right conduct. And yet the word 'norm' has often been used more broadly to indicate standards which are not specifically ethical in character. In particular it has been used for the standard embodied in any existing code of laws in a community. Laws are not always obeyed; hence we may say that they are not so much something to which people in fact conform, as something to which they are required to conform. Thus, as well as a positive study of the operation and the effects of the enforcement of law, there can also be a normative study of law as a system of rules and of the relation between these rules. But though questions of law may be distinguished in this way from questions of fact, they are in no sense ethical in character.[3] They form part, though a somewhat special part, of a factual social enquiry, and we should not be misled by the use of the word 'norm' into putting them into the same class as ethical questions.

The tendency to confuse the legal and the ethical is enhanced by the fact that the word 'law' is sometimes in its turn used in an extended

---

[1] See A. D. Lindsay—*The Modern Democratic State* (Oxford, 1943) Ch. 1, pp. 37–38, for a discussion of 'operative ideals' in which these questions do not appear to be kept clear.

[2] Note that in the use of the word 'ideal' there lurk further ambiguities. (*a*) It may be used merely for the unrealized, without reference to what is good. (*b*) It may be used for the perfect—the 'ideal type' or standard, by which we can grade things in some respect, whether that respect be goodness or anything else.

[3] Unless, of course, ethical words (like the word 'justice', for example) are in their turn defined naturalistically in terms of the existing law.

sense. In making laws, those who exercise political power may be said to be prescribing rules of conduct—stating in general what people are to do. Where these rules are criticized, appeal is made to other rules of conduct—ethical rules about what people ought to do or ought to be allowed to do. It is very easy to regard this as an appeal from a lower to a higher law—from political to moral law, or from positive to natural law. What is in accordance with moral or natural law is of course an ethical question, but because of the twofold use of the word 'law', it is made to appear like a higher-order legal question. The danger of confusion is increased still further when 'law' comes to be defined entirely in ethical terms, and the political rules of any community only called laws in so far as they satisfy ethical requirements such as conformity to natural law. This has been done quite generally throughout the history of political theory.[1]

Factual Support for Ethical Statements

The illustrations we have given of the interconnection between the factual and ethical uses of words show how easy it is to confuse one with the other. But even when the required distinctions are clearly made, there may still be confusion of another kind. This is the confusion which arises when we seek to support ethical statements by an appeal to facts.

Where ethical words are used in an exclusively naturalistic way, such an appeal is of course perfectly legitimate. But in other cases it is not. And yet it is precisely in these other cases that we feel difficulty about how our ethical statements are to be supported. When we make recommendations, we wish to justify them, but we cannot justify a recommendation by producing evidence in its favour. We may of course produce evidence to show that our policy has certain consequences, but we are still left with the recommendation that we accept these consequences. Again when we claim something to be good, we wish to substantiate our claim in some way other than merely subsuming it under a more general claim of the same kind. In such circumstances there is a natural urge to support our conclusions by appealing fallaciously to factual premises. For here we have something for which, in theory at least, we are able to produce evidence.

Of this type of fallacious argument we will give two instances.

Actions and institutions are sometimes justified as being in accordance with human nature. When people speak of human nature, they clearly intend to refer to facts; they are thinking of the general way in which human beings are constituted. From their natures it follows that

---

[1] This use was made explicit long ago by Thomas Aquinas. See *Summa Theologica, Prima Secundae,* Qu. 93, Art. 3, reply to Objection 2. 'Human law has the nature of law in so far as it partakes of right reason' (Vol. 8, p. 32 of the Translation by the Fathers of the English Dominican Province).

they have certain needs, and existing social arrangements or activities may or may not contribute to the fulfilment of these needs. If they do so, the tendency is to infer from this fact that they are good, while what prevents their fulfilment, being unnatural, is correspondingly condemned as bad. Thus it is that social co-operation has been approved of on the ground that man is by nature a social animal,[1] and the limitation of the powers of governments insisted upon on the ground that man is by nature free.[2]

The second fallacious argument which we will mention is that implied in the appeal to history. In order to justify actions or institutions, it is sometimes assumed to be sufficient to point out that they are in line with the general course of historical development. As in the parallel case of the appeal to nature, history does not here include everything that happens—for if it did the appeal to history would justify everything. What is appealed to is rather the general order which occurs in history, and many social changes may not conform to this order. It is easy to think of the general course of history as a movement forward, or an advance. When this is done, we may be led to suppose that the way to justify anything is to show that it is part of this advance, and the way to condemn it is to show that it is an attempt to put the clock back, and return to what human beings have grown beyond.[3]

It will be clear that any argument of this kind depends on the surreptitious use of an ethical principle. In the appeal to human nature, it is assumed that the fulfilment of needs is a good thing. In the appeal to history it is assumed that what comes later in time is in general better than what comes earlier. Such assumptions may be defended, but they can be defended only in the same way as other ethical statements. We must avoid the mistake of supposing that such a defence is unnecessary and that the establishing of certain statements of fact about social life will do instead.

It may be that some of those who have made these appeals to nature and to history have intended to define their ethical words naturalistically in terms of the fulfilment of needs, or of social trends. If so, the confusion resolves itself into one which arises from failure to adhere strictly to this use. Again, in the appeal to human nature, the word nature may at times be given an ethical rather than a factual use—a man's nature being that which is good in him—his 'true nature'. If so,

[1] The phrase is Aristotle's, and the type of argument a common one among those who follow him. Cf. for example Thomas Aquinas—*Summa Theologica* I, Qu. 96, Art. 4.

[2] See Locke—*Second Essay on Civil Government*. The 'appeal to nature' has often taken a more comprehensive form, 'nature' being identified not merely with the general way in which human beings are constituted, but with the general way in which the world as a whole is constituted.

[3] This type of argument is implicit, for example, in the writings of many Marxists, though by no means restricted to these.

the confusion becomes one which arises from a shift between factual and ethical uses of a word. It may in fact be impossible to find a pure case of ethical conclusions being supported deliberately and self-consciously by an appeal to facts. But confusions, from their very nature, are not easy to distinguish sharply from one another.

Our purpose in pointing out these confusions has been primarily to make sure that the relation between factual and ethical questions is seen in its true light. Their presence makes much easier the acceptance of the anti-scientific view that the facts of social life cannot be studied by themselves, and to point them out is to remove some support which that view has improperly acquired.

It may be suggested that it also serves the secondary and more practical purpose of encouraging social enquirers to avoid them. Where such encouragement is needed, however, it is doubtful whether it would have much effect. The very persistence of confusions of this kind should warn anyone against overconfidence. Such confusions are often firmly rooted, if not in personal prejudices, then at least in the structure of our language and prevailing habits of thought. They bring up, in fact, in quite a sharp way the problem of objectivity in social enquiry.

VII

THE DENIAL OF OBJECTIVITY

THE straightforward way to criticize a statement is to assert that there is insufficient evidence in its favour. If someone tells me in good faith that the reason why the Prime Minister spoke of reducing taxation was that there was an election coming, I may deny this on the ground that the Government had consistently had a low-taxation policy irrespective of elections, and that there was no evidence that the Prime Minister was doing more than giving expression to this.

I might, however, argue in a less direct way. I might point out that, although he believed what he said, the man who made this statement about the Prime Minister was a man of bad judgment, apt to jump to conclusions without sufficient evidence. Or, without doubting his capacity to draw the right conclusion from the evidence at his disposal, I might point out that he did not have some important evidence at his disposal. Or, finally, without questioning his capacity or his access to evidence, I might say that his statement should be discounted because of his anti-Government sympathies or because he was predisposed by his background to be cynical about politicians.

All these arguments are forms of what has traditionally been called *argumentum ad hominem*. In each case a conclusion is drawn concerning the truth of a statement not by referring to evidence directly for or against the statement, but by referring to evidence about the intelligence, information, interests, character or circumstances of the man who makes it. It is the type of argument we use whenever we challenge anyone's assertion on the ground that he is stupid or that he is not an expert in his subject, or that he has an axe to grind. We have suggested three forms which it may take. To put them briefly: we may say of someone who makes a statement either that he is lacking in intelligence, or that he is lacking in access to evidence, or that he is lacking in objectivity.

It is with the third of these forms of the argument that we are here concerned. We are concerned with it not as it is directed against particular statements or theories made or maintained by particular people, but rather as it is directed against the whole body of statements which are made in the course of a social enquiry. There is no reason to suppose that social enquirers are less intelligent than others. Whether they are inherently lacking in evidence is something we have already considered. But it has been argued that they are of necessity less objective than other enquirers, and this is a charge with which we have yet to deal.

In the conduct of any enquiry there are always occasions when people fail to be objective. A physicist or a biologist, for example, may cling to a theory because his prestige is bound up with it, or because it is the official theory. But it is often held that social enquirers, because of the very nature of their subject-matter, are affected by lack of objectivity in a much more wholesale way than natural scientists. They themselves are human beings who live in societies, and hence have social interests, participate in social movements and accept certain ways of life. Hence, it is suggested, we should expect that their theories will be influenced by their interests, by their position in society, or by the characteristics of the age in which they live. This being so, it is argued that we should discount the claim of any such theories to be true, and should interest ourselves rather in how it comes about that different theories are held by people in different circumstances and at different times.

Objectivity, it will be recalled, is the fifth of the features we have set down as characterizing a scientific procedure. In an important respect it is different from those which we have so far considered. In the previous cases, no one would wish to deny that it is *possible* to proceed in the scientific way. Those who maintain the anti-scientific view recognize that social enquirers if they wish to do so can abstract, generalize, rely on empirical evidence, and keep to facts. What they do is to criticize such ways of proceeding as ineffective, not deny that they are possible. But in the case of objectivity the position is reversed. They do not wish to criticize a procedure in which objectivity is maintained— they wish rather to deny that it is possible. They recognize that it is desirable for social enquirers to take account of evidence, but they assert that the general circumstances of a social enquiry are such as to prevent even the most intelligent from using the evidence at their disposal.

THE RELEVANCE OF THE DENIAL

A short way of meeting this challenge would be to say that it is irrelevant for anyone who is concerned with the *logic* of social enquiry. The view that it is irrelevant is not often stated, but it is frequently assumed, and it is as well for us to make it explicit. For if it were true we could not regard the denial that social enquirers are objective as an anti-scientific view, and there would be no need to discuss it further.

The view can be presented most simply by pointing out that to ask how a person comes to hold a belief is one thing and to ask whether there is sufficient evidence for it is another. The question whether some-one is being objective is a question of the first kind. To hold a belief is to have a disposition to make statements on various occasions which, as we say, 'express' it, and to claim these statements to be true. To ask whether social enquirers are objective is to ask how they come to acquire such dispositions. This is a causal question and one which should be sharply distinguished from the logical question about how their beliefs can be established.

It is important that this distinction should be made, and confusion often arises from ignoring it. But once it is made, it is very easy to take a further step and maintain that the causal and the logical questions are not only distinct but independent. Thus people are led into saying that it does not matter how social enquirers have come to hold the views they do, for this can have nothing to do with the way in which these views can be established. The study of the causes of beliefs, including the beliefs held by social enquirers, is admitted to be an undoubtedly interesting branch of social enquiry. But, it is said, the only proper way to challenge the beliefs themselves is to deny that there is sufficient evidence in their favour; to deny the objectivity of those who hold them is, from this point of view, interesting gossip and no more.

It seems obvious to common sense that there is a mistake here. If we have established that someone has really taken account of the evidence before making a statement, we can point to this fact as evidence in favour of what he says even though we have not investigated the matter for ourselves.[1] We have reason to respect the beliefs of those whom we know to have thought about a question and whom we know to have been objective in their treatment of it. If an economist, for example, who we have reason to believe has been both intelligent and objective in his approach to the evidence, asserts that higher taxation is necessary to curb inflation, we would be foolish not to accept this as *some* evidence in favour of this statement being true.

If we now ask why it is that a statement about the cause of a belief can be taken as evidence in favour of that belief, we will see that it is due to a simple but peculiar fact about beliefs to which we have already referred in discussing the explanation of actions.[2] Beliefs are peculiar in that the evidence for them may also be part of their cause. This is the case whenever the person who acquires the belief takes account to a greater or lesser extent of the evidence. Beliefs so formed we called rational beliefs, recognizing of course that the rationality of a belief is always a matter of degree. In the case of such rational beliefs the evi-

---

[1] How we can establish this fact is a further question. Difficulties in the way of establishing it, which we will refer to later (p. 84 et. seq.) in no way affect the force of the present argument, in which it is supposed that it is established.

[2] See pp. 43–45

dence has, as it were, a dual role. It is not only what justifies us in accepting the belief, it also determines the character of the belief of anyone who takes account of it. It follows from this that if we can be sure that someone *has* taken account of it, we can use this fact about the cause of the belief as an argument in its favour. This is the point which is missed by those who regard questions about the causes of beliefs as logically irrelevant.

It is true that we are concerned at this point only with the converse form of this argument—one which is based not on the assertion of objectivity, but on its denial. And this, though it is quite as often used, has admittedly less force. If we know that a person is lacking in objectivity and has therefore *not* taken account of the evidence, all we can do is discount the claim to truth implied in his belief. In doing this, we are not producing any evidence against the belief. But we are at least showing that in the absence of any further evidence which we can acquire for ourselves, there is no evidence for it. Thus if someone puts forward a theory and appears to present evidence for it, it is relevant to challenge it by claiming that he is biased or that he is in some way adversely influenced by his circumstances. For if this is true, it follows that despite appearances he has not taken account of the evidence in propounding the theory.

In the case of particular theories, this procedure of 'debunking' does not take one very far, since it is always open to anyone to consider the evidence on its merits. But when it is made to apply to all social theories it becomes much more effective. For in this case it ceases to be possible for anyone to consider the evidence for any theory on its merits. If anyone appears to do so, it can always be pointed out that he, like everyone else, can be charged with lack of objectivity. The beliefs of at least some people must result from their taking account of evidence before social enquiry can occur at all. Those who assert the irrelevance of the question about the causes of beliefs fail to see this only because they surreptitiously set themselves apart from all other social enquirers and assume their own beliefs to be exempt.

It must be admitted, then, that it is relevant to consider how social enquirers come to hold their beliefs, and that the challenge to their objectivity is one which cannot be by-passed but has to be met. In recognizing this we must of course avoid assuming that the success of the challenge is a foregone conclusion. Explaining a belief and debunking it are not the same thing. People have sometimes found it easy to assume that they are because they have forgotten that explanations of beliefs, unlike other explanations, *may* be in terms of the evidence for them.[1] What we have to decide is the extent to which this is in fact the case where social enquirers are concerned.

[1] See p. 44.

76

THE DENIAL OF OBJECTIVITY
INFLUENCES AFFECTING BELIEFS

Since the challenge to the objectivity of social enquirers cannot be dismissed as irrelevant nor yet upheld on *a priori* grounds, we must go on to consider it in more detail. First, we must consider more precisely what those circumstances are which may prevent social enquirers from taking account of the evidence at their disposal.

We are assuming here that social enquirers in general are sufficiently intelligent to take account of evidence. No one, of course, is perfect in respect of intellectual capacity, and for this reason alone enquirers are liable in a greater or a lesser degree to fall into error. Some are better than others at noticing or searching out the relevant facts and judging when they are sufficient to establish the conclusion. And in so far as people fail in this, they cannot be said to take account of the evidence at their disposal.[1] But in discussing objectivity we are not concerned—except in one case incidentally—with this type of deficiency. We are concerned rather with those adverse influences which may affect the beliefs even of those who have no special lack of intellectual capacity.

These influences we may sum up as the adverse influence of one's motives, of custom and of one's social situation. It is when a person's beliefs are subject to these influences that we speak of him as lacking objectivity. Objectivity, in the sense in which we are discussing it here, is thus to be defined negatively. To be objective in the conduct of an enquiry is *not* to have one's beliefs influenced adversely by one's motives, by custom, or by one's social situation. Objectivity in itself will not ensure that a person holds rational beliefs. He may be objective and still not take account of the evidence at his disposal, since for this intelligence is also required. But failure in objectivity—that is, the presence of the influences mentioned—is something which will prevent him holding rational beliefs, however intelligent he may be.

The Influence of Motives

Having some end in view, when conducting an enquiry, is clearly in itself in no way inconsistent with taking account of relevant facts and accepting the conclusion to which they point. It may be said in fact that the normal case is that in which our motives predispose us to do this. For in order to achieve our ends, whatever they may be, it is usually necessary to find out as much as we can about the means of achieving them, and this involves taking account to the best of our ability of the evidence about the means. In short, it generally *pays* to be objective.

[1] It would be interesting to consider, in the case of this kind of failure, what it is that leads to one belief being held rather than another. It is commonly assumed that in this case the particular error committed can be accounted for in terms of incidental circumstances which vary with the occasion. If, however, we were to follow up the suggestion of Freud about the causes of error, (see *Introductory Lectures on Psycho-Analysis*, Chs. 2 to 4) we might find the same type of influences operating here as in the case where the control of the evidence over belief is not weakened by intellectual incapacity.

And yet we know very well that motives do sometimes affect beliefs adversely. At times they lead us to adopt beliefs without considering evidence at all, in which case we normally speak of prejudice; and at times they lead us to make a defective estimate of the evidence, giving reasons for our beliefs but not good reasons, in which case we normally speak of bias.[1] How is it that these effects occur?

The answer to this is that we gain satisfaction not only from actual achievement, but also from imagined achievement. In this respect, prejudice and bias are like fantasy—they are the result of a tendency to avoid facing realities—to believe what it is comforting to believe even though it is of no further practical value.

When our motives predispose us in this way to believe without good evidence, we are, of course, never aware that this is so. No one is irrational enough to accept a conclusion when he has been brought to realize that there is not sufficient evidence in its favour. Thus prejudice and bias survive only so long as they escape detection. Mere prejudice is especially vulnerable in this respect; a request for evidence can in this case be met only by dogmatic reassertion. This is why prejudice will always tend to be converted into bias by a process of rationalization. Some reasons will be given, and so long as the standard of sufficiency for evidence is not clear-cut, it will be relatively easy to believe that the reasons given are sufficient. We may thus defend our beliefs almost indefinitely without slipping over into dishonesty.

The Influence of Custom

There are many cases of irrational belief in which it would be a mistake to look for a motive—even the motive of avoiding social disapproval. At any time there is a large stock of beliefs which are commonly held and which any individual simply takes over. Where this occurs, there is clearly no question of his considering the evidence for his beliefs. In this respect such beliefs resemble prejudices, and in fact they are often classified as such. But they differ in that in the absence of a motive there is not the same resistance to the invitation to consider the evidence. And when the evidence is considered, there is not the same reason for regarding this as rationalization and for expecting the conclusion to be biased.

This being so, it might be thought that these customary beliefs would be easily eliminated, at any rate by anyone who was conducting a

[1] The word 'prejudice' is often used to cover both these types of effect and sometimes even more broadly, to cover the influence of custom as well. G. C. Field, for example, in *Prejudice and Impartiality* (Methuen, 1932) includes bias under prejudice in Chs. 1 and 2, and extends the use of 'prejudice' in Ch. 4, to include the effects of habit.

Note that prejudice and bias, in our sense, should both be distinguished from dishonesty. Though there is often a very narrow borderline between 'self-deception' and deception of others, the practice of the latter has nothing to do with social enquiry.

systematic enquiry in any subject. This, however, is by no means the case. At any time there are many habits of thought which, simply because they are generally accepted, are not easy to detect. The beliefs which they imply are presupposed in the sorts of questions we ask and the ways in which we answer them. Furthermore, they are often presupposed in the very structure of the language which we learn as we grow up.

But however much emphasis is placed on the influence of custom, we have to recognize that it is never by itself enough to account for the presence of any set of beliefs. For customs must themselves be accounted for. If we ask how one set of beliefs and not another comes to be generally accepted, we have to fall back at one stage or another on a reference to other factors. We may say for example that the existing stock of beliefs, though unreflectively held, is nevertheless rational in origin, since it has arisen through various people, in the course of time, having either in a systematic or in a piecemeal trial-and-error way taken account of the evidence.[1] Or we may say that these beliefs have arisen at one time or another from the distorting motives of at least some members of society. Or, again, we may refer to a type of influence which we have still to discuss—that of the social situation.

The Influence of the Social Situation

Those who speak of the social determination of beliefs rarely make clear how it is that a person's social situation—the social class to which he belongs, for example, or the historical period in which he lives— affects the beliefs which he adopts.[2] To speak, as has often been done, of beliefs being a reflection of social conditions, or an outgrowth from them, or a superstructure based upon them, is to use metaphors without taking the matter further. When we ask how this effect takes place, we come to realize that this type of explanation is in many cases not an alternative to the ones already mentioned, but a supplement to them.

There are in fact cases where the effect of the social situation is in no way inconsistent with objectivity. For all it may do is to impose limits on the availability of evidence. People's views change as with changing circumstances new information comes to light. But this does not mean

[1] This is the explanation we commonly adopt in the case of the accepted beliefs of the natural sciences. In the case of social beliefs it was eloquently expressed, for example, by Edmund Burke when he defended the prejudices of Englishmen as enshrining the wisdom of the ages. See his *Reflections on the French Revolution*.

[2] It is not made clear, for example, by Marx, or by those who, like Karl Manheim, have pursued an enquiry into the social origins of beliefs under the name of the 'sociology of knowledge'. For an examination of Mannheim's statements on the matter, see R. K. Merton—*Social Theory and Social Structure* (Glencoe Free Press Illinois, 1949) Ch. 9, pp. 254–258.

either that their earlier or their later views are unreasonable ones to hold given the evidence at their disposal.[1]

In other cases an effect adverse to objectivity is produced when a person's situation gives rise to certain interests, and in this way to prejudice or bias. The influence here is in the first instance that of motives, and to refer to the social origins of the beliefs in question is to explain how the motives have arisen.

There are also cases, however, where an effect adverse to objectivity arises in another way, without any interests being involved. There is a common form of intellectual error which consists in placing undue weight on evidence which is near at hand. And the evidence which is near at hand varies with a person's social situation. What happens in our immediate environment is what catches our attention, and it is easy to conclude without sufficient evidence that it happens generally. Hence it may come about that different social theories, each of unrestricted generality, may be held by people living under different social conditions, and it is not unreasonable to speak of such theories as 'reflecting' the social conditions in which they arise. In this case, it is true, a degree of intellectual incapacity is presupposed. If people were clever enough, the distorting effect of a social point of view would not arise. But people are not normally as clever as that—hence an effect on the weight they give to items of evidence which is in many ways parallel to the bias of motives.

There is no guarantee that this account of the possible adverse influences on beliefs is a comprehensive one. But it seems to cover those influences which people normally have in mind when they discuss a person's objectivity. Are they such as to render objective social enquiry impossible?

THE ESTIMATION OF OBJECTIVITY

If we consider these influences we will realize at once that objectivity is a matter of degree, and hence that no cut-and-dried answer can be given to our question. No one doubts that each kind of influence has some effect on the beliefs of social enquirers. What is meant by those who deny objectivity to them can therefore only be that the influences are so great as to prevent quite generally the achievement of worthwhile results. And all that can be done to refute them is to point out that the influences have been over-estimated. The onus is on the critic to establish his case, and it will be sufficient if it is shown that he fails to do so.

We may approach the estimation of objectivity in two ways. We may ask in general terms what effect the general circumstances of social

[1] I neglect here the point that is often made that social conditions affect the sort of questions people ask. We are concerned not with differences which the social situation makes in the subject-matter of enquiry but rather with the differences it makes to the beliefs which are held about that subject-matter.

enquiry are likely to have on the objectivity of those pursuing it. Or we may start with particular social theories, ask what influences have contributed to their acceptance, and attempt to generalize from this. If we follow these two lines of approach in turn, we will see that the general considerations against objectivity are either irrelevant or inconclusive, and that attempts to back them up by reference to particular theories are either unreliable or self-defeating.

General Considerations

Some of the general considerations which have led people to doubt the possibility of objectivity in social enquiry may be dismissed at once as beside the point.

Thus, in the first place failure in objectivity is sometimes attributed to the simple fact that the social enquirer is himself a social being participating in social affairs. It is true that this is a fact which we must not ignore, but taken by itself it has no relevance for the present question. The biologist is himself an organism interacting with other organisms, and the physicist is a body of given mass and volume interacting with other bodies. We do not assume for this reason that the theories of biologists and physicists must be unduly subject to the influences of the biological or physical environment at the expense of the evidence. And we should no more assume that the interaction of the social enquirer with his social environment need in any way interfere with the rationality of his beliefs. No one is causally detached from the subject-matter he is investigating. If any particular causal relationship is alleged to have a damaging effect on an investigation, it must be pointed out in each case what this effect is.

In the second place, the influences we have enumerated have been assumed to be specially damaging for social enquirers because of their involvement in ethical questions. Those who regard social theories as socially determined ideologies have in fact always regarded them as incorporating statements about policies and ideals, and it is against these statements that their criticisms have been primarily directed. Whatever view is taken about ethical statements, it is admittedly much easier to account for them in terms of interests, traditions and social view-points than is the case with factual ones. But there is no reason for carrying such an account over from one kind of statement to the other simply because they often happen to be made in close connection by the same people.

In the third place, those who speak of the lack of detachment of social enquirers from their social environment generally point to the special strength of the interests and emotions which are centred round their relations with other people. But to do this is to forget that strong interests and emotions do not necessarily give rise to prejudice or bias. They only do so where satisfaction is gained by means of escaping from difficulties rather than overcoming them. The real issue therefore is not about strength of interests or intensity of feeling, it is whether such interests and feelings are liable to have a specially distorting effect on social beliefs.

It is at this point that we pass on to those considerations which *are* relevant. For in the first place, interests do easily involve us in prejudice and bias when we are dealing with social questions, and we may suggest a reason for it. It is that individuals do not generally find it easy to alter the course of events to their liking. Where there is a practical programme to be carried out, a realistic appraisal of means is essential. But where there is nothing effective which can be done, we can afford the luxury of prejudice. We may find consolation in different ways. We find it in a conservative way, for example, when we believe that what we want is more adequately realized in the existing state of affairs than is actually the case. And we find it in a radical way when we believe that what we want can be more easily achieved than is actually the case.

A complex but specially important case of this effect of powerlessness on belief arises from the fact that people frequently desire incompatible things. It may be that either of two ends can be achieved separately, but that there is insuperable difficulty in achieving them both together. Because of the multiplicity of social interests, these interests constitute a case in which this situation is specially likely to arise. Conflict of motives is peculiarly painful, and instead of facing the issue and rejecting one end in favour of the other, we may find relief in believing the state of affairs to be such that both can be realized at once.

It is this which explains the effect of 'vested interests' on beliefs. Those who possess wealth or power under an existing system are likely to wish to maintain it. But this in itself would in no way distort their views about how the system works or how it affects other members of the population. Where such views are distorted, it is because of the presence of other and incompatible motives such as a concern for their fellow-men who, let us suppose, can only be helped by changing the system. A simple way to avoid the conflict is for them to suppose that the system works not only for their own profit but for the welfare of all. In the same way it can be pointed out that it is the ruthless tyrant who is a realist, and the tyrant with a conscience who practises self-deception.

In the second place we have to admit that both social prejudices and custom-based beliefs may have their own peculiar form of survival values, irrespective of their truth. Despite what has been said earlier, social prejudice does sometimes pay. Those who are blind to difficulties develop an irrational faith in the success of their cause, and this may provide the very impetus which is needed to carry it through; whereas an unbiased appraisal of evidence may well provide just that discouragement which leads to failure. To the extent that this occurs, comforting beliefs cannot be eliminated, as they can in the natural sciences, through their failure to produce results in real life.

Similarly with beliefs which arise from custom. In this case it is not that they are a spur to action, it is rather that they ensure social cohesion. The acceptance of a common stock of beliefs, however irrational, has a stabilizing effect, and this makes them less susceptible to challenge.

Finally, we may point to the obvious fact that social beliefs are specially susceptible to the influence of point of view. In so far as social situations are more varied than physical ones, it will follow that the tendency to generalize from evidence which is near at hand will have more serious consequences. We must recognize the danger, therefore, that people belonging to different social classes or living in different periods will have their social theories subjected to a distorting effect not paralleled in the natural sciences.

Not only are these considerations relevant; they must also be admitted to apply generally. There is no reason to suppose that there are special circumstances in which the distorting factors do not operate. It has been suggested, for example, that the detached intellectual who has no special class position and participates in no social movement will be able to achieve an objectivity which others lack.[1] From this kind of detachment, however, there is no guarantee that the result will follow. Like everyone else, the intellectual has a special social situation which may distort his view of evidence. And he has his own social interests, ranging from the need to maintain his standard of living to his love of prestige and even his desire to preserve his detachment. Where the achievement of these ends is in conflict with his desire to find out the truth, the difficulty can be removed by a resort to orthodoxy. In this way the specialists in social enquiry may be said to be tied to their social roots just as firmly as others.

With such considerations before us, we may now ask what conclusions we can reasonably draw from them. It should be clear enough that they are insufficient to establish the general inability of social enquirers to base their conclusions on evidence. What is shown is that there are special dangers which beset social enquiry. But it is quite another thing to show that social enquirers generally succumb to them. The only way to show this would be to examine the origins of particular social theories and to point out the predominant influences of motive,

---

[1] This suggestion was made explicit by Mannheim—*Ideology and Utopia*, pp.137 ff. (English translation, Kegan Paul, 1936). Another, and less plausible, suggestion is found among Marxists who assign the privileged position to those theorists who adopt the point of view of the working-class, on the ground that these are the forerunners of a future free and classless society, in which the distorting effects of social interest and social situation disappear.

custom or social situation which have given rise to them. We are thus led on to consider the second line of approach in which tests are applied to particular cases.

Particular Tests

The trouble here is that there are no reliable tests which do not beg the question. It would be simple if we had merely to find out whether the person who holds the theory can produce any evidence for it. But this will not do for two reasons. In the first place, he may have arrived at his conclusions intuitively; that is, he may have taken account of evidence and yet be unable to set it out explicitly. And in the second place, even if he does produce evidence, he may still be biased. As we have pointed out, most people will find reasons for their beliefs when pressed.

One thing we can do is to see whether the theory which a person in fact holds is the one which he would hold if he were lacking in objectivity. We can see whether the theory he holds is one which would be consoling to a person with his interests, whether it is similar to theories currently held, whether it is one he would naturally be led to hold if he were to notice only those facts with which his situation immediately confronts him. If we notice further that the differences between theories correspond with differences in interests, customs or situations, this would give further support to the view that in each case they were dependent on these influences.

This kind of test has often been applied in the case of economic theory, and has been held to show its lack of objectivity. Classical economic theory, it has been said, clearly suited the interests of the employers, while opposed theories put forward by socialists suited the interests of the workers. Those whose own interests were not obviously involved tended to adhere to one or other of the rival orthodoxies, as one would expect if one took account of the effects of custom. Again classical economic theory is what one would expect from those presented with the capitalist economy of 19th century Britain, and post-Keynesian developments in economic theory are what one would expect from those who live in a period of partial state-control.

It must be remembered here, however, that a person's views may happen to coincide with his interests or with current beliefs or with his point of view, and yet they may in fact be based on a proper consideration of evidence. We must not suppose that a person's theories have to be heterodox or in conflict with his interests or unexpected for one in his circumstances before he can claim to be objective. What is required is an independent estimate of the extent to which he takes account of evidence, and this is what is so difficult to obtain.

Admittedly, the argument is more cogent where there are different views on the same question each of which could be explained in terms of adverse influences. This is not so much because tests applied in a number of cases are more effective than those applied only in one; the number of cases we are able to refer to in this sort of argument would hardly be enough to offset the weakness of each individual test. It is rather because the very fact of there being differences suggests lack of objectivity. It does so because we know that the more account is taken of evidence the more likely it is that an agreed conclusion will be arrived at by different people. The absence of an agreed conclusion is thus a sign that some at least of the persons concerned have not taken full account of the evidence.[1]

It is not a sign, however, that *no one* has taken account of the evidence. Where one person is prejudiced and another not, their views will differ in just the same way as if both were prejudiced. Where there are competing theories, it is well known that the upholders of each theory will charge their opponents with lack of objectivity, but they will claim themselves to be exempt. Pointing to the difference between the theories will not help us to refute this claim.

In the absence of reliable direct tests of objectivity, the usual thing is to fall back on a simple procedure which we have not so far mentioned. This is to ask whether the theory is or is not a reasonable one to hold. If someone puts forward a theory for which we recognize that there is insufficient evidence, and if we also know that he is unlikely to make mistakes through failure in intelligence, it will follow that it is his objectivity which is at fault. That this is a common way of arguing is brought out by the fact that we tend only to concern ourselves with objectivity in cases where we think people have made mistakes. Thus we may point to the deficiencies in classical economic theories and argue from this that their exponents must have been prejudiced or influenced by their special situation.[2]

The use of this kind of test, however, presupposes that we can consider the evidence for ourselves and that our own conclusions will be unbiased. It is therefore quite useless for establishing the lack of objectivity of social enquirers in general, since we ourselves must be included in this number. That this type of argument is a common one is a sign that we do not normally take the general challenge seriously enough to influence our conduct. If we did we would have to avoid the argument as circular.

[1] Even this is not an infallible sign, since there always *may* be two or more different and rival theories between which, on the evidence, there is nothing to choose.

[2] A good example of this method of argument is to be found in the treatment of economic theories by J. A. Hobson in Part II of his *Free Thought in the Social Sciences*. (George Allen & Unwin 1926). In illustrating the ubiquitiousness of bias Hobson explicitly assumes the role of the unbiassed scientist who asks how the various theorists came to make their mistakes.

THE CIRCULARITY OF THE DENIAL

It would seem then that we must dismiss as inconclusive all attempts to establish that there is a general failure of objectivity among social enquirers sufficient to render their enquiries futile. This being so, we might feel it unnecessary to take the matter further. But we cannot conclude without pointing out that those who make the attempt are in danger of succumbing to their own charge. For the investigation of the origins of social theories is itself a branch of social enquiry, and any theory which is put forward about the origins of theories must therefore apply to itself. The critic of objectivity is thus involved in a circularity which is more deep-rooted than the one we have just mentioned. So long as his own theories are not about the origin of social theories, he can afford to include them in his criticism, even if people in general tend not to follow this course. But in the case of his theory about the origin of theories he cannot afford to do this without involving himself in inconsistency. For if in the presenting of this theory, he is so influenced by interests and situation as to make the defence of it futile, he is not justified in presenting it at all.

To make this point, of course, does not help to establish the objectivity of social enquirers. It might still be the case that everyone was so subject to adverse influences as to make enquiry futile. The point is that if this were the case, no one could possibly establish it. The alternative to admitting objectivity is not denying it, but rather lapsing into a sceptical silence.

The only way to avoid this difficulty would be to assert that statements about the origins of theories form a special class by themselves and are therefore exempt from the general charge. It is true of course that theories about theories differ in their subject-matter from theories about other kinds of social facts. The theories of classical economics, for example, have to do with the economic relationships of men; the theory that the theories of classical economics arose from a desire to defend the existing system has to do with certain of the economists' ideas. But there is no reason to suppose that this difference is relevant when we come to estimate the degrees of objectivity of those who put them forward. We all recognize that it is very comforting to explain away the theories of our opponents, for if we can do so we avoid the difficulty of having to meet their arguments. This no doubt is why this form of polemic is so frequently indulged in. It can hardly be claimed therefore that those who investigate the origins of social theories must have an objectivity which others lack.

With all these considerations before us, we may say that a case has not been made against the possibility of an effective degree of objectivity in social enquiry. The dangers, however, are there, and if we accept the possibility of proceeding scientifically we may ask what are the best means of avoiding them.

From what has been said, it will be clear that it will not do to try to avoid them by seeking a special position of detachment. Those who try to keep themselves above the battle cannot avoid having their own social interests and their own point of view. Whether in the study or the market-place, no one lives in a social vacuum, and no one can afford to ignore the adverse influences on his beliefs.

This is why it may be said that the true remedy is rather to make oneself conscious of these influences. To take seriously the investigation of the origin of social theories has value precisely because it helps people to do this. To show that one's theories are socially conditioned does not of course in itself stop those theories from being socially conditioned. But it may help to alter them, for the simple reason that neither prejudice nor bias nor the influence of custom survive detection.

The value of this remedy should not be over-estimated. For it does not help to overcome distortions which are due simply to the limitations of one's social situation. And even in the case of the other influences, though it is true that they do not survive detection, we must remember that they are often extremely difficult to detect.

For these reasons it may well be necessary to fall back on a remedy of a different kind, namely, controversy.[1] If all who had the same evidence at their disposal took perfect account of it, all would arrive at the same conclusions and there would be no disputes between them. But this, as we know, does not happen, and one of the reasons for this is that different people are subject to the influence of different motives, customs and situations. The best way to eliminate these influences, it may be suggested, is to bring the holders of the different theories together and ensure that they are able to engage in open criticism of one another without fear of consequences. Left to ourselves we are an easy prey to influences adverse to objectivity. We do not easily become aware of our own bias, our own unreflective presuppositions, or the limitations of our own point of view—we need to have them pointed out to us by others. Ensuring that social enquiry is a competitive collective enterprise is thus the best guarantee of such objectivity as is within our reach.

[1] See K. R. Popper—*The Open Society and its Enemies*, Volume II, Ch. 23, pp. 206–211 (Routledge, 1945) for a forceful statement of this point.

PART II

The Logical Peculiarities of Social Enquiry

VIII

INTRODUCTION

THE decks are now clear for the second stage of our investigation. Of the five basic features in terms of which we defined a scientific procedure, we have shown that there is none which is inapplicable in a social enquiry. Furthermore, we have shown that in no case has a social enquirer any other alternative but to adopt a procedure which has these features. They provide the framework within which he *can* work, and within which he *must* work.

The framework, as we have seen it emerging, is a simple one. There is a certain limited number of statements which the social enquirer can establish simply by observing the things which go on around him and distinguishing their features—the expressions and movements of people, the things they make such as buildings, books and tools, the natural surroundings in which they are placed. There is an even more limited number of statements—those about his own experiences—which he can establish simply by having those experiences. With this empirical evidence at his disposal, he can provide inductive support for general statements of various kinds. And by using these general statements he can bring the empirical evidence to bear in support of statements about what he has not observed or felt, whether this be in the past or the future or the unobserved present.

We have here a framework which is common to all empirical science, whatever its subject-matter. Our next task is to consider some of the complexities which arise when a procedure of this general kind is used in social enquiry. Though differences in subject-matter make no difference to the logical rules which determine how one should proceed in any empirical enquiry, they may nevertheless make a great deal of difference to what can be done within the limits imposed by these rules. And there is no doubt that there are general differences between the subject-matters of the social sciences on the one hand and the natural sciences on the other which are greater than any of the differences within either of these fields. We shall here be concerned with the consequences of having to cope in an enquiry with the special and peculiar features of social life.

91

IX

PSYCHOLOGY AND THE SOCIAL SCIENCES

IN the social sciences we are concerned with people, not with things. Just as atoms and other individual material particles are the units of physical study, so individual human beings—their experiences, their dispositions and their behaviour—are the units of social study.

One problem which immediately arises from this fact is how any of the social sciences is to be distinguished from psychology. For the investigation of the experiences, dispositions and behaviour of human beings is commonly regarded as the task of the psychologist. It may be said that psychology is itself one of the social sciences, but whether or not it is so classified is not a matter of great importance. What is important is that politics, economics, anthropology, sociology, and so on, cannot be simply identified with psychology. On what principles, then, if any, is the subject-matter to be divided? And how closely are the two kinds of enquiry related?

There has been much confusion on these questions. As a first step towards removing it, we may point out that three alternatives present themselves. In the first place the division might be so made as to defend the claim that the social sciences and psychology are independent, being concerned with different kinds of fact which can be explained with the use of different sets of general statements. On this alternative there would be social facts which were in some sense ultimate and irreducible to psychological facts, and social laws which were in some sense *sui generis*. In the second place the division might be made in such a way as to make social enquiries dependent on the psychological, though not vice versa. On this alternative, the social sciences would be treated as if they were branches of applied psychology. Or finally, it might be held that there is no clear-cut division and that there is a general interdependence, there being various branches of enquiry concerned with human beings which it is convenient to distinguish as social and as psychological respectively, so long as the distinctions are not taken too rigidly.

Those who adopt the first alternative are commonly said to be defending the autonomy of the social sciences. Those who adopt the second are said to be denying this, and asserting that all the social sciences have their basis in psychology. It is easy for each to show that the other is mistaken. This is not surprising, because both *are* mistaken. The way out of the impasse so created is to recognize that there is the third alternative.

THE ALLEGED INDEPENDENCE OF SOCIAL ENQUIRIES

There appear to be two possible ways of dividing the subject-matter, which may serve as a basis for asserting the independence of social from psychological enquiries. Let us consider these in turn.

Individuals and their Social Relations

The simpler of the two ways of making the division would be to say that psychology is concerned with individual human beings and their characteristics—their experiences, dispositions and behaviour—while the social sciences are concerned with those relations between them which arise from their having these characteristics. It is these relations which we call 'social' relations, and it therefore seems natural to say that it is the business of the social sciences to study them. If we were to accept this distinction, it would mean that if there were a hundred human beings each living by himself on a desert island, we might make a psychological study of them, but there would be no social science at all, since there would be no society. Whereas, if the hundred were all on one island in proximity to each other, we could make two studies—a psychological study of their personalities, their experiences and their behaviour, and a social study of their effect on each other. The psychological study would be like atomic physics which is concerned with the internal constitution of atoms, and the social study would be like molar physics—the study of the impact of atoms on one another.[1]

To this simple way of making the division there is an equally simple objection. It must be accepted as a general empirical fact about human beings that the experiences, the dispositions and the behaviour of any individual are very greatly influenced by the presence and the behaviour of other individuals. No individual that we are aware of has ever lived in a completely separate Robinson-Crusoe world, but we have plenty of evidence that if he did, he would be completely different from the people we know and have to study. In other words, what happens to a human being cannot be effectively explained without reference to his social environment. We can make this assertion without saying how

[1] See, for example, Radcliffe-Brown—*A Natural Science of Society* (The Free Press, Illinois, 1957), pp. 45–50 for a division made on these lines.

great these influences are or attempting to take sides in fruitless controversy about the relative extent of the effects of heredity and of environment on human beings in general.

It will prevent an under-estimation of the effect of social environment, however, if we bear in mind that social influences on an individual need not necessarily be either intended or direct. An orator may be said to have an influence on the members of his audience even when he unintentionally produces a reaction against his policy. Someone who constructs a road may be said to be influencing the future generation, even though the influence is less direct than that, say, of the schoolteacher. Furthermore, people may be influenced by others even when they are unaware of what those others are doing. When someone buys less because the price has risen, it makes no difference whether or not he knows of those actions of other people which have led to the rise in price. Often in fact the effect on a person depends on his being unaware of it, as in the case of the influences of custom and of social situation on beliefs, which we have mentioned in discussing objectivity.[1] When we reflect on this great variety in the possible kinds of influence which people have on one another, it becomes a truism to say that they cannot be neglected.

In this respect there is a significant difference between the individual human being and the atom. They have a superficial resemblance to one another as units to be studied. In general both persist as undivided wholes, though on occasion a human personality, like an atom, can be split. What makes them very different is that an atom is a closed system in a way in which a human being is not. What happens outside an atom makes very little difference to its characteristics or to the internal arrangement of its parts—the difference made is predominantly to its direction and rate of movement and its position in relation to other atoms. Thus it might be said that in explaining changes in atomic structure, heredity is of prime importance, and this makes it possible to study such changes without reference to the mutual relations between atoms. Whereas, in the case of a human being, we are unable to explain changes in experiences and mental dispositions without taking into account the mutual relations between human beings.

It follows from this that to make a division between psychological and social enquiry on the lines suggested would be a very inconvenient thing to do. For the two enquiries would be interdependent at every point. Because of this interdependence we would find it more reasonable to regard them as a single enquiry—a psychological-cum-social enquiry concerning socially related human beings.

Individuals and Social Structure

The other way of making the division avoids this obvious objection.

[1] Pp. 78–80.

According to this view there need be no attempt to distinguish between the characteristics of individuals and the social relations between them. All facts about individual human beings, including those about their social relations, may be treated as psychological facts. And if this were all that was to be found on the island where the hundred were gathered together, they would be matter for nothing more than a psychological enquiry.

It is likely, however, that there would be something else to be found. The individuals would fall into groups, there would be various institutions, customs and laws, with individuals filling special roles—in a word, there would be a social structure. The study of the actions and reactions that took place when individuals were angry with one another or took food from one another or made love to one another would be the task of the psychologist—perhaps we might call him here a social psychologist. But in so far as they formed tribes or families or classes, or there was a system of retributive punishment, or property or marriage, we would have on this view a situation containing what might be called specifically social facts, the study of which would fall to the social scientist. Social scientists, it would be pointed out, are able to describe such facts without mentioning individuals. Further they are able to explain or predict changes which take place in them by using laws or other general statements which make no mention of individuals. Here, then, it will be said, there is a field of enquiry in which social scientists can work without having to concern themselves with facts or generalizations of a psychological kind.

There is an apparently extreme form of this view according to which social structure is itself thought of as mental in character, and a division is made between the study of the individual mind and the study of the social, or collective, mind. This way of putting it is made to seem natural by the fact that in describing social groups we frequently use the same phrases that we use in describing individuals—as when we speak of political parties holding beliefs, nations defending their interests, or a government depending on the will of the people. Psychology thus becomes the comprehensive science and the division becomes a division between individual and collective psychology.[1]

When the division is presented in this way, however, the change is largely a verbal one. It would only be more than this if it were seriously maintained that groups had experiences and performed actions which were different from and additional to those of their members. For such additional experiences and actions there is no evidence whatever, and it is extremely doubtful whether those who have spoken of a general will or a group mind have ever thought that there was. What they have

---

[1] Cf., for example, William McDougall—*The Group Mind—a Sketch of the Principles of Collective Psychology*, Ch. 1. (Cambridge University Press, 2nd Edition, 1926).

wished to maintain is that groups have enduring structural features which manifest themselves in the experiences and actions of various individuals—for example in the laws that are made or the way people feel towards one another—just as the dispositional features of an individual's personality manifest themselves in his experience and behaviour. In expressing this point about social structure, they have stretched usage unduly, and, led on by the natural tendency to personify groups, have emphasized an analogy at the expense of obscuring manifest differences. Hence in discussing the sense in which groups, institutions and so on are to be spoken of as social facts, it is as well that we should avoid treating them as large-scale mental facts.

Now there is a perfectly ordinary sense in which we do speak of facts about groups and their structure. In describing what goes on, we constantly make statements about them, as when we say that the United States was at war with Japan, or that the market for Australian wool is highly competitive, or that the House of Commons in Great Britain has the Prime Minister as a member. Further, in explaining what goes on, we constantly make general statements about them, such as that industrialization contributes to the growth of democracy or that tariffs tend to produce inefficiency in domestic production or that religion serves the function of ensuring social unity. Much social enquiry is conducted on this level, as when students of politics and of anthropology, for example, investigate the changes which take place in political and social institutions, in cultures and in ways of life. It is no doubt this fact which suggests the view under discussion according to which social facts of this kind are different from facts about individuals, and social laws independent of laws concerning individuals.

Such a view, however, does not follow from this fact. Though statements about social structure are constantly made, it may still be the case that they can be elucidated in terms of statements about individuals. And though general statements about social structure are commonly used in giving explanations, they may themselves still be capable of being explained in terms of general statements about kinds of interaction between individuals. To establish the independence of social enquiry, conceived as a study of social structure, the possibility of such elucidation and such explanation must be denied.

The questions at issue then are, firstly, whether facts about social structure[1] are different in kind from facts about individuals, and secondly, whether there are social laws (or other general statements) which could not themselves be explained, if we went far enough, in terms of laws about the social behaviour of individuals.

---

[1] Since, on the view we are discussing, these would be classified simply as 'social facts', in opposition to psychological ones, we will refer to them as such in what follows.

(a) The Status of 'Social Facts'

Let us take any social group such as a football club, a political party, a family, a school or a nation, and ask what we mean when we say it is a group and has a structure. At once we see it is *possible* to give an account of such social wholes in terms of the individuals concerned and the effects they have on one another. The first thing is to give such an account, and then we can consider whether it is adequate.

The account would run roughly as follows. When we speak of a group, we would say, we mean that there is a set of people, all of whom regularly expect each other to act in certain ways, which they all recognize as proper. Each expects the others to conform to certain rules, and disapproves of those who do not. In some cases such as families the rules are unformulated, and will only come to light when expectations are not fulfilled; in other cases such as football clubs and nations, they are written down and can be read. In no case is it necessary, for membership of a group, for an individual invariably to act in the prescribed ways. The important thing is that every one accepts them as prescribed. It is this which makes irregularities not mere exceptions but deviations from a standard.[1]

If we accept an account on these lines, it becomes clear why it is in connection with groups that we speak of customs, institutions, and social roles. To say that it is a custom in a family to have dinner at seven-thirty is to say that this is a recognized way of behaving, applicable to all members. To say that private property is an institution in a community is to say that within that community there is, despite occasional theft and some government ownership, a generally recognized arrangement whereby individuals have exclusive control over certain material things.[2] To say that different people perform different roles within a group (such as teacher in a school or teller in a bank) is to say that they, as sub-classes of the total membership, are regularly expected to behave in certain special ways. When we say that one group shows a higher degree of organization than another, we generally refer to the greater explicitness of its customs, the greater complexity of its institutions, and the greater degree of differentiation between its roles. It is the standing relationships between the members of a group which are comprised in its customs, its institutions and its roles, that we speak of as social structure.[3]

On this account there will be no difficulty in showing how it is that we

[1] Cf. Radcliffe-Brown, op. cit. pp. 55–58, for an account of social structure in terms of social usage which is of the same general kind as this.

[2] The word 'institution' is of course used variously; in particular it is sometimes used to refer to groups themselves (e.g. schools or hospitals) rather than to recognized structural arrangements within them.

[3] This may be expressed by saying that customs, institutions and roles are 'dispositional properties' of *sets* of individuals. It is in virtue of their possession of such dispositional properties that they are called groups.

can describe groups without mentioning the characteristics of their individual members. For all we need to do is to describe the standing expectations which constitute their structure. Because of this structure we can treat them to some extent as wholes, or units, just as we can treat stones as wholes or units, without mentioning individual atoms. Further, when the structure persists, we can say that the group persists, even though the individual members change—so long, that is, as the change of membership is not a sudden and a wholesale one.

In giving this account, we have not mentioned various other kinds of mutual influence which are to be found among members of a social group. In particular we have not mentioned the desire on the part of each to promote an end which all have in common—something which must be recognized as a powerful influence holding many groups together.[1] Nor have we mentioned the effects of personal acquaintance and friendship which are to be found in small 'face-to-face' groups like families and social gatherings, but not in political parties or nations. But we have said sufficient to make it clear that it is possible to give an account of social structure solely in terms of individual human beings and the ways in which they influence one another. The expectations, the recognition of what is proper, the approvals and disapprovals are all attributable to individuals. All we need say is that these are manifested regularly in given circumstances, and that what each individual does will be influenced by what others expect, recognize as proper and approve of, taken together with the individual's own belief about the regularity with which these expectations and approvals will be manifested.

It may be objected, however, that this account of social structure is inadequate. According to it the elements—namely, individual human beings—constitute a social whole solely by virtue of the fact that they are interrelated in certain ways. But, it will be said, a social whole is more than the sum of its parts, and by this we surely mean not merely that these parts interact, but that the whole is more than the parts *plus* their interaction. It is the characteristics which social groups possess as wholes which our account omits.

Now there are undoubtedly cases where something's having a structure appears to imply that it has characteristics which will not be mentioned in any description of its parts and the relations between them. Thus a house built of cards may be said to be square, but this squareness will not reappear in description of the separate cards and the way they are placed in relation to each other. In general, spatial wholes may be said to have a pattern, and the pattern is a feature only of the whole. On analogy with this it may be suggested that social wholes have features of the same kind. Thus when a political system is called democratic, it may be said that this democratic character is a pattern

---

[1] There are some, indeed, who would define a group in terms of common purpose, rather than in the way we have done.

belonging to the system as a whole, and will not simply reappear in a description of the individuals who take part in it and the regular expectations they have about each other's behaviour.

It may be doubted whether this analogy holds—but if it does it need not worry us. For a pattern, though not the same thing as the interrelation of the parts, is nevertheless entailed by this interrrelation. If you describe the relative positions of all the cards, you can deduce the squareness of the house. So, by the analogy, if you described the amount of influence each person had on the government and on the others in the group, the expectations each had about voting procedure, and so on, you could deduce the democratic character of the system. So that even if statements about groups could not be treated merely as statements about the interdependence of individuals, anything more in the way of distinctively social facts could be immediately deduced from statements about such interdependence.

What would cause real difficulty would be if social groups, as structured wholes, had features which were not deducible from facts about individuals and their relations. In speaking of social structure we compared groups with physical objects like stones. A stone might be said to possess, as a whole, a structural pattern depending on the arrangement of its atomic parts. But it also possesses further features—for example, greyness and hardness—which are not deducible from the arrangement of its parts, though they are known empirically to be associated with certain kinds of atomic structure. The same may be said of individual human beings who, as experiencing and acting units, possess parallel non-structural features. Just as a stone may be grey or hard, so likewise may an individual be intelligent or angry. If features of this kind were also possessed by social wholes, there would be good reason for speaking of social facts as a distinctive kind.[1]

Social wholes, however, do not appear to have such features. Small groups, like families, may be said to possess 'atmospheres' of their own,[2] but these seem evidently metaphorical and easily analysable into the attitudes of the members to each other and to outsiders. The same may be said of the 'national character' sometimes attributed to the larger and more comprehensive geographical units. It is of course perfectly proper to speak of group atmosphere and national character. But if anyone is asked to explain what he means when he does this, he will not be stuck for an answer as he would be if asked what he meant by a stone being grey. He will proceed to tell us what the individuals are like and how they react to one another.

[1] When Kurt Lewin, in discussing social groups, speaks of the 'dynamic properties' they have as wholes it is not clear whether he has properties such as these, or merely structural properties, in mind. See Lewin—*Field Theory in Social Science.* (Tavistock, 1952) esp. p. 146.

[2] Cf. Lewin op. cit. p. 63, where atmospheres are referred to as properties of a social field as a whole.

It would seem, then, that our 'individualist' account of social structure is adequate. We may now go on to point out that it has certain obvious advantages.

In the first place it makes it easy for us to accept the undoubted fact that social groups overlap. Any individual may be a member of various groups—of a family, for example, of a church, of an economic class and of a nation. Again some groups may fall entirely within others. A community, comprising as it does within its structure all those living within a given area—town, region, country, as the case may be—is clearly an important group of a comprehensive kind, but it remains one kind of grouping among many others.

In this respect social groups are once again unlike stones and unlike individual human beings. For these are exclusive structures. Whereas an individual may belong to more than one group, an atom cannot belong to more than one stone, nor can an experience or a motive belong to more than one individual. One great danger in speaking of 'social wholes' is that it leads easily to this important difference being neglected.

On our account this overlap of social groups is something which we would expect. For any individual is very likely to have relations of the systematic and regular kind we have described, with various different sets of people. But if a group were to have non-structural features of its own, it is not easy to see how different groups could have some of their members in common. We would have to think of them as exclusive structures, like stones and individual human beings. And it is to be noted that those who take this view of social structure tend to regard them in this way. They think of social enquiry as the study of exclusive 'societies', and assume that if anyone belongs to one society, he cannot belong to any other.

The avoidance of this danger, however, is not the only advantage of our account. It also relieves us of the necessity of treating the facts of social structure as in a class by themselves, to be distinguished sharply from other facts about the relationships between human beings. Human beings may influence each other in a great variety of ways, and it is, to say the least, a considerable convenience to be able to treat the mutual influences which, on our account, constitute group membership simply as one kind of influence among others. Furthermore, when fadts about groups are set in a class apart as the specific subject-matter of social enquiry, there is a grave danger that other facts about the relationships of human beings will not merely be set aside as 'psychological' but will be ignored.

One important way in which people influence each other without forming into groups is by coming into conflict. We may say there is conflict whenever two people seek to achieve incompatible ends and each tries to stop the interference of the other. Obvious cases of such incompatible ends are those in which two people both seek exclusive use of material things, or both seek to be in a position to control the actions of the other. Wealth and power, in other words, are crucial causes of conflict. But they are of course not the only ones, and no one doubts that conflicts of various kinds play an important part in human affairs.

In so far as people come into conflict with one another, they do not form into groups or become elements of a social structure. Hence, if social enquiry is to be the study of social structure, it cannot include a study of the effects of conflict. This in itself is a strange limitation. But it is made worse by the fact that conflict and group-membership are often very closely associated. In the case of groups which have not only agreed rules but also a common purpose—political parties, for example —the ends sought respectively by the members of two groups may well be incompatible, and in these circumstances we will start speaking, in a secondary way, of conflict between the groups themselves. Conflict, again, may take place not only between groups but within groups, the members being divided on certain issues—as when different parties are in conflict within a parliamentary political system. Most conflicts, in fact, are limited in this way, taking place only within a framework of institutions recognized by the members of both parties.

It is not only that conflict and group-membership are intermingled. It is also the case that the borderline between them is often very thin. A custom which is recognized by some may be imposed on others. A law which many accept as an established way of behaving in a political system may be obeyed by others only under threat of force. Even in the case of one and the same person, both kinds of influence may be felt. In view of this, it becomes extremely awkward to distinguish the study of the institutional features of groups from the study of the non-institutional relations, and especially the conflicts, of human beings.

Furthermore, with the making of this distinction, there goes the very considerable danger that the element of conflict in human affairs will be ignored. Attention is at once focused on the things which unite people at the expense of the things which divide. For it is the uniting of people into groups which has the prestige of being the proper object of social enquiry.

This tendency to ignore conflict is assisted curiously enough by the way in which we commonly use the words 'social' and 'society'. We speak of people being social, or forming a society, only when they are members of groups. People who fight, are not regarded as being in society, and people who do not recognize group standards are spoken of as being anti-social. It becomes natural, therefore, to exclude consideration of them in our study of society, just as we would exclude consideration of solitary human beings living on desert islands.

It will be clear, however, that there is a very great difference between being in conflict and being solitary. Those who are in conflict influence one another, and even if such people do not form a 'society', there is every reason for classifying these influences as 'social' in a broader sense of the term. This will at least ensure that they are not passed over in silence. Social enquirers cannot afford to neglect 'anti-social' behaviour, and any view about the subject-matter of social enquiry which suggests that they may do this is to that extent suspect.

(b) The Status of 'Social Laws'

We may now pass on to our second question—the question whether there are social laws (or other general statements)[1] which cannot themselves be explained in terms of laws about the experiences, attitudes and behaviour of individuals. For even though the facts of group structure are not distinguishable as a separate kind of fact from facts about individuals, it may still be the case that there are laws about the character and changes of group structures which are not deducible from laws about the relations of individuals.

Consider, for example, the statement that industrialization leads to democracy, or the well-known 'Iron Law of Oligarchy' which states that power in any group always becomes concentrated in a few hands.[2] These are general, and unrestricted, statements about institutions. According to the first, when we find one set of institutions in a community, we will find, or tend to find, another. According to the second there is one kind of institution which is to be found in any group whatsoever. To speak of an institution is, on our view, to speak of the regularity of occurrence of certain kinds of expectation and action among a particular set of individuals. It follows that general statements about the connections and character of institutions are to be understood as general statements about individuals, having only the peculiarity that they are doubly general, being concerned with the regularity with which regularities occur. It does not follow, however, that they are thereby deducible from the simpler and more straightforward general statements about individuals which, on the division under discussion, would be classified as psychological laws. It would be a case of deriving a social law from a psychological one if someone were to argue, for example, that the connection between industrialization and democracy was due to the fact that people obtain power more easily when they are brought together into one work-place and taught to read and write—or (to turn to our other example) that concentration of power was due to a widespread human tendency to submit to authority or to shelve responsibility. It is at least conceivable that explanations of this kind could

---

[1] When we speak simply of 'laws' in what follows, it is for the sake of brevity; other types of general statements are not thereby meant to be excluded.

[2] For the formulation and defence of this, see Michels—*Political Parties* (trans. E. & C. Paul, Jarrold).

not be given. Hence we still need to consider the question of the possible independence of social laws.

We have already pointed out that such laws are frequently formulated, and frequently used for the explaining of social events, without any further explanations being given in terms of general principles of individual behaviour. If a government extends the franchise we may be content to point to the growth of large-scale industry as a cause, or at least as a contributing factor, without asking precisely how this growth of industry influenced the individual members of the government. If a leader emerges in a trade union, we may account for this simply by referring to a general law about oligarchy. We may point to types of social theory in which this avoidance of further explanation appears to be adopted as a matter of principle. There are the Marxists, for example, who seek to explain changes in economic structure solely in terms of 'laws of motion of human society'. There are anthropologists like Malinowski who seek to explain institutions in a social group in terms of functional laws which show how they contribute to the unity, or stability, or survival of the group.

There might, however, be two quite different reasons for failing to give further explanations of social laws. It might be maintained that the giving of such explanations is in principle impossible, in which case the social laws would have a genuinely independent status. But it might also be maintained that such explanations, though possible in principle, are often impossible to give in practice, and at any rate unnecessary for the purposes of a particular social enquiry. From the complex interaction of large numbers of human beings, certain stable patterns emerge, and it might be held that social enquirers should concentrate on these, thereby by-passing altogether the intricacies of the intervening psychological 'mechanisms'. Social laws, it might be said, are like Boyle's law about gases, or the 'law' that stones, when dislodged, roll downhill—laws which can be relied on in themselves by people who do not concern themselves with the laws about atoms and molecules from which they can be deduced.[1]

This second reason for limiting social explanations to the level of institutions is one which it is in many cases reasonable to accept. It is a fact that, despite the great complexity to be found in the interactions of human beings, there are social structures which are relatively stable and exhibit regularities that are relatively easy to detect. There is no reason why we should not make use of this fact for making a convenient division within the general body of psychological-cum-social enquiry. We may, therefore, regard the study of social institutions as a relatively self-contained portion of that enquiry, and one that undeniably deserves the epithet 'social'.

---

[1] Which of these two alternatives is in fact accepted by Marxists and by functional anthropologists is a matter of dispute which we will not go into here.

The point of making this division is brought out if we consider what is normally done on the one hand by students of institutions, such as political scientists, and on the other by social psychologists. The term 'social psychology' has no standard use.[1] But one of the things which is done by those who speak of themselves as social psychologists is to study the behaviour of people in groups. Why then, it may be asked, should not the study of political institutions come within their scope? The answer is that they naturally stop short with the consideration of the direct mutual influences of members of a group, such as are found in 'face-to-face' groups like families, work-teams, meetings and crowds. If they discuss the 'psychology of politics', they concern themselves with such things as the effects of political propaganda, not with constitutions and party systems. Whereas political scientists, being concerned primarily with social structure, do not normally pay much attention to the direct influences which members of a group have on one another, and therefore regard their subject as relatively independent of psychology.

To make this division, however, is one thing, and to insist that further explanation of laws of social structure is in principle impossible is quite another. Even though political science is different from social psychology, a political scientist may still be prepared, if need be, to try to explain his generalizations about political institutions in terms of the mutual influences of individual human beings. But when it is said that, from the nature of the case, he cannot do this, the situation is altogether different. He is left with a set of laws about institutions unrelated to laws about the individuals in whose regular and accepted ways of behaving the institutions consist. Against the view that social laws have such an independent status, there are very strong objections.

To begin with, we must point out something about which everyone will be agreed. This is that the particular actions of individuals are sometimes to be explained, at least in part, by reference to social structure. Thus it may be said of someone that he spoke with authority, because he was the Prime Minister—that is, filled a certain role in the political system. Or again, we may explain someone's shaking hands with a friend by saying it is the custom. We accept institutions as dispositional features of a person's social environment which are rarely absent from any explanation of any part of his behaviour. Even those who regard them as irreducible social facts are quite happy about this.[2] In their

---

[1] For reference to other uses, see this chapter, pp. 95 and 108.

[2] Maurice Mandelbaum, in an article entitled 'Societal Facts' (*British Journal of Sociology*, 1955, pp. 305–317), goes further and uses this point as a basis for an argument in favour of the irreducibility of social facts. He points out (pp. 307–9) that to explain a bank-teller's action in cashing a cheque, we must refer to his role in the banking system. He goes on to argue that we cannot mean by his having this role that others regularly expect him to behave in certain ways, since we can only

(Continued at foot of next page)

terms, we may say that there are always social as well as psychological factors involved in the explanation of the actions of individuals.

But, though this is freely admitted, it is sometimes forgotten that the converse kind of explanation is also freely given. Not only do we explain features of individual actions in terms of social structure, but we also explain features of social structure in terms of individual actions. People not only conform to social rules but contribute to their alteration. If asked to explain certain democratic institutions, for example, we may well refer not only to the presence of other institutions, but to the actions of those who have struggled to get the democratic ones established. It is true that most institutions grow gradually and are not set up by any clearly defined set of people. This, however, does not mean that their growth has not been influenced by the actions of various individuals over a period of time, and we frequently point to influences of this kind.

This being so, those who maintain the independence of social laws are involved in rather odd consequences. Institutions can be explained either in terms of other institutions in accordance with independent social laws, or they can be explained in terms of individual actions, in accordance with laws about the interaction of individuals. There will be social and psychological factors involved in the explanation of institutions, just as there are social and psychological factors involved in the explanation of the actions of individuals. If the two sorts of factor were of the same general kind and the social laws were explicable in terms of the psychological, there would be nothing peculiar about this. But if the two kinds of explanation are regarded as irreducibly different, we will be put into the position of having to make an odd kind of choice. We will have to ask questions like—To what extent is democracy due to industrialism and to what extent to the agitation of reformers? And we will have no guidance, from the character of the institutions themselves, which of these two quite different kinds of explanation to accept.

Though this might be odd, it might, of course, still be the case. But here we come to the more straightforward objection that in the case of many laws of social structure, we do in fact have little trouble in suggesting at least the broad lines of an explanation in terms of influences on individuals. We have already suggested what the explanation might be of the connection between industrialism and democracy—any individual who is made literate and brought together with others of similar

---

explain the expectations of these others once again by their recognition of his role. This threat of circularity, however, need not worry us. It is quite consistent to explain any individual's expectation that the teller will cash a cheque in terms of his recognition that the teller is *generally* expected to do so (by employers, customers, etc.). The relations between the members of a group are reciprocal. *Each* expects something because he recognizes that it is regularly expected by the rest—not because it is part of a social framework which is above them all.

economic interests more easily increases his share of power. Similarly the connection between tariffs and productivity could easily be explained in terms of a general human tendency to relax when competition is removed. In such cases, as we say, we can 'see why' the connections hold. And if we see why in some cases it is reasonable to assume that, if we were clever enough and looked hard enough, we could see why in all.

The reasonableness of this assumption is brought out if we compare human groups with certain non-human groups such as bees in a hive. We are strongly inclined to assign an independent status to some of the laws of beehive structure, since we have no idea at all how they could be explained in terms of the effects of bees on one another.[1] But in reflecting on this, we see that human groups are different and the difference consists precisely in the fact that we see how further explanations can be given in terms of principles of individual behaviour, even if we are often unable to follow out these explanations in detail.

We conclude then that we must dismiss as unsuccessful the attempt to establish the study of social structure as a specifically social enquiry independent of the study of individuals. To assert this independence is to place more weight on a convenient and rough-and-ready distinction than it will bear.

THE ALLEGED DEPENDENCE OF SOCIAL ENQUIRERS

Once we deny that there are specifically social facts and independent social laws, it might seem that we are committed to the view that all social enquiry is dependent on psychology. If we take psychology to include the whole study of individual human beings and the influence they have on one another, this is indeed the case. In fact we might go further and say we have shown all social enquiries to be part of psychology, the study of the structure of social groups being one relatively isolable part of it—but still a part of it.

At this point, however, there is a danger of making a fatal mistake. The word 'psychology' is here being used in a very broad sense. From saying that all social enquiry comes within the orbit of psychology in this sense, it is very easy to pass over to the view that all social enquiry is dependent on psychology in a narrower sense. We must see how the transition to this indefensible position can take place.

We have said that all the social sciences are concerned with individuals. But we have always been careful to add that this includes the

[1] See J. W. N. Watkins, note on *The Principle of Methodological Individualism*, in the British Journal of the Philosophy of Science, Vol. 3 (1952–3), p. 188, for a quoted illustration of this. In this Note which includes modifications of the position taken in an article on *Ideal Types and Historical Explanation* in the same Journal, Vol. 3, pp. 22–43, the issue under discussion is presented with unusual clarity.

effects they have on each other. In the case of any given individual, this means that a social enquirer is interested in two things—first, how what he does affects others, and second, how what others do affects him. The trouble comes when we assume that, in tracing social enquiries back to the study of individuals, we are concerning ourselves only with the first of these things. If we do this, we have to regard the characteristics of individuals in themselves as the *starting-points* of social enquiry, and we have to say that the task of the different branches of social science is to examine the consequences, direct or indirect, intended or unintended, of the actions of these individuals—including under these, of course, the kind of groups and institutions which are found among them. If it is asked who is to examine and explain these characteristics of individuals from which the social consequences flow, the answer will then be that this is the proper task of psychology—psychology now in the narrower sense. Psychology in this sense will be said to provide the data about individuals and the elementary laws of human nature. Ultimately all social explanations will have to be in terms of these.[1]

Even if the consequences of people's actions always turned out as they intended, there would, on this view, be still quite a lot for the social sciences to do, in tracing the means whereby they achieved their ends. But it can be pointed out that when many people act together, the actions of each may also have many unintended consequences, and these are likely to figure more prominently the more indirect they become. Hence those who think of the social sciences as derived from psychological premises sometimes conceive of them as having, as their important distinctive function, that of tracing all the unintended consequences of the actions of individuals.[2]

The obvious objection to this view is that it appears to involve a reversion to the simple and untenable division with which we started—a division according to which psychology is concerned with the characteristics of individuals taken in themselves, and the social sciences with their effects on one another. What it does is to make this division

---

[1] J. S. Mill (*System of Logic*, Book 6) is a case of one who believing correctly that 'all phenomena of society are phenomena of human nature' (Ch. 6, Sect. 2), finds himself slipping over into this position, the trouble starting with a confusion about the relation of psychology to what he calls 'Ethology' in Ch. 5, Sect. 4. The position is one which appears also to be adopted by F. A. Hayek—*The Counter-Revolution of Science* (Free Press, Glencoe, 1952). It is associated by this writer with the use of the term 'methodological individualism'. It is criticized by K. R. Popper—*The Open Society and its Enemies* (Routledge, 1945), Vol. 2, Ch. 14 as 'psychologism'. Popper reserves the term 'methodological individualism' for the acceptable view, which he defends, that the actions of groups are to be understood in terms of the actions of individuals. Despite his sound and important distinction between these two 'doctrines', it is a sign of the persistence of the confusion that he should still regard his criticism of 'psychologism' as constituting a defence of the 'autonomy of sociology'.

[2] Cf. Hayek, op. cit. p. 25. 'The aim (of the social sciences) is to explain the unintended or undesigned results of the action of many men.' See also p. 39.

look more acceptable by telling only half the story. It recognizes that the states of mind of individuals have social effects, but it makes no mention of their social causes. This is what enables it to give the impression that these states of mind can be the subject-matter of an independent psychological study. Yet it is clear that social effects imply social causes. We cannot assert that individual actions have social consequences without admitting some degree of reciprocal dependence of individuals on their social environment. For what is a social consequence from the point of view of one person is social environment from the point of view of another.

There is, however, one point at which this circle of interdependence is broken. In order to explain some of the characteristics of individuals, we need to refer not only to the influence of other individuals but also to the influences of heredity and of natural environment. This suggests a way in which the objection just made can be partially met. It can be done by making the division between psychological and social enquiry in a new place. Psychology, we might now say, is not concerned with all the characteristics of human beings—it is concerned only with those characteristics which can be explained in terms of heredity and natural environment. Psychological explanations are to be restricted to those which can be given in these terms, and in so far as we take account of social environment we may be held to be giving not psychological but social explanations. By making the distinction in this way, we can retain a field of psychological enquiry which is independent of the social, and at the same time maintain with reason that social enquiries are at least partly dependent upon it.

Those who speak of the dependence of the social sciences on psychology frequently appear to have this division in mind, though they rarely make it explicit. The elementary laws of human nature are usually found to be concerned with what is innate in it. And when it is said that the human motives which are the starting-points for social enquiry are themselves to be explained psychologically, this is usually made to make sense by concentration on those motives which are unaffected by social circumstances. Again, it is to the study of those hereditary features of human nature which are more especially relevant for the understanding of the behaviour of people towards each other that the name 'social psychology' is sometimes given.[1]

We have here a sense in which some dependence of the social sciences must be admitted. But it can never be more than a partial dependence. It is in fact logically impossible for *all* social happenings to be explained in psychological terms. For if hereditary (or natural environmental)

---

[1] This, for example, is the type of study made by William McDougall in his *Introduction to Social Psychology* (Methuen, 1908). McDougall himself admittedly thought of 'social psychology' as something much more comprehensive; hence the often neglected phrase 'An Introduction to' in the title of his book.

influences were the sole influences on individuals, each individual would be in a state of monadic isolation. Their actions could have no social consequences, and there could be no social science at all.

One device for avoiding this absurdity while continuing to insist on the complete dependence of the social sciences, would be to push the monadic isolation back into the past. It might be admitted that what happens to people of the present generation is partly due to the influence of others. But if we were to trace the causal sequence of mutual social influences back far enough, we might eventually get to the origin of society—that is, to a time at which human beings first began to influence each other. These first influences would then have to be explained entirely in terms of the heredity features of the men who lived in a pre-social state. We would thus have got to the original starting-point of all social enquiry.

That this device should ever have been taken seriously is a tribute to the persistence of the confusion which makes it appear necessary. It is easy to speak in terms of the 'origin of society'—of what happened when people first came together—as the one-time prevalence of 'social-contract' theories shows. But there is of course no reason to suppose that men were ever solitary. The supposition could only be due to the sound feeling that all social events can only be understood in terms of the actions of individuals, and the fatal misconstruing of this to mean that they can only be explained in terms of certain ultimate and innate characteristics of human nature.[1]

There is no absurdity, however, in admitting a partial dependence of social events on innate characteristics. The trouble that arises here is rather that of deciding how much can be explained in these terms. The extent of the dependence is itself a matter of dispute, and this dispute in its turn can only be settled by the empirical investigation of social enquirers. Some, for example, will maintain that incest taboos and international warfare are to be explained largely in psychological terms, others that they are to be explained in social terms. Such questions have to be settled for each particular case before the present distinction between the psychological and the social can be applied to them. And they are, moreover, questions which it is peculiarly difficult to settle.

In this predicament, those who look for a psychological basis for the social sciences tend to make a very general assumption about where the line is to be drawn—an assumption which enables them to regard the 'psychological', or hereditary, influences as fundamental though not all-embracing. This is that there are certain basic innate motives which affect everyone's behaviour—these may be called instincts or drives or

[1] Cf. Popper, op. cit. p. 89. 'This theory of a pre-social human nature which explains the foundation of society . . . is not only a historical myth but also, as it were, a methodological myth.'

elementary human needs. In their attempts to satisfy these, individuals come into contact with each other, either in conflict or in co-operation or in some other way. The influence they have upon each other will, on this view, determine the specific forms which these innate tendencies take and the extent to which they are satisfied. These are the social consequences which it is the business of the social sciences to examine. But in all this the basic tendencies themselves are unaffected, and must be taken as axiomatic. Thus human beings have, for example, sexual, self-assertive, gregarious, and aggressive tendencies, they are naturally suggestible, they seek wealth, and they seek power. The question that is presented is what kinds of relations between human beings follow from the fact that a given individual is motivated in these ways, when it is taken together with the fact that others with whom he comes in contact are likewise motivated.

So long as we can be sure about given innate motives, and can trace their effects in this way in relative independence of the effects of other features of individual character, there is no doubt that this scheme provides us with a useful form of enquiry—a social enquiry based on psychological presuppositions in the present narrow sense of 'psychological'. The science of economics is in fact commonly regarded as being an enquiry of precisely this kind. The basic motive in this case has usually been taken to be the desire for wealth, or, less vaguely, the desire to maximize money gains. Other more specific psychological premises may be substituted for this without changing the principle.[1] If we have two people in contact, one wishing to sell a commodity at as high a price as possible and the other wishing to buy it at as low a price as possible, the resulting price at which it is exchanged may be regarded as the perfect example of a consequence following from the psychological preference-scales of the participants. With this simple model in mind, we can see how various economic facts—such as the prices people pay, the wages they get, how much they invest, how many are unemployed—might all be explained in terms of certain basic characteristics of human nature, taken as axiomatic and assumed to be innate.

It is not surprising then that those who think of all social enquiries as conforming to this scheme usually start with the example of economics in mind.[2] Economics is quite naturally regarded as the most mature of the social sciences. Its maturity is no doubt due to the concentrated character of the explanatory framework we have just described; it is one which suggests at once the possibility of developing a deductive system of theory. But because it is mature, it is thought natural that the

[1] Cf. J. M. Keynes' account of the psychological factors involved in the 'propensity to consume', 'liquidity-preference', and in expectations of future yield, in *The General Theory of Employment, Interest and Money* (Macmillan, 1939).

[2] This is the case, for example, with writers we have referred to—Mill and Hayek.

other social sciences should follow in its footsteps, and adopt the same kind of explanatory framework. If, for example, it is the business of the economist to trace the consequences of the desire for wealth, why should it not be the business of the student of politics to trace the consequences of the desire for power?

There are, however, two things to be remembered here. The first is that in the case of economics we are in a peculiarly favourable position for giving explanations of this kind. As a field of enquiry economics has, as we shall see, some very special features; hence it does not follow that what can be done within this field can be applied universally. In particular it so happens that what people do when they seek to maximize their monetary returns can be studied in relative independence of the effects of their other motives and of the effects of the context of accepted institutions in which their actions occur. The same thing cannot be said when we ask what people do when they seek power. In the study of power-seeking we immediately find ourselves having to take account of policies and ideologies and the character and changes of political institutions.[1]

In the second place, we can never be certain about the innate character of the fundamental motives. What is taken to be natural to men may always on further investigation turn out to be to a greater or lesser degree a social product. Thus it has been maintained that even the psychological premises from which economic conclusions are deduced are not so much statements about the general hereditary dispositions of human beings as statements about how people behave in a given social environment—in the environment of modern European civilization, for example, or in that of the business class in the community. When J. M. Keynes accepts as a 'fundamental psychological law' the statement 'that men are disposed, as a rule and on the average, to increase their consumption as their income increases, but not by as much as the increase in their income[2], it may be suspected, as his own cautious wording indicates, that this is not a law which could be regarded as holding under all social conditions.[3]

This does not mean that there is no place for the kind of enquiry which takes certain kinds of human motive as given and traces their consequences. All that it means is that there is no guarantee that even this kind of enquiry is dependent on psychological laws of human nature in the narrow sense. Thus, even the admission of a partial dependence of the social sciences on psychology tends to break down.

---

[1] In Mill's terms, the conclusions of a science of government are greatly affected by 'ethological considerations', cf. Mill, op. cit., Book 6, Ch. 9, Sect. 4.

[2] J. M. Keynes, op. cit. p. 96.

[3] For a study of the institutional influences on economic motives see Talcott Parsons—*The Motivation of Economic Activities*, in *Essays in Sociological Theory*, Revised Edition (Free Press, Glencoe, 1954.)

THE INTERDEPENDENCE OF PSYCHOLOGICAL
AND SOCIAL ENQUIRIES

With the removal of two separate sources of confusion, we are left with a healthily untidy situation. In the general body of enquiry concerning socially-related human beings, certain convenient lines of division have emerged, but nothing which will prevent us admitting a general inter-dependence of all branches of the enquiry.

In particular we can point to two kinds of enquiry which undeniably deserve the name 'social', and which demand a degree of independent recognition. The first is the study of social institutions—of the structural features of social groups which persist even though the members change. The second is the study of the effects which people have on each other when each is characterized by some very general set of human motives, innate or acquired.

On the other side we may regard as undeniably psychological any investigation of those facts about human beings which are found to be relatively independent of their social environment. These are the facts we study when we concern ourselves with the hereditary features of human nature and with the effects on these of our merely natural sur-roundings. It is only in so far as these hereditary features are referred to for the explaining of the actions of people who are in contact with one another that we can speak unambiguously of social enquiries being dependent on psychology.

It would be a great mistake, however, to suppose that these divisions cover the whole field. Human beings influence one another in many different ways. There are, for example, influences of a direct face-to-face kind, which do not fall under any of our headings and might be classified as the proper subject-matter of 'social psychology' in a not uncommon meaning of this phrase. In considering further the effect on our procedure of the peculiar features of socially-related human beings, we must keep all these kinds of social influence in mind, leaving on one side as far as possible only those questions which we have classified as undeniably psychological.

X

THE USE OF GENERAL
STATEMENTS: INTRODUCTORY

IN the social sciences, we have said, we are concerned with the ways in which people influence each other, the effects they have on each other, the interactions between them. The task of the social enquirer, that is to say, is to find out what people feel, desire, believe or do by considering their social surroundings, and to explain what they feel, desire, believe or do by reference to their social surroundings. And we have pointed out that in order to make these discoveries and give these explanations, he can, and indeed must, make use of general statements.

We have seen, however, that general statements may be of various types. Moreover they can be used in various ways. The time has come, therefore, to consider their use in more detail.

Theories

In the illustrations we have given of establishing and of explaining what happens, we have taken simple cases in which only one general statement is referred to. Thus, in the case of establishing that there was privilege in Ancient Egypt, we suggested that the appeal would be to some such principle as that tombs of a certain kind are built only for privileged people. In the case of explaining a rise in price, we said, it would be necessary to introduce some general statement like 'Price rises when there is a rise in costs'.[1]

Such illustrations, however, fail to bring out an important point. This is that the general statements of which we make use rarely stand on their own, unconnected with others. Any given statement can usually be deduced from some combination of others, and if it itself is taken in combination with others there are usually further statements which can be deduced from it. Because of these ramifications we often find that we have at our disposal not single statements, but sets or systems of state-

[1] See Ch. III, p. 17.

ments logically interconnected in various complex ways. Such systems of general statements are commonly spoken of as 'theories'.[1]

It is a feature of any theory that some of the statements which comprise it are more general than others, in the sense that they are concerned with wider classes of objects. The reason for this is that when one statement is deduced from others, it is normally the case that at least one of those from which it is deduced is more general than it is itself.

Consider, for example, the archaeologist who finds an ornate and massive tomb, and says that tombs of this kind are built only for privileged people. He may argue that such tombs require wealth for their building, and where there is wealth there is privilege. In doing this he is showing that his original statement can be deduced from two others taken together. The first classifies tombs of this kind as special cases of objects requiring wealth. The second states the general principle that anything which requires wealth is associated with privilege. The argument thus takes us back from a more special principle to a more general one.

Similarly, someone who wishes to explain why the price of a commodity rises when its costs rise may point out that, other things being equal, a rise in costs means a fall in supply, through marginal firms going out of business, and where supply falls, then, other things being equal, price rises. Here again the original statement is brought under the more general principle about supply and price, by it being shown that rising costs are one of the things which tend to shorten supply.

These illustrations are rudimentary, and, as we shall see, the relation between the more special and the more general statements in a theory may take various forms. Furthermore they give us only one small cross-section in the structure of a theory. The more general statements may themselves be deducible from further statements, including still more general ones, until we come to a set of very general principles which are accepted without their being deduced from anything else. These will then be regarded as the key statements of the theory. They will be

---

[1] The word 'theory' has of course other uses. Any general statement, and in particular any law, may be called a theory, in opposition to statements about particular things and events, which are said to 'state facts'. Again there is the sense in which theory is opposed not to fact, but to practice; in this sense any activity aimed at establishing conclusions and giving explanations would be called theoretical. On 'the relation of theory and practice', see Ch. XVI. We are neglecting both these senses of 'theory' here.

We are also neglecting a more special sense of 'theory' in which a theory is not any system of general statements, but only a system of general statements about unobservable entities like electrons and unconscious complexes. Norman Campbell is a case of a writer who uses the word 'theory' in this more special sense (Cf. his *What is Science?* Methuen, 1921, Ch. 5.) Such 'theories' must be related to statements about what can be observed before they can be used, but in sciences like physics they can be developed extensively on their own account. We may have occasion to refer to such theories; in fact motives (as distinct from intentions) and other people's experiences may be regarded as unobservables. But we will not restrict the use of the word 'theory' in this way.

logically connected, directly or indirectly, with all the other statements of the theory, and these can be visualized as ranged below them in a hierarchy of generality.

To have at one's disposal a body of theory in the sense described is clearly a very great advantage in any enquiry. For in the first place, if we are to use a general statement to establish some unobserved fact, that general statement must itself be established. It may be possible to establish it independently on the basis of its own evidence. The arch-æologist would do this, for example, if he were to have observed various massive tombs in various circumstances and were to have noted that in every case they were built for someone belonging to a privileged class. But vast additional support is at once obtained if it can be shown that the statement in question is logically connected with a number of others each of which has some independent evidence in its favour. In other words, where there is a theory, the evidence for all the constituent statements is pooled, and it can all be drawn upon in support of any given statement. This is why the suggested argument of the archæologist immediately strikes one as more convincing than his citing of instances.

In the second place the presence of a theory makes possible a much more satisfactory explanation of any particular event than we could ever obtain by relying on one single general statement. To say that where costs rise price rises is undoubtedly to contribute to an explanation of a rise in price, and it is a perfectly good contribution as far as it goes. But we are always tempted to ask why price rises with costs, that is, to demand a further explanation of the original general statement, or to ask why the effect of the rise in costs was not offset on this occasion, that is, to demand that the explanation itself be completed. In doing either of these things we are requiring an appeal to other general statements, in other words an appeal to the background of theory lying behind the original statement. In so far as further explanations can be given or existing explanations completed, we feel that we have gained a better understanding of the particular event.

In view of these advantages, it is obviously of considerable importance to consider the extent to which systematic bodies of theory can be developed in social enquiries. It is often felt that without such bodies of theory we could not properly speak of 'social sciences' at all; we would have instead only a large number of small-scale isolated enquiries all concerned with the same subject-matter. To say this would be to give a more special meaning to the word 'science' than we have done. Social enquiries could be conducted after a fashion without theories, and so long as they possess the features we have enumerated in Part One, we would not want to deny them the epithet 'scientific'. But they would be very much less effective. Hence we need to raise the question: how far are theories possible in social enquiry?

The Questions to be Considered

In discussing the use of general statements, then, we have two questions before us. The first concerns the way in which general statements can be applied in the discovering or the explaining of what happens in particular cases. The second concerns the extent to which they can be incorporated into supporting theories. Though these two questions are closely connected it is as well to keep in mind that there is a difference between them.

So far we have spoken, without discrimination, of general statements and of theories as systems of general statements. We must now remind ourselves of certain of the distinctions we have drawn between types of general statement. For there are important differences between the ways in which statements of these different types can be applied to particular cases. And there are also important differences between kinds of theory according as they are composed of, or include, statements of one type or another.

It will be remembered that we made a distinction between laws and statements of chance and a further distinction among laws between those which are straightforwardly universal and those which we spoke of as 'theoretical' laws, or tendency statements.[1] Taking these two distinctions together, we have three types of statements to consider— *straightforward laws* which concern what always happens in given circumstances, *statements of chance* which concern the chances of something happening in given circumstances, and *tendency statements* which concern what always happens in given circumstances in the absence of interfering conditions.[2] Let us now take these types of statement in turn and ask in each case how they can be used for establishing and explaining particular facts, and how far they make possible the construction of theories.

[1] Cf. Ch. III, pp. 18–19. We neglect in this context the distinction between restricted and unrestricted statements.

[2] Where it is necessary to emphasize that tendency statements are a kind of law, we will continue to speak of them as 'theoretical' laws. But where we use the word 'law' by itself it is to be understood that we are speaking of laws of the straightforward type. This is admittedly contrary to the usage of some, who reserve the word 'law' or 'law of nature' for laws of the 'theoretical' kind, and speak of the others as 'empirical generalizations'. J. S. Mill sometimes does this; the laws of nature are, for him, 'the laws of the separate causes'. See also Toulmin—*Philosophy of Science* (Hutchinson, 1953) Chs. 2 and 3. Toulmin contrasts 'laws' with 'natural history generalizations'. But there is no standard terminology here.

XI

THE USE OF
STRAIGHTFORWARD LAWS

ONCE a law of the straightforward type has been established its application to particular cases is a very simple matter. If it is the case that every *a* is a *b*, then it follows that a particular instance of *a* will be a *b*. If we can say that wealth invariably leads to privilege, with no allowance for exceptions and no allowance for interfering conditions, then from the fact that any person or class is wealthy we may straightaway deduce that he or it is privileged, whether it be in Ancient Egypt, present-day America or the Trobriand Islands. Similarly, where we are aware of the privilege we can explain it immediately and completely by referring to the wealth of those who possess it. As we have pointed out,[1] it is this automatic way in which laws can be applied that makes them superior to general statements of other kinds for the purpose both of discovery and of explanation.

Law Theories

Just as it is a simple matter to deduce particular conclusions from laws, so also is it a relatively simple matter to deduce some laws from others. It is in doing this that we develop the first and simplest of the different kinds of theory, one in which all the constituent statements are laws. In this kind of theory the ways in which the statements are related to each other stand out clearly. To begin with there is a very simple pattern in accordance with which one statement can be deduced from two others, one of these being a more general one. Given that all *a*'s are *b*'s, the more specific statement that all *a*'s are *c*'s can be seen at once to follow from the more general one that all *b*'s are *c*'s. A great number of our ordinary arguments have at least the appearance of conforming to this pattern. It is very easy to assume, for example, that it is this kind of logical connection between statements which is revealed in our illustrations about privilege and about a rise in prices. Whenever

[1] See Ch. III, pp. 19–20.

117

such a connection is found we can say that one law is a special case of another or is subsumed under another.

Given this type of logical connection, it is, furthermore, easy to see how a theory can be developed as a hierarchical structure of general statements, all the statements of one level being subsumed under general statements of a higher level. Suppose that we represent any statement of the form 'All a's are b's' or 'Whenever a is present, b is present' by writing '$a \rightarrow b$'. We could then present a simple pattern for a theory in the following way:

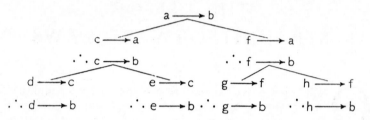

It will be seen here that any evidence for a statement on the bottom line will be evidence for the statements from which it is deduced, right up to the most general statement of the system, and hence also it will be evidence for all the other statements which can be deduced from these. Similarly where any statement on the bottom line is used in explaining particular facts, the explanation can be followed up by a reference to all those statements above it in the body of the theory from which it is deduced.

The pattern presented here may of course be varied in a large number of ways. At any point in the system, combinations of statements may occur which will give rise to new deductions. It may be, for example, that $c \rightarrow k$, and since in the system $d \rightarrow c$, this will give rise to a further statement of the form $d \rightarrow k$. And so on, more or less indefinitely.

This, however, is not the only sort of deduction to be found in systems made up of laws of the straightforward type. The possible kinds of logical relationship holding between such laws are various. In particular there is the kind of logical relationship which holds between statements in a mathematical proof. If we have the statements that income = consumption + investment and that saving = income − consumption, we may deduce that saving = investment.[1] If we have the statement that all freely falling bodies near the earth move towards it with an acceleration of 32 feet per sec.^{2}, we may deduce that any such body starting from rest moves $16\ t^2$ feet in t seconds. In the first case use is made of simple algebra, the second requires the integral calculus.

[1] Cf. J. M. Keynes—*General Theory of Employment, Interest, and Money* (Macmillan, 1939) p. 63.

In physics, a great deal of the deduction takes the form of mathematical calculation, and for this reason physical theories of this kind bear little resemblance to the simple pattern we have set out. In so far as there are social theories of this kind, this would not be true of them to nearly the same extent. But whichever form the deduction takes, the laws of such a theory will tend to form a hierarchy in which large numbers of specific laws will be derived by stages with the aid of intermediate premisses from an ever-decreasing number of ever more general laws.

Where such theories can be framed, they will evidently have great advantages. For, on the one hand, the laws of which they are composed fufill the purposes of discovery and explanation more effectively than any others; and on the other hand, the relations between these laws are of a kind which is relatively easy to grasp. The question remains, however, to what extent there can be social theories of this kind.

In the social illustrations we have given it is, as we have said, very easy to assume that we have been revealing small cross-sections of such theories. Moreover, it has often been supposed that social theories of this pattern can be constructed on a more extensive scale. Suppose, for example, we take as a key general principle that wherever there is unequal wealth in any group, there is privilege. From this, with the aid of various statements about wealth and about privilege, we could deduce various others, among which the statement that massive tombs indicate privilege would be quite subsidiary. Thus by associating privilege with class conflict, we might deduce that unequal wealth leads to class conflict. By asserting that wealth depends on ownership of the principal means of production, we might deduce that wherever there is such ownership there is privilege. We could apply this last statement to various types of case by specifying the means of production as consisting principally of human labour, or land, or capital, and we could deduce further that where there is common ownership privileges vanish through becoming available to all.

This illustration, suggested by the Marxist social theory, and bearing some resemblance to part of it, is taken from the study of social institutions. Another and more obvious one may be taken from that kind of study which traces the effects of the operation of basic human motives. This is the system of classical economics. This has often been thought of as an elegant example of the type of theory we have been discussing. The key general principle in this case is that all men desire to maximize their money gains. Given this principle we can deduce what different people will do in various circumstances. We can deduce, for example, that any seller of perishable commodities will desire to dispose of his stocks, hence that greengrocers will lower their prices when stocks accumulate, hence that the price of beans will fall when there is a glut. And we will be able to make large numbers of other deductions of a similar kind.

Limitations on the Use of Laws and Law-Theories

It is not hard then to find apparent illustrations of the use of social laws and social theories composed of them. In all these cases, however, the trouble comes when we ask ourselves whether the statements which make up the theories are really laws of the straightforward type. Do we really mean that they have no exceptions, and that they have to be abandoned if we find any single case in which they do not hold? In the case of most of them, the answer is clearly—No. People frequently seek to maximize their money gains, but they do not always do so; it is recognized that the pure 'economic man' is only an ideal, and that this key generalization is, after all, only an approximate one. Similarly, those who assert the association of wealth with privilege are not put off by the existence of some cases of wealth without privilege such as that, perhaps, of Jews in Nazi Germany or of the well-to-do in general in Russia in the 1920's. It is very easy and natural to frame our general statements in the form of laws. For laws have a certain bold simplicity about them, and there is no need to worry about their application to any given case. But we should not be misled by this. If we are to have laws of the straightforward type we are considering, we must be sure that we are ready to reject them if there are any exceptions.

In the social sciences, it is not easy to find laws of this type against which no negative instance could be produced.[1] The obvious regularities which we find in social life are hardly ever exceptionless. We expect human beings to act in similar ways in similar circumstances, but this does not always happen. Where they form groups, we expect them regularly to abide by the customs and institutions of the group, but on occasions customs may be broken and institutions ignored. We expect certain institutions to be associated together—the industrial, for example, with the democratic—but this cannot be relied on in all cases.

In order to pass from such approximate regularities to laws, one thing we may do is to start incorporating a statement of the circumstances in which exceptions will be avoided. People always seek to maximize their money gains, we will say, except where they are influenced in certain ways, which we might specify, by a love of their work for its own sake, a desire for leisure, or patriotic fervour. Or again, industrialization always leads to democracy, so long as natural resources are not too meagre or social traditions too rigid. But in the perpetual struggle to exclude cases where the general statements do not hold, these statements will become more and more complex. They could be better represented by a formula like 'Whenever $acdefg$—, then b' than by the simple formula 'Whenever a then b'. The time may come when we arrive in this way at a genuine law. But if we do, it will be a very specific one and for that

---

[1] Cp. Kaufmann—*Methodology of the Social Sciences* (Oxford 1944), p. 174. Kaufmann is more sweeping—'There are, as I see it, no empirical laws established in social science.'

reason not very serviceable. It is true that where we find a particular case in which all the conditions are satisfied, the law can be automatically applied to it. But the more conditions we have to include, the fewer will be the cases to which the law can be applied. Further, if we only have such specific laws, we will be unable to construct a law-theory. For these laws are in place only at the lowest level in the deductive system of such a theory, and if there are no laws of greater generality from which to deduce them, the connecting superstructure of the theory will be missing. We will thus be left with a heterogeneous collection of laws, each of them applicable on comparatively few occasions.

There is of course one infallible way of preserving a higher-level law, and that is to make it true by definition. Definitions and laws are frequently expressed through the use of the same kind of sentence. Thus we may say that where there is a fall in demand less is bought at the existing price, and also that where there is a fall in demand there is a fall in price. In this case it is easy to see that the former statement must be true in all conceivable circumstances, since we are doing no more than making clear how the phrase 'fall in demand' is being used, whereas the latter statement has to stand the test of evidence, and if it were to be a straightforward law it would have to be shown to be free of exceptions. In many cases, however, the distinction is not so clear, since the common use of the crucial words is vague, and tends to shift from person to person and context to context. Thus when J. M. Keynes asserts that savings = investment, we may need to look carefully to see that he is making the statement true by definition and not establishing an equality which other economists had denied.[1] Again, when someone says that in a democracy there is individual freedom, we may be uncertain whether he is explaining what he means by 'democracy', or asserting the invariable connection of two different features of a political system.

Because of such uncertainties, it is very easy for anyone to slip unawares into defending a law against refutation by making its truth dependent on the meanings of the words used. Words like 'wealth' and 'privilege', for example, have the required vagueness, and they are also matters of degree, the degree being left unspecified in the general statement of the law. Hence it becomes possible to exclude any alleged exception by saying that the people concerned are not really wealthy or not really unprivileged or not sufficiently wealthy or not sufficiently unprivileged. Furthermore it may be said that what is really meant is that privilege always goes with wealth in the long run, so that their dissociation over short periods (the actual length of time being left unspecified) proves nothing against the law. If a procedure of this kind is persisted with, it becomes clear that the alleged empirical law is one which could not be refuted under any conceivable circumstances.

[1] Cf. J. M. Keynes, op. cit. Chs. 6 and 7.

It is notorious that a defence of this kind has often been given for the key principle of classical economics. The trouble, it may be said, is that in speaking of the maximizing of money gains, we have not taken the principle broadly enough. We can include all cases by saying that everyone desires to maximize their satisfaction, for this leaves it open whether they obtain satisfaction through increasing their money incomes, through love of work, through leisure or even through the most extreme self-sacrifice. We arrive in this way at a completely exceptionless principle. But it only becomes exceptionless because the word 'satisfaction' is being so used that it stands for anything that a person may desire.

So long as we recognize them for what they are, statements whose truth depends on the way the words are being used are by no means valueless. For they give us information about how the words are being used, and it is most important that we should know this. Furthermore, we can deduce some such statements from others, thereby making clear how the uses of numbers of words are related. This is what is being done by Keynes for 'income', 'consumption', 'savings' and 'investment', in the example we have quoted. Finally, we can incorporate such statements, or logically connected sets of such statements, into the body of a theory, thereby enabling ourselves to pass from one way of expressing a given statement in the theory to another.

But for all that, it is clear that the function of such statements in a theory is a subsidiary one. They may help to clarify what is being said, but they tell us nothing about social life. To say that everyone wants to maximize his satisfactions may help to relate the uses of 'want' and 'satisfaction', but no verifiable economic consequences follow from this. Hence if we try to preserve the strict universality of laws by converting them into statements of this kind, we will be left with a verbal amework for a theory, but no theory.

When we say that it is not easy to find genuine empirical laws of the exceptionless type in the social sciences, we do not of course mean that there are no such laws. In fact, if we cast our net widely enough, we can bring in a large number of them. And we can do this without having to resort either to narrowing them down into highly specific laws, or to treating them as definitions.

For instead of narrowing down their subjects, we can adopt the reverse procedure of generalizing their predicates. If the features we ascribe to individuals or to groups are made sufficiently general, we will soon get to statements which no one would wish to dispute. We can safely say, for example, that everyone who understands the use of money is affected to *some* degree on *some* occasions by the desire to increase the amount he holds, or again, that in every community there is some differentiation, however slight, in the amount of power possessed by its members. Here we have completely universal statements which we can conceive to be false, but which we are pretty sure are true.

This point can be put another way. Any law can be cast into a negative form by obverting it. That is to say, instead of saying that all a's are b's we can say that no a's are non-b's. Hence we could express the statements just mentioned by saying that no one is entirely unaffected by the desire to increase his money gains, and that in no community is there complete equality of power. In doing this, we are substituting for the assertion of very general features the denial of their opposites which are correspondingly specific. We thus bring out the point that in making statements of this kind, we are setting certain broad limits to what is socially possible. If the limits are extended far enough, we make it quite safe to say of what lies outside them that it *never* happens.

When the matter is put this way, we can also see why it is that it is often easier to retain laws stating necessary conditions for occurrences than those stating sufficient conditions. A necessary condition of an event of a given kind is that without which it will not occur, while a sufficient condition is that in the presence of which it will occur. Thus a statement of a necessary condition may be represented by the formula 'Whenever not -a, then not b', and a statement of a sufficient condition 'Whenever a, then b' Where b is relatively specific, we have said, it will be hard to find social laws of the latter kind. But where b is specific, not-b will be correspondingly general. Hence the stating of the conditions (positive and negative) under which the event b will not occur will present less difficulty. Thus if someone were to say that without a reasonable degree of social unity there could never be stable parliamentary government he would be making a universal statement which could at least be plausibly defended. But if he were to be asked for those conditions given which stable parliamentary government would invariably ensue, he would be hard put to it to find an answer.

It will be seen then that the possibility of establishing social laws will always remain so long as we are prepared to be sufficiently cautious and restrict ourselves to either asserting very general features or denying very specific ones of whatever it is we are discussing. But anyone who follows this path of caution must resign himself to being unilluminating. Though the general laws which we manage to retain in this way are applicable to many particular cases, no social enquirer will be particularly interested in so applying them. It will not be of much help to an economist to know that the profit motive will have some effect on a given person's behaviour sometime during his life, and if this is a fact, it is not the sort of fact he will feel called on to explain. Though the denial of complete equality of power may be useful for countering a naïve political assumption, it stops short of the crucial question about the extent of the differentiation. The establishing of the necessary conditions for the occurrence of events undoubtedly has more point, but even here it remains the case that the primary purpose of the establishing of laws is to establish and to explain what *does* happen rather than what does *not* happen, and for this the statement of sufficient conditions is required. In short, if a social enquirer has to play very safe in order to operate with laws, he will not get very far.

This being so, it will be evident also that there will be little point in a social enquirer developing law-theories in which laws of this kind are incorporated. There is nothing in the nature of the laws to prevent the construction of such theories. But if the laws themselves have to be framed so cautiously that they become uninteresting, no one will wish to waste time providing them with equally uninteresting theoretical support.

We may conclude then that such genuinely empirical straightforward laws as can be established in social enquiries are of no great value when taken by themselves, and hence also that little use can be made of simple theories of the law kind. This makes it important that we should consider the use of other kinds of general statements and other kinds of theory.

XII

THE USE OF STATEMENTS
OF CHANCE

IF it is the case that laws are hard to come by, why should we not be content with approximations? We may know very little about what always happens, but we know a great deal about what usually happens. Why should we not use this knowledge as a guide to what to expect in particular cases? If wealth is generally, though not always, associated with privilege, may we not still reasonably infer the existence of privilege in Ancient Egypt or in any other society in which we know that there is inequality of wealth? And again, why should we not construct theories by accepting statements like 'People maximize their money gains' as approximate ones and deducing approximate consequences from them? This may be less satisfactory than working with laws, but the question remains whether we should not accept it as a reasonable substitute.

It will be remembered that we classified such approximations as one kind of statement of chance, or statistical generalization.[1] Instead of saying 'Nearly all a's are b's', we could say that there is a good chance of an a being a b, or that a high proportion of a's are b's. In these cases, the chances or proportions are not stated with any precision; all that is said is that they are high. But it would be possible to increase their precision, the ideal being to state an exact number, by saying, for example, that 95% of a's are b's. In this respect they are similar to any other statements of chance, for these may be more or less precise and refer to chances which vary on a scale between high and low. In considering, therefore, how to make use of approximations, we must regard this as part of the wider question about the use of statements of chance generally. By regarding it in this way, we bring out the point that, though we may think of statements like 'Wealth generally leads to privilege' as just falling short of laws, they nevertheless differ only in degree from more precise statements of more even chances, such as 'There is a 51% chance that any baby born will be a boy'.

[1] See Ch. III, pp. 18–19.

Let us then ask about statements of chance the two questions distinguished in the previous chapter. In what way can they be used in establishing or explaining particular facts? And how far is it possible, when using them, to develop social theories?

THE APPLICATION OF CHANCE-STATEMENTS TO PARTICULAR CASES

In the case of straightforward laws, we have pointed out, application to the particular case is a simple matter. To establish that all a's are b's is automatically to justify any inference from a thing's being a to its being b, or any explanation of a thing's being b in terms of its being a.

Once our general statements fall short of being laws, however, we are no longer in this happy position. However good the chance is of an a being b, it does not *follow* that any particular a will be b. Hence doubt has sometimes been thrown on the propriety of using chance-statements at all when we wish to find out or to explain what happens in particular cases. This may seem extreme and even obtuse. But in view of the comparative unavailability of laws in social enquiries and the consequent reliance which has to be placed in many cases on chance-statements, it is as well that we should at least be clear about the principles which are presupposed by their use.

We may present our problem formally in the following way. Suppose we write P (a, b)=p for 'The chance of any a being a b is p', p being a fraction between 0 and 1.[1] The question then is: Given that P (a, b)= p, and that a particular thing A is a, in what way does this provide evidence for or against a statement of the form 'A is b'?

It is clear that the argument—P (a, b)=p and A is a, therefore A is (or is not) b—suffers from two defects, as compared with the application of a straightforward law. In the first place, there is the simple point that, however high (or low) the value of p, we cannot conclude that A is (or is not) b without recognizing that A may be one of the exceptions. Though there is a good chance of a trade-unionist voting for a Labour candidate, we cannot conclude that Mr. Smith, who is a trade-unionist, will do so without recognizing that he may be one of those who will not.

In addition, however, there is a second defect which is less easily noticed. The particular case, A, may always possess features other than a, in virtue of which it will fall under a further rule in which the value of p is quite different. Thus, A may be c as well as a, and though P (a, b) $=\frac{3}{4}$, say, P (ac, b) may equal only $\frac{1}{4}$. If Mr. Smith is not only a trade-unionist but also has a personal dislike for the Labour candidate, this will, as we commonly put it, 'reduce the chances' of his voting Labour.

---

[1] The symbolism is that adopted by W. Kneale. See his *Probability and Induction* (Oxford 1949), Section 25, pp. 118 et. seq. The letter 'P' is used because Kneale speaks of 'probability' where we speak of 'chance'.

This difficulty, it should be noticed, does not arise in the case of the application of laws. If there were a law that every trade-unionist voted Labour it would make no difference whatsoever to our argument what other features Mr. Smith possessed.

In order to meet the situation in which these two defects are present, we may formulate two principles:

(1) The value which the general statement P (a, b)=p possesses, as evidence for the statement that A is (or is not) b, increases as p varies from $\frac{1}{2}$ upwards (or downwards).

(2) The evidential value of the statement increases the greater the number of features of A it takes into account.

These principles seem clearly to be presupposed by the judgments we commonly make on social questions. Let us consider them in turn.

Raising Chances

The first principle is the ground on which we accept approximate generalizations as being 'nearly as good' as laws, while refusing to draw conclusions about what will happen when the chances are more or less even. There has seemed so obvious a correspondence between the increase in the chances stated in a rule and increase in the evidential value of the rule that it has often led to a confusion between the chance of any a being b and the likelihood on the evidence that some particular instance of a will be b.[1] Though the identification is a mistake, it bears witness to the ease with which we accept the principle which asserts their connection. Given the principle we may base on it the recommendation that wherever we have to rely on considerations of chance, we should try to use rules in which the chances stated are as high as possible.

Yet despite its apparent obviousness, this principle has sometimes had doubt thrown upon it. Such doubt is thrown by people who query whether statistics have any value for estimating what will happen in individual cases. Even if we know that 70 out of every 100 trade-unionists vote Labour, it may be argued that there are so many special circumstances involved in any individual case that it is impossible to tell whether the case will be included in the 70% or not. If we knew more about Mr. Smith we might be able to use some law from which we could deduce that he would *not* vote Labour. Or at any rate we might arrive at some rule of chance which would make it very unlikely that he would do so. Are we not then merely guessing when we say that he will?

The trouble with this line of argument is, firstly, that if we are demanding a straightforward law from which we may deduce a con-

[1] On this confusion see, for example, Carnap—*Logical Foundations of Probability* (Chicago, 1950) Ch. 2; Sects. 9–10; also Kneale, op. cit. Sect. 25.

clusion, we will very rarely find one, and hence will very rarely be able to draw any conclusions at all. This would be decidedly alarming, since we commonly assume that we can estimate the likelihood of events occurring even when we cannot get beyond approximate generalizations. If, on the other hand, we are merely demanding some further rule of chance which takes account of as many features as possible of the case under examination, we do not avoid the difficulty. The attempt, in other words, to rely solely on our second principle while abandoning the first is doomed to failure. For we are still left with the need to apply a chance-statement, and if we doubt the first principle we cannot do it. If, for example, we find that Mr. Smith belongs to a class of people who, though trade-unionists, have declared their intention of voting against the Labour Party, and if we estimate the chance of such people voting for it as about 1 in 10, this would leave us, on this view, with no better evidence as to what Mr. Smith was going to do than we had originally. The application of chance-statements to individual cases would be ruled out in the one case as in the other.

Those who seem prepared to accept this conclusion do in fact attempt to mitigate its severity by regarding it as holding only when we are speaking of individual cases, and not when we are speaking of large sets of things. A set of things, such as that comprising the students entering a given university in a given year, or the transactions arranged at a given stock-exchange during a given month, may be regarded as a 'particular case', and conclusions about the proportions in such sets of things having such and such features, may be regarded as one kind of conclusion about particular cases.[1] Against the drawing of this kind of conclusion there is rarely any objection raised, and the applicability of chance-statements is to that extent saved. Thus, if we have the statement that 75% of university students with an I.Q. of more than 120 obtain degrees in minimum time, it will be said that this will tell us nothing about the performances of any individual student who happens to be in this category, but that it will give us a very reliable conclusion about the number of degree-obtaining students in a particular group of 2,000, say, who have the required I.Q.—the number, we will say, will be something about 1,500. Similarly, an insurance company which accepts, let us suppose, that 80% of people of the age of 40 will die before they reach the age of 85, will not be prepared to stake its profits on Mr. Jones, now 40 years of age, dying before that time; but it will be quite happy to take a risk on about 8,000 of the next 10,000 40-year olds they insure dying before that time. The evidence for chance-statements is, after all, derived from the proportions which we find in sets of observed in-

---

[1] They may, of course, also, in their turn, be regarded as restricted chance-statements. A 'particular set' and a 'closed class' are the same thing, and all restricted statements may be said to be both particular and general. See Ch. III, p. 19. But this does not alter the point.

stances. Should we not therefore expect that when the statistical knowledge so gained is applied, it will be applied to proportions in sets rather than to individual cases?

Now there is obviously a good point in discriminating between these two types of case, but it is important that we should be clear what the point is. In order to draw conclusions about large sets of things, we make use of a logical relation which holds between two kinds of chance-statements. From a statement of the form P $(a, b)=p$, we can deduce various statements about the *chances* that *any* large set of things of the a kind will contain such and such a proportion of things of the b kind. In particular we can deduce that the chance of any large set of a's containing a proportion of b's approximating to p, is high. This is the gist of a well-known logical principle about chances which is commonly referred to as the 'law of large numbers'. As the size of the sets under discussion is increased or the required approximation to p made less close, the chances referred to in the second kind of statement can be made higher and higher. But it is important to remember that they always remain statements about chances. Given that we have derived a statement of this kind, we will commonly say that it provides fairly good evidence for statements about *particular* large sets of a's—for the statement, for example, that the large set, S, of a's contains a proportion of b's which approximates to p. And there is no doubt that it does provide evidence of this kind. But it should be noted that this evidence is of precisely the same kind as that provided by any rule stating high chances for a particular case falling under it. Just as the individual case, A, may always be an exception to a chance-statement of the first kind, so also the large set, S, may always be an exception to a chance-statement of the second kind, in that the proportion of b's which it contains is nowhere near p. Hence the move from the one kind of chance-statement to the other should make no difference to anyone who is sceptical about the first principle.

For anyone who accepts the principle, however, the advantage gained in making statements about large sets is clear. For whatever the chances given in the first statement, the derivation enables us to deal in chances which are high. The insurance company has *some* evidence that Mr. Jones will die before the age of 85; the trouble is that the shareholders may not think the evidence good enough. By dealing modestly in approximate proportions of deaths among large numbers of clients it raises its chances until they approach indefinitely close to 1. And the evidence so provided is enough to satisfy the most prudent investor. The preference for applying chance-statements to proportions in sets is therefore an excellent illustration of the acceptance of the principle.

It is admittedly impossible to meet a critic of this principle by attempting to derive it from anything more elementary. We are tempted to support it by pointing out that the chance of any case being an exception becomes less and less as the value of p increases, and using this in favour of the particular case, A, not being an exception. But this is merely to convert P (a, b)=p into P $(a, -b)$=1-p (-b standing for 'not-b'), and to use the principle as before, with the rule in its new form. And so on with other considerations of this type. If we feel it necessary to justify the principle at all, we have to do it in some other way. The problem of justifying it, in fact, raises precisely the same sort of issue as the problem of justifying the use of inductive evidence in support of a law or chance-statement. We have agreed not to discuss the question how this problem is to be solved, or whether it is a problem at all.[1] So we will likewise be content here to accept the principle, recognizing that it is in honourable company.

Specifying Chances

We come now to the second principle. This is the one we have in mind when we seek not to use chance-statements which are as high as possible but ones which include as many as possible of the relevant features of the particular case we are concerned with. In estimating whether a particular student is likely to graduate, it is natural to ask not only about his I.Q. but also about his previous education and his interest in his subject. As well as enquiring about Mr. Jones's age, an insurance company will seek, at the very least, to make sure that he is not suffering from cancer and that he is not a test pilot. What is happening in such cases is that general chance-statements are being replaced by more and more specific ones—P (a, b)=p by P (ac, b)=p and P (acd, b)=p. The particular case is examined with the purpose of selecting a specific rule which is applicable to cases of that special type. For it is recognized that the more specific rule, where applicable, is more to be relied on than the general one; it takes account of circumstances which might make the case an exception to the general rule. Thus, to revert to the case of trade-unionist Smith, if we can use such rules as 'The chance of a trade-unionist who is an active member of the Labour Party voting Labour is $\frac{9}{10}$, or 'The chance of a trade-unionist who dislikes the Labour candidate voting Labour is $\frac{1}{3}$', we will be well advised to do this rather than rest content with the general rule, 'The chance of a trade-unionist voting Labour is $\frac{2}{3}$'.

It must be clear that this applies whether the specific rule states a high chance or a low chance, and even when the general rule states a high one. If A is both a and c, and there are rules P (a, b)= $\frac{99}{100}$ and P (ac, b) =$\frac{1}{2}$, we must accept the second and (applying the first principle) refuse to commit ourselves as to whether A is b. It is of course the case that, given the first of these two chance-statements, the second, though true,

[1] See Ch. III, p. 21.

will be rarely applicable, for it can be shown that there is very little chance of an *a* being a *c*. P (*a*, *c*) must in fact be less than $\frac{1}{50}$. Hence if we do not know already that A is *c*, we can argue legitimately that it is unlikely that it will be. But if we do know that it is *c*, this removes the likelihood of being *b*, which it has when we take into account the first statement alone.

Here then we have a procedure by which we are driven to the use of ever more specific chance-statements, applicable on an ever-diminishing number of occasions, of which the occasion under consideration is one. Unless we already know that many of the characters of A are irrelevant, it is a procedure which may go on indefinitely. It may, of course, end with the discovery of a law which is applicable to the case. If so, we are taken beyond considerations of chance altogether, and no further specification is necessary. But, as we have seen, this is not likely to happen in any social enquiry.

This being so, we can clearly see an objection to the second principle parallel to the objection that was raised against the first. If there may always be conditions present which require us to replace the chance-statement we are using at any stage by some other chance-statement in which the value of p is quite different, can we say that the first one, however many characters it takes into account, is of any value at all as evidence of what is going to happen? To this we can give no better answer than before, namely, that the objection is of the same type as that which can be raised against the use of inductive evidence for laws or chance-statements themselves, and hence that the justification of the principle, if it is felt to be required, must stand or fall with the justification of induction.

Even assuming the principle, however, the need to search for more and more specific chance-statements is clearly a defect in any procedure which makes use of them. For it is not only that there may always be further conditions present which may alter the chances. It is also that the more specific the statement, the fewer the cases (other than the one under consideration) to which it can be applied, and hence the greater the difficulty in obtaining evidence sufficient for estimating the chance even in the roughest way. This is a difficulty which is not found in the parallel case of establishing specific laws. For in the case of laws we are not so dependent on numbers of supporting instances. We can at least quickly exclude a law by finding a single exception, and each failure to find an exception helps. Whereas with chance-statements, so long as we have to establish them separately, we have to rely on counting proportions in as large and as varied a number of cases as possible. And in the case of very specific kinds of people or events, such cases may be hard to find. It will not be easy, for example, to estimate the chances of a Labour vote coming from a trade-unionist of conservative upbringing who dislikes the Labour candidate but has expressed himself in favour of the nationalization of banking, since we will not be able to find many people belonging to this class.

For this reason, it often becomes advisable to rely on the first principle rather than on the second, and seek to use rules which are both general and state high chances. For, as we have seen, once we know that A has the general character a and that P (a, b) is high, we already know that there is only a slight chance of any a (A included) possessing other features which will radically alter the chances. Thus, once we know that Mr. Smith is a member of the Labour Party and that the chances of members of the Labour Party voting Labour are high, we already know that there is only a slight chance of such a person having his chances of voting Labour reduced by his possession of other features such as having a conservative upbringing or disliking the Labour candidate. Hence it is only when we are unable to employ general rules stating high chances that the application of the second principle, with its attendant difficulty, becomes important.

Further, it must be kept in mind that the procedure of resorting to more and more specific chance-statements is of no avail when taken by itself. For specific chance-statements, like general ones, have to be applied to particular cases and their value as evidence will depend in the last resort on whether the chances they state are low or high. It follows from this that when specifying chances leads to reducing them, we are in a worse position than before for drawing positive conclusions about the particular case. We are only helped in that we are prevented from drawing the wrong conclusions.

It is in this connection that we must notice a further advantage in drawing modest conclusions about approximate proportions in large sets rather than straightforward ones about individual cases. By drawing such conclusions we do not avoid the need to employ the second principle, or the difficulties which this involves, any more than we avoid the need to employ the first. Any particular set, S, of a's, may always contain such proportions of things possessing other features—c, d and so on—as will require us to replace a rule about the chances of approximate proportions of b's in a set of a's by another which makes reference to these other features. Thus, given that the chance of a manual worker voting Labour is $\frac{2}{3}$, we may have as our first rule 'The chance of any set of 1,000 manual workers containing a proportion of about $\frac{2}{3}$ Labour-voting members is high'. If, however, a particular set, S, happens to contain a large proportion of active Labour Party members, it will come under a new rule in which this chance will be reduced, the high chances moving in favour of some higher proportion. It is clear that our second principle is operating here, only in a more complex form.

And yet we do gain a considerable advantage, in considering approximate proportions in large sets, from being able to rely on dealing in general rules giving chances which are high. For this ensures that there is only a small chance of the chances of the approximate proportion holding for any set being seriously altered by its having some special constitution. In any sufficiently large collection of manual workers, there is not much chance that there will be such an undue proportion either of active Labour Party members or of people who dislike nationalization or whatever it may be, as will greatly alter the chances of such and such an approximate proportion of them voting Labour. This can be put in a common-sense way by pointing out that while the individual members of a set may have a variety of features which would bring them under various specific rules of higher and lower chances, it becomes more and more likely, as the size of the set increases, that these deviations will cancel out. Thus, by dealing in sets, we short-circuit to some extent the multiplicity of relevant conditions which would otherwise force us into using ever more specific rules.

Precision in Statements of Chance

In our discussion of these two principles we have found it convenient, for purposes of illustration, to take chance-statements in which precise values are given to the chances. It will be recognized, however, that it is rarely possible for a social enquirer to establish chance-statements of this determinate kind. The statistical evidence at his disposal does not usually justify him in stating more than a fairly rough range within which the chances are to fall. It is in fact only on the assumption that precise values are not given to chances, that chance-statements can be said to be easier to establish than laws. We may know a good deal in general terms about what usually happens, but we know very little about what happens in, say, precisely 90% of the cases. In compiling statistics, we will, of course, be able to give exact percentages for the *observed* cases, but the number of our observations would have to be very large and very varied if we were to be safe in generalizing from this and to say that the same percentage held for all cases. If we observe a large number of university students, and find that exactly 75% of those with an I.Q. of more than 120 obtain degrees in minimum time, all we can safely infer from this is that the percentage among students generally is something *in the neighbourhood of* 75%.

For the application of chance-statements, however, this lack of precision makes no difference in principle. We can make an estimate of what will happen in a particular case without using precise fractions. All that is needed is that we should be able to grade chances from high to low, and to speak of raising them or reducing them. We may, if we like, obtain a somewhat arbitrary precision for any chance-statement by naming certain exact limits within which the chances fall—between 70% and 80%, say, or over 80%. In doing this we make it clear that, though our considerations are not based on exact chances, they are based on a more or less extended range of chances. When we use phrases

133

like 'high', 'fairly high', 'not much more than even' and so on, we admittedly do not normally have even precise limits in mind. But unless we are prepared to give precise limits, or at least some further ranges within which the limits are to fall, our statements may as well be abandoned as of no use to anyone. For under those circumstances the necessary grading would become impossible.

There is of course a difference between dealing in precise values and dealing in ranges of values. If we do not know quite how high the chances are, we also do not know quite how good the evidence is that a particular event will occur. Hence, the more extended the range of chances, the less basis we have for drawing conclusions about individual cases or about particular proportions in sets of cases. This is why it remains an ideal not only to find chance-statements in which the chances are as high as possible, but also to find them in which they are stated as precisely as possible. But precision here has to be recognized as a matter of degree. Furthermore, the higher the lower limit of the range, the less important does precision become since we can then rest more and more content with the minimum evidence which the chance-statement provides.

We may conclude then that, though social enquirers can rarely use laws, there is no objection to them resorting to the more easily available alternative of drawing particular conclusions from more or less precise statements of chance. They cannot deduce such conclusions, even when they are concerned with proportions in large sets, but so long as they are guided by the two principles we have been discussing and take the necessary precautions, they can make reasonable estimates, similar in kind to the estimates made by any scientific worker when he engages in the inductive confirmation of laws or chance-statements themselves. The only difference is that in the case of chance-statements the procedure of estimation enters in at two points instead of one. Not only do we have to judge of the truth of a chance-statement on the basis of evidence; we also have to estimate whether, given the chance-statement, something will or will not happen in a particular case to which it applies.

THEORIES AND STATEMENTS OF CHANCE

So far we have been considering the use of chance-statements taken separately. We must now ask what possibility there is of finding logical connections between them and thereby developing deductive systems of social theory. If we can do this, we will be able not only to give more adequate explanations in terms of them, but also establish them more securely by pooling the evidence in their favour. We have seen that if they are not too precise and not too specific, we can often find reasonable independent support for them. But, as with laws, this support would be vastly increased if they could each be incorporated into a body of theory. In particular, this would be of special importance for those specific chance-statements to which the employment of the second principle leads us. For if these statements were to find a place at the lowest level of a deductive system, they would be saved from being a mere heterogeneous collection and would be provided with the support which their few ascertainable instances fail to give them.

What Cannot be Done

In considering this question, we must start by pointing out two things which we would like to do but cannot do. In the first place, we cannot merely substitute chance-statements for laws in a deductive system such as we have described in the previous chapter. Those who speak of starting off with approximations and deducing other approximations from them are inclined to miss this point. If there is a $\frac{3}{4}$ chance of any student with an I.Q. greater than 120 obtaining a degree in minimum time, we cannot deduce from this that there is a similar chance of this occurring among those of such students who show a special interest in their subject. In such a case we realize that further enquiry is needed to find out what difference interest makes. Similarly, if we take as our general principle the statement that there is a 95% chance of any person seeking to maximize his money gains, it does not follow from this that there is a 95% chance of any retail tradesman seeking to maximize his money gains, or of any clergyman doing so. We may have an idea that in the first case the chances will be higher and in the second case they will be lower. If we are asked how we know this, we will have to confess that we have found it out quite independently of the general principle, by observing the behaviour of the classes of people in question. The higher-level rule will not have helped at all unless we have independent reason to believe that the lower-level one does not concern a class which contains a high proportion of exceptions to it. And this applies, however high or low, and however precise or imprecise, the chances which are stated in the higher-level rule.

This point may be put formally in the following way. From P (a, b)=p and $c{\to}a$, it does not follow that P (c, b)=p, or, for that matter, that P (c, b) has any particular value whatever. And the same will hold, *a fortiori*, if we substitute the chance-statement P (c, a)=p for $c{\to}a$. For, clearly, if there is a 95% chance that employers will maximize their money-gains, and, say, a 60% chance that retail tradesmen will be employers, nothing whatsoever can be deduced about the extent of gain-maximizing among retail tradesmen. Hence we must rule out the possibility, when working with chance-statements, of constructing simple subsumptive systems of the type we set out at the beginning. And since such systems are the easiest to construct and the easiest to grasp, this at once implies a serious limitation on the use of chance-statements in theories.

The second thing which we often feel inclined to do is to take the separate chances of an event of a given kind occurring in two or more different sets of circumstances, and deduce from these the chance of it occurring when these circumstances are all present together. To put it formally, we feel inclined to deduce a specific statement of the form P (ac, b) from the general ones P (a, b) and P (c, b).[1] If we could do this, then, knowing the chance of a student of given intelligence quotient obtaining a pass, and the chance of a student of given previous training obtaining a pass, we could tell without further investigation what the chance would be of a student passing if he had both the I.Q. and the previous training. Or again, from the chance of a trade-unionist voting Labour and the chance of a person of conservative upbringing doing so, we would be able to deduce what the chance would be of a Labour vote coming from a person who combined these features. Our tendency would be to suppose that if the two chances were both favourable—that is, greater than half, they would combine to give a still more favourable one, that if they were both unfavourable they would combine to give a still more unfavourable one, and that if one were favourable and the other not, the combined chance would lie somewhere between the two.

Unfortunately, however, we cannot make deductions of this kind. We can perfectly well conceive a combination of a and c giving rise to a chance which bears no relation to the constituent ones. Consider, for example, the case of trade-unionists with conservative backgrounds. We may suppose that the chance of a person of conservative upbringing voting for a Labour candidate is small and that the chance of a trade-unionist doing so is high. We might therefore wish to infer that the chance of a Labour vote from a person who is both a trade-unionist and of conservative upbringing must lie somewhere between the two. But we may well find that the chance of a Labour vote coming from such people is even greater than that found among trade-unionists in general. For when people of conservative upbringing become trade-unionists, they may react in a wholesale way against their former political views. It is clear therefore that, whatever the value of P (c, b), the addition of the feature c to things of the a kind may have the effect either of raising or of reducing their chances of being b, and which it does can only be settled by further enquiry into the value of the specific chance P (ac, b).[2]

---

[1] Note that chance-statement theories constructed on this model would have an analogy not with subsumptive theories, but with the factor theories to be discussed in the next chapter.

[2] John Stuart Mill was one who argued that specific chance-statements could be deduced from general ones in the manner described. Cf. *System of Logic* Book 3, Ch. 23, Sect. 6. (He admittedly had doubts about his argument in the 7th edition, but subsequently reinstated it.) If the rules used in his argument are formalized, it will be seen that he is led into absurd consequences.

It may be asked why we should feel so inclined to compound chances in this way. That we should be so inclined appears to be due to a confusion between two quite different things—the consideration of evidence for or against a given statement and the tracing of logical relations between chances. No one doubts that two pieces of evidence in favour of a statement corroborate each other; if this were not so, in fact, there would be no point in constructing theories at all. And similarly no one doubts that we can weigh one piece of evidence against another. The mistake comes when these processes are interpreted as if they were a matter of calculating composite chances from simple ones.

What Can be Done

From the fact that these two possibilities are excluded it does not follow that it is impossible to construct any deductive system of chance-statements. For there remain various logical relations which do hold between such statements. The logical principles which are embodied in these relations can be set out in a formal logic of chance-statements—the so-called 'calculus of chances'—which is as extensive in its range as the formal logic of universal statements. But the principles are different and deductions which conform to them have an altogether different kind of pattern. So we must ask what use can be made of deductions of this kind when we are developing a body of social theory.

There is one important principle to which we have already referred—the 'law of large numbers'.[1] It is this, we have seen, which enables us to associate chance-statements of two different types—those which concern the chances of occurrence of individual events of given kinds and those which concern the chances of occurrence of certain proportions among large numbers of events of these kinds. From any statement of the first type we may deduce various statements of the second type, each concerned with different possible proportions in sets of different sizes (always including some, it will be remembered, in which the chances stated are very high). It follows that any evidence for any of these statements about the chances of there being certain proportions in sets will also support the general chance-statement from which it is deduced and hence also the other statements which in their turn can be deduced from it. Similarly, the general chance-statement may be offered as an explanation of any of the deduced ones.

The classic example of the use of this principle in the construction of a theory is to be found in the kinetic theory of gases. Given that there is an even chance that any molecule of gas in a container will move in one direction rather than the opposite one, it can be deduced among other things that there is a very high chance that among a large number of

[1] See above, p. 129.

molecules, almost exactly half will move one way and half the other, thus making the pressures in the two directions almost exactly equal. Because of the largeness of the numbers, the chances, in this second statement, are so high and the approximation to a half so close that it has been regarded as a law, but it is only as a chance-statement that it can be deduced from the first.

The principle illustrated here can clearly be applied in any social enquiry in which we are interested in proportions among large collections of people or large numbers of events of a given kind. If there is a fifty-fifty chance of any member of the Roman Catholic Church in the United States voting for the Democratic Party, it follows that there is a very good chance that in any group of 10,000 Roman Catholics, say, about half will vote in this way and half not. If the chances of anyone buying in the cheapest market are 10 to 1, there is a very good chance that in any country in any month, the number of occasions on which this is done will be about ten times greater than the number on which it is not done. Whenever deductions of this kind are made, the general chance-statement may be regarded as the key statement of a theory, unifying and explaining those which are derived from it.

These deductions about proportions, however, constitute a rather special case. If we wish to find out what can be done with chance-statements generally, we must go back to the more elementary theorems in the calculus of chances, and see how far these can be used for the construction of theories.

Let us take as an example the simplest of these—the 'conjunction theorem'. According to this, if we are given that $P(a, b) = p$ and $P(ab, c) = q$, it follows that $P(a, bc) = p \times q$. To illustrate how this principle might be used, let us take the case of Roman Catholics in the United States, and consider what might be done in the course of an enquiry into their political and economic affiliations. If we take the chance of a Roman Catholic voting for the Democratic Party and the chance of a Roman Catholic who votes Democratic being a trade-unionist, we can see, at any rate if we refer to the formula, that there is a logical relation between these two chances taken together and the chance of any Roman Catholic being both a Democratic voter and a trade-unionist. The third chance would be lower than the first two by an amount which would vary according as the first two were high or low. If, for example, the first two were 60% and 70% respectively, the third would be 42%; if they were 30% and 40%, it would be 12%.

Again, to move from the sphere of restricted to that of unrestricted statements, suppose that the chance of anyone seeking to maximize his money gains is high, say 95%. And suppose that among those who seek to maximize their gains, the chance of avoiding mistakes in judgment in pursuit of this end is also high, say 90%. From these two statements it follows that the chance of anyone both seeking to maximize his gains *and* avoiding mistakes in judgment will still be fairly high, but not as high as the other two; given the figures suggested it will be $85\frac{1}{2}\%$.

There is no doubt that the tracing of such connections will on occasions be useful, and it will remain useful even where the chance-statements concerned lack precision. Yet we need go no further with the illustration of the logic of chances in order to realize that there is an obstacle to its extended use for the construction of deductive systems. The principle we have illustrated is one of the simplest available, and yet it is evident that the connections it makes possible are considerably more complicated and less easy to grasp than those which are found in deductive systems of laws. It is to be noted that these connections only hold if we introduce complex classes (represented by *ab* and *bc* in the formula) into two of three statements. This means in the first place that the number of possible statements which we can bring into any system is severely limited. After two or three steps we are likely to find ourselves with statements concerning combinations of features which we are unable to provide with independent support or which are of no interest for us. And it means in the second place that we are often prevented from simply 'seeing' that a given connection holds. It is in fact usually · necessary to refer to a formula which has been extracted by reflection on specially devised cases. If this is not done, it is easy to commit logical errors through treating the connection as simpler than it really is. Conspicuous examples of such errors are the two illegitimate ways of deriving chance-statements which we have discussed. Indeed, these may be said to arise out of the false assumption that it is possible to operate with chance-statements in the straightforward and easily intelligible manner with which we are familiar in the case of laws.

It appears then that it is such practical difficulties rather than any impossibility in principle of constructing systems of chance-statements, which puts a gap in the social sciences between statistical enquiries and theoretical enquiries. It is these difficulties which seem to account for the fact that, except where we introduce the somewhat special principle of the 'law of large numbers', we usually expect statistical generalizations to be supported by their own independent evidence, and do not seek to provide them with additional support by showing that they are logically connected with other statistical generalizations. It is to be noted that logical relations of the kinds we have been pointing out have aroused interest mainly in connection with those deliberately contrived situations which are found in games of chance. It is more natural to illustrate them by referring to dice and cards than to the actions of human beings.

If we are to have social theories, then, with all the advantages they carry with them, it is desirable that we should have laws. And since straightforward laws are difficult to establish, this brings us to the alternative of using laws of the other kind—those which we have called theoretical laws or tendency statements. If we cannot replace statements about what usually happens with statements about what always happens we can at least replace them by statements about what would always happen in the absence of interfering conditions. Let us now consider the extent to which it is possible to have social theories which include statements of this kind.

XIII

THE USE OF
TENDENCY STATEMENTS

TENDENCY statements and chance-statements have one notable feature in common; they each leave open a way of dealing with exceptions. A law of the straightforward empirical type must be rejected if we find any single instance in which it does not hold. In a chance-statement this consequence is avoided by exceptions being admitted in the statement itself. In a tendency statement the consequence is also avoided, but in another way, by the exceptions being accounted for by interfering conditions. The form of a law is thus retained, while at the same time it is recognized that there are circumstances under which the law does not hold.

For this reason it is always possible to replace any chance-statement by a corresponding statement about a tendency. Instead of saying that tariffs usually lead to inefficiency in home production, we can say that they invariably tend to do so. Similarly, trade-unionists tend to vote for the Labour candidate, those with high I.Q. tend to pass, and people tend to buy in the cheapest market. So easy is it to make this transition that the phrases 'usually happens' and 'tends to happen' are often used almost interchangeably. The extra implication when we say that something tends to happen is that the exceptions could be accounted for in some way or another. But that is all.

Kinds of Tendency Statement

Statements of this kind are in very common use. In particular they include most of the statements that are made about causes in social enquiries. To assert a straightforward empirical causal law we have to do one or other of two things. Either we have to specify a set of conditions given which an event will always occur whatever the circumstances or we have to specify some condition (or set of them) without which an event will never occur whatever the circumstances. To do the

141

first, we have seen,[1] is to state a sufficient condition for the occurrence of an event, and to do the second is to state a necessary one. To emphasize that there must be no exceptions, we may speak here of stating absolutely sufficient conditions and absolutely necessary conditions. We have argued that it is not easy to do either of these things, though it is easier to do the second than the first. Whenever we demand a *complete* causal explanation of an event, it is the absolutely sufficient condition we are asking for. Already in the discussion of motive explanations it was pointed out that we are not likely to get this,[2] and in the light of our discussion of laws we may now add that this is true of social explanations generally.

Hence what we normally do in assigning causes is to point to certain conditions, and say that when they are present the event will follow, so long as the other unspecified conditions are favourable. Likewise, in the case of necessary conditions we say of certain conditions that when they are absent the event will not follow, so long as the other unspecified conditions are favourable to this negative outcome. In other words, we distinguish between various relevant causal factors, and say of each of them that it is a sufficient, or a necessary, condition in the absence of interference by other factors. Thus we say that a rise in costs will cause a rise in the price of a commodity, though an actual rise in price may on various occasions be prevented by other features of the situation. And we say that the introduction of labour-saving machinery will cause unemployment in an industry, though this result may be offset by the effects of counteracting causes.

What applies to discussion of causes applies also to discussion of influences. When we say that one person has an influence on another, we may mean that what he does will be followed by a change in the other person whatever the circumstances. But more usually we assume that any influence may be offset by another, which is the same thing as saying that any law asserting some kind of influence is understood as not necessarily holding under all conditions. A threat of violence, we may say, will have an influence on any person's conduct, though we admit that this will not take effect if he has strong moral convictions.

The same applies in the case of another very common way we have of speaking about social situations—that of the operation of forces. Though the word 'force' has an original social use, it has also acquired a new and different use in social enquiries, which has been taken over from physical dynamics.[3] Thus we speak of the economic forces operating in a market and the political forces which determine the out-

---

[1] Ch. XI, p. 123.
[2] See Ch. IV, p. 32.
[3] This has in fact led to serious confusions. See my article on *Social Forces*, The Journal of Philosophy (New York), Vol. LV, No. 11, pp. 441–455.

come of an election, to say nothing of our use of such allied expressions as 'inflationary pressure' and 'international equilibrium'.[1]

An important difference here is that whereas statements about causes and influences are normally to be taken as tendency statements, statements about forces are invariably to be taken in this way. In physical dynamics, when a force acts on a body, the body does not always move in the direction of the force; whether it does or not depends on whether there are other forces at work. Hence when the terminology of forces is adopted in the development of a 'social dynamics', social forces come to be substituted only for influences or causes conceived as tendencies, and not for the complete sufficient or necessary conditions for the occurrence of events.

The phrase 'other things being equal' is often used when we wish to isolate a tendency and discount the effects of other factors in a situation. But it is not always used in this way and care has to be taken to avoid ambiguity.

For 'equal' may be taken to mean 'stable' or 'unchanging'; and, if it means this, a statement about what happens 'other things being equal' will be a straightforward empirical law. Take, for example, the statement that, other things being equal, price rises when demand increases. This may be interpreted to mean that if demand increases and no other changes occur—in particular no changes in supply—then the price will rise, whatever the situation may be. The statement would then give an absolutely sufficient condition for a rise in price, namely an increase in demand taken together with the absence of other changes, and it would have to be rejected if a single case were found in which this condition held and no price rise ensued. Similarly, the statement that, other things being equal, price falls when supply increases, may be interpreted to mean that with an increase in supply and no other changes—in particular no changes in demand—a fall in price will invariably ensue. Both of these statements would be straightforward empirical laws, each applying to its own type of case.

It is clear, however, that though we might start with this interpretation of the phrase we do not normally adhere to it. For one thing, if we were to do so, both statements would have to be rejected if we were to find a case in which there was a rigid and effective system of price control. For such a system would be a stable factor in the situation, and yet if it were present neither an increase in demand nor in supply would be followed by a change in price. Obviously we would wish to discount the presence of the controlling agency as a counteracting factor even though an unchanging one and would continue to uphold the laws of supply and demand in spite of it.

Again we would normally wish to uphold these laws even in cases

---

[1] Examples of writers who have made much use of such terminology are Karl Marx, William McDougall, and, more systematically, Wilfredo Pareto and Kurt Lewin.

where various changes were taking place. We would say that changes in demand always have an effect on price, even though the effect may on occasions be counteracted by other changes, such as changes in supply. Thus it is that we move from 'equal' in the sense of 'unchanging' to 'equal' in the sense of 'discounted' or 'allowed for'. When this happens, statements about what occurs, other things being equal, cease to be taken as straightforward empirical laws and become tendency statements.[1]

Factor Theories

It is clear then that tendency statements are frequently resorted to in social enquiries, and must be taken seriously. But it is equally clear that no single tendency statement is of any use when taken by itself. It may be said in fact that to replace a chance-statement by a tendency statement is to take a retrograde step. For in a chance-statement a limit is set to the number of exceptions which are to be admitted. Whereas in a tendency statement there is no such limit. When 'tends to happen' is taken as a substitute for 'usually happens' the assumption is made that interference from other factors is infrequent. But this is an extra assumption, not included in the tendency statement itself. To take the extreme case, we may continue to assert that something will happen other things being equal, even though they are never equal. This in fact is what is commonly done when we speak of forces in physical dynamics. A body, we say, will move uniformly in a straight line if perfectly free from friction, but there is always friction. Similarly, price will always equal cost of production under perfect competition, but competition is never perfect. It follows that such statements taken by themselves can never be refuted and will explain nothing. They will only begin to be of use if we are able to say something about the operation of the other factors.

If we are to resort to tendency statements, then we *must* have a theory. We can only work by taking a number of such statements together, each of them stating the effect of some given factor in a situation, and arguing from these to what will happen in their combined presence. It is because tendency statements do not stand on their own, but can only function in this way as parts of theories, that they may suitably be spoken of as 'theroretical' laws. Different tendency statements are not subsumed under one another in a hierarchy with a key general principle at the top. They are rather set side by side as the laws of the different factors, a more special law being derived from them by estimating their resultant. It is not so easy to represent this kind of logical relationship in a sym-

---

[1] Note that John Stuart Mill (*System of Logic*, Book 3) failed to appreciate this distinction, with resulting confusion in his account of 'causal laws'. He thought of these ultimately as tendency statements (the 'laws of the separate causes'), yet he also assumed they could be established separately, like straightforward laws, by the observation of changes occurring under stable conditions.

bolic pattern, but the following will help to bring out the contrast with the subsuming type of theory:

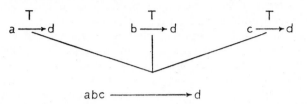

The laws represented by the formulae in the first line are to be understood as theoretical laws or tendency statements, and the statement represented in the second line is a specific one which is derived from them. Wherever we find this type of pattern appearing we will say there is a theory of the factor type, as distinct from a theory of the straightforward law type.

It will be clear that it is this type of theory which is used when the operation of forces is studied in physical dynamics. It is in fact a type of theory which has much to recommend it. The theoretical laws dealing each with a different tendency are all simple and by combining them in various ways it is possible to derive large numbers of different statements about what happens in large numbers of special cases. The system of laws taken as a whole is supported by our ability to derive from it specific statements which are found to hold in particular cases. Once it is sufficiently supported in this way, it can be used for finding out what would happen in various other cases. Likewise we can explain what happens on a great variety of occasions by showing, in each case, that it is a resultant derivable from certain laws of the system.[1]

Those who speak of social forces and of social dynamics imply that this type of theory may be used in a similar way in social enquiries. The time has now come to consider the extent to which this can be done.

The Use of Factor Theories

We have said that tendency statements are commonly used in the discussion of social events. Since they cannot be used to any effect except in combination, it follows from this that some theorizing of the factorizing sort is constantly being presupposed in such discussions. In discussing democratic institutions, we may ask what factors contribute to their growth or maintenance. In discussing international warfare, we may

[1] Some logicians have assumed that this is the most satisfactory type of explanation, more satisfactory, that is to say, than an explanation in terms of straightforward empirical laws. Mill (see Note 1, p. 144) may be said to be one of these. He felt that to state a merely 'empirical' law was not really to answer the question 'Why?' To do this, it was necessary to give a further explanation in terms of the 'laws of the separate causes'. There appears, however, to be no real reason in principle for this discrimination between the two types of explanatory theory.

point to various tendencies which lead to its outbreak, and others which tell against it. It is in economic argument, however, that this analysis of factors is most systematically applied. We have pointed out that the laws of supply and demand are theoretical laws. Changes in price may be regarded as the resultant of changes in supply and changes in demand—so long, that is, as there are not also other factors affecting the freedom of the market. It may then be asked further what are the factors affecting supply, and what are the factors affecting demand. And so on. To take another and more complex illustration, consider the answer to the question why there has been a general rise in prices—or whether there will be one. It will normally be couched in terms of various 'inflationary pressures' such as those arising from full employment, credit expansion and restriction of imports, and these will be weighed against counteracting deflationary pressures.

Again, we have already referred to the fact that explaining individual behaviour in terms of motives involves us in this kind of theory.[1] A person's motives are various and each implies a tendency to act in certain kinds of way. What he does is therefore to be looked on as the resultant of these tendencies.

It is clear, then, that theorizing in terms of factors and their resultants is a common practice in social as in physical enquiries. It remains to be seen, however, how widespread and effective it can be. In considering this we must first bring out more definitely than we have done so far some of the implications of the procedure.

In the first place, in abandoning straightforward empirical laws and operating instead with theoretical ones, it need not be supposed that we abandon subsumptive theorizing altogether. For it may still be useful to show that one theoretical law is a special case of another, or can in some other way be deduced from another. There is in fact nothing to stop anyone from incorporating within the framework of a factor theory, a whole subsumptive system of theoretical laws. This is what is done when people start with certain 'unrealistic assumptions', such as that everyone seeks to maximize his money gains, or that everyone acts rationally, or that everyone seeks power, and proceed to deduce consequences from these in the same way as they would deduce consequences from straightforward empirical laws. The only thing needed is that the propounders of such theories should be aware of what they are doing. The statements at each level of the deductive system have to be 'corrected' by a consideration of other factors before they can become effective. Furthermore, the corrections cannot be made once and for all at the level of the initial assumption and automatically repeated for all the special assumptions deduced from it. For the influence of other factors may vary greatly from case to case. Personal friendship, for example, may affect very greatly the decisions of housewives on where

[1] See Ch. IV, p. 32.

to buy vegetables, but will have little effect on brokers in the stock market. Hence it is necessary to apply the factor-combining procedure independently to the different statements of such a system.

In the second place, a glance at our symbolic pattern at once suggests that theories of the factor kind will be very much less concentrated in their structure than subsumptive ones. Instead of each statement of a lower level being derived, with the aid of a minor premiss, from some single statement of a higher level, it is derived from a set of statements not necessarily connected with each other. There will therefore be no key principle from which all the other statements of the theory can be deduced; there will only be a set of theoretical laws, none of which need have any logical priority over the others.

It may be, of course, that we can devise theories depending on sets of laws which are limited and relatively self-contained. Where this is done, the factors to which we appeal in drawing conclusions will all operate in accordance with a few laws which will be used over and over again in different contexts. The neatness of the system of Newtonian dynamics depends largely on the fact that it is a factor theory of this special kind. Though the number of forces acting on bodies in special cases which come up for consideration is usually large, it is nevertheless the case that they are all conceived as conforming to certain general theoretical principles, such as the laws of momentum and of gravitation. This simplifies the theory, though we may still be left with a difficulty in applying it.

It will be clear that the laws of supply and demand play a similar key role in the system of classical economics. They are applied and re-applied in numberless special cases, thus giving to the theory a relatively well-knit structure. Yet even here a certain diffuseness begins to emerge when we ask about the factors which determine supply and the factors which determine demand. And when we start asking about the relevant factors affecting the growth of democracy or territorial expansion or a decline in the birth-rate, we realize at once that the theoretical laws we have to draw upon are very various. Though we theorize in the factorizing way, it does not seem possible in such cases to build up self-contained bodies of theory.

This fact is of importance for our understanding of the relation between the various social sciences. The question whether any set of enquiries can be conveniently marked off from others as constituting a separate 'science' depends very largely on whether the theoretical laws that are drawn upon can be kept within a given field. In economics, this is done to some extent. But other 'social sciences' are very much interconnected, in the sense that factor theories which are used to establish or explain some given kind of fact, remain inadequate unless they include a reference to factors of various other kinds. Such factors may of course be discounted and 'other things being equal' inserted as a preamble to the whole theory. But unless it is already known how much difference is made by the neglected factors, this will put us on the way to reducing the whole theory to the same futility that we pointed to in the case of single theoretical laws.

This leads on to a third point. An explanation in terms of influencing factors may well be incomplete. It would only be complete if we were sure that all relevant factors were mentioned. We would then have a set of theoretical laws from which we could derive a straightforward empirical law about what would invariably happen when all the factors were combined. The difficulty of doing this, however, will be precisely the same as the difficulty of establishing an empirical law direct. If we cannot guard ourselves against exceptions in the latter case, we cannot guard ourselves against the presence of possible further factors in the former. In resorting to the factor-combining procedure in social enquiries, therefore, we will have in the main to rest content with incomplete explanations.

It may be said that if this is so the procedure will remain ineffective. For we will still be left with an 'other things being equal' clause attached to our stated set of theoretical laws. If we do not state how much difference is made by the presence of further, unmentioned factors, we will never be able to draw any conclusions from combining those whose effects we do state, and hence also any explanation in terms of those factors alone will remain an empty one.

This difficulty must be admitted. It is avoided, however, if we *do* state how much difference is made by the presence of further unmentioned factors. It is perfectly possible to do this without mentioning or even being aware of what the other factors are or how they operate. Suppose we take as our theory a certain set of theoretical laws and derive conclusions from them. We may then find that these conclusions do not hold invariably, that they are chance-statements and not straightforward empirical laws. This means that there is something wrong somewhere for we cannot derive a chance-statement from a set of theoretical laws taken by themselves. It may be that something is wrong with one or more of the theoretical laws we have included in our theory, and if this is so we must modify the theory accordingly. But if these laws can be used effectively in various combinations for deriving conclusions which hold at least approximately, this would be an unreasonable thing to do. Instead we would retain the theory and add to it an extra statement—a chance-statement—to the effect that there is such and such a chance that further unmentioned factors will affect the result. The whole theory, including this extra statement, may then be said to be supported by the chance-statements which are derived from it. And by continually using the laws of the theory together with their supplement to derive more and more chance-statements which are found to hold, the laws will become progressively more and more firmly established, without our ever deriving a complete empirical law from them.

Consider, for example, the central theory about supply and demand in economics. Suppose that, given the laws about the effect of supply on price and the effect of demand on price, we can derive a conclusion about a change in the price of a commodity. And suppose that we know nothing of any other factors which might affect the price. It may well be that the actual price change does not always conform to the one which is deduced from the theory. In these circumstances we might challenge one or another of the laws of supply and demand. But this would be unreasonable since many conclusions can be derived from these laws which at least hold approximately. Hence we add to our theory that there is a chance of other factors affecting the price, and in this way we correct the discrepancy in the conclusion. With this addition the laws of the theory can be retained intact, and further confirmed as more approximate statements about price changes are derived from them.

Once it is recognized that factor theories can be established in this way, it is possible to accept the incompleteness of most social explanations with comparative equanimity. The ideal, no doubt, is to bring in all the relevant factors, thus making it possible for us to derive the absolutely sufficient condition for the occurrence of an event of a given kind. But if we know what the separate effects of different circumstances are, a mention of even one of them will be the beginning of an explanation. Thus we have said something useful when we have pointed out that a rise in price is partly due to an increase in demand, or that obedience to the laws is partly due to threat of punishment. And the more factors we mention the better our explanation will become.

What applies to explanation, however, does not apply in the same way to discovery. For an explanation of our lower-level general statements, we will be reasonably satisfied if the main contributing factors are mentioned. But for establishing them this will not be enough. If we are to derive a conclusion about what always happens, we must introduce all the relevant factors. Where this alternative is ruled out, we may still derive a conclusion about the chances of something of a certain sort happening, but only so long as we add to our incomplete list of relevant factors a statement about the chances of other factors making a difference. And the trouble with this additional statement is that it cannot normally be established independently of the conclusion. It is rather to account for the conclusion being no more than an approximation that we introduce it into the theory at all. Hence, when we introduce factor theories in social enquiries, they will be of more use for explaining what happens in given circumstances than for discovering what happens in given circumstances.

This point may be illustrated from the case of motive-explanations. In an earlier chapter we pointed out that motive-explanations of the unrestricted kind were likely to be incomplete.[1] To account for a person's action completely in terms of motives we would have to refer not only to all relevant motives but to all relevant occasioning circumstances. We are not normally able to do this. Nor are we normally able to make an independent estimate of the chances of unmentioned counteracting motives or circumstances being present. Hence we are not normally able to predict actions by considering motives, though we are happy to give partial explanations of them by referring to motives.

Since ability to predict has sometimes been regarded as the hall-mark of science, there have been some social scientists who have taken this conclusion very hard. But they have no cause to regard themselves as unique in this respect. Even in the simple self-contained factor theory of Newtonian dynamics, the number of forces acting on a body is commonly so large as to prevent calculation of the resultant beforehand. Prediction in terms of such theories is for the most part only possible in the laboratory and in the convenient emptiness of astronomical space.

Limitations on the Use of Factor Theories

We now come, however, to a final point about factor theories, and this time it is one which involves a definite limitation on their use in social enquiries not found in the case of Newtonian dynamics. If we are to deduce the resultant of the operation of different tendencies, we must assume a rule for their combination. In dynamics we have such a rule, which we incorporate without question into the theory itself—the principle of the composition of forces. Forces are 'vector quantities'—they have both magnitude and direction. Where two forces act on a body in different directions, the effect will be the same as that produced by their vector sum. If the two component forces are represented in magnitude and direction by the two sides of a parallelogram, their vector sum will be represented by its diagonal. In the special case where the forces act in the same or diametrically opposite directions, this will be the same as their ordinary arithmetical sum. Can we point to a corresponding rule for estimating the combined effect of different tendencies or factors in social enquiries?

It will be clear that there are important differences. In the first place, since we are concerned with various kinds of change and hardly at all with mere motion, we cannot speak of tendencies operating in different spatial directions. There is no question therefore of the summation of vectors. All that we could be expected to do would be to estimate the outcome of opposed tendencies—that is, of those which favour a change and those which interfere with it.

In the second place, we have no common standard, like the dyne in physical dynamics, in terms of which we could compare the strength

[1] See Ch. IV, p. 32.

cf any social tendency with any other. We have nothing to put in place of the spring-balance. Nor can we compare tendencies by looking to the amount of effect produced, as we do when we measure forces by reference to acceleration produced in a body of given mass, since the effects, being of various kinds, cannot be assembled on a single scale like that of amount of acceleration. Thus it would not be sensible to ask which was the greater influence—the influence of a rise in costs on the price of potatoes, or the influence of trade union agitation on a government's policy. We could only be expected to compare influences in so far as they led to events of the same kind, for example the influence of a rise in costs and of a fall in demand respectively on the price of potatoes.[1]

To these limitations, we must now add a third. Acceleration is something which admits of degree; it can be either greater or less. Hence the effects of different forces acting in a given line can all be stated in terms of the *amount* of acceleration produced. But when we speak of the tendencies which tell for or against any social change, we may not wish to restrict ourselves to changes which admit of degree. Admittedly we deal in variations in amount in many important cases—in the case of prices, for example, volumes of goods bought and sold, levels of employment, numbers of votes obtained, even of power. But we are also inclined to ask about the factors which tell for or against someone making a speech, or a given kind of law being passed, or the achievement of a military victory. In such cases, either the event in question will occur or it will not, and any talk of variations in amount does not make sense.

In the case where effects admit of degree, we can see the possibility of using a rule of combination similar in kind to that of the composition of forces. This is the rule that the effects of different factors be simply added or subtracted to give the total effect. This may be represented by the following version of our original symbolic scheme:

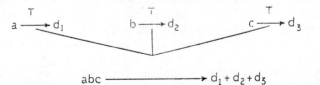

where d_1, d_2 and d_3 are specific quantities of d and may be positive or negative. Suppose, for example, that we were to consider the combined effect on the demand for beer of an increase in price of 3d. a glass, a

---

[1] Note that we can compare influences on the prices of *different* commodities, so long as we take account of their different elasticities of demand, just as we compare physical forces exerted on different bodies, so long as we take account of differences in their mass or inertia. 'Inertia of demand' would in fact have been a more appropriate metaphor for economists to use than 'elasticity of demand'.

publicity campaign about its being bad for the health, and an extension of hotel trading hours. And suppose we were to take as our premisses that the first factor would decrease the demand by, say, 10,000 gallons, that the second would decrease it by 5,000 gallons, and that the third would increase it by 7,000 gallons. If there were no other relevant factors we could then use our rule to deduce that the combined effect would be a reduction in demand of 8,000 gallons. In practice, of course, no one would attempt to give precise quantities, but in making a rough estimate they would still be assuming the same rule of combination.

There is no doubt that this rule—called by J. S. Mill the principle of the 'composition of causes'[1]—is freely accepted and used in all social enquiries which have to do with quantities. Since economics has to do very largely with quantities—quantities of money and quantities of goods—it is particularly evident as a constituent principle of economic theories. It may be said further that it is the availability of the principle in this field which accounts for the free use there made of theoretical laws and theories of the factor type.

For it will be clear that where effects do not admit of degree there can be no question of adding or subtracting them. If all factors are favourable to the occurrence of an event this will admittedly not matter. We will only need a slightly modified version of the addition rule to conclude that in their combined presence the event *will* occur. It was in fact because the symbolic scheme as originally presented suggested this version that it appeared to harbour no difficulty. But as soon as we take account of interfering conditions, or counteracting causes, we are presented with a problem. If *a* favours the occurrence of *d* and *b* tells against it, how can we deduce anything about its occurrence or non-occurrence when *a* and *b* are both present? If the advice of economists, for example, will, other things being equal, lead to a banking reform, and press agitation will, other things being equal, prevent it, how are we to estimate their combined effect? If the army with superior equipment will tend to win a battle, and the army with the less capable leadership will tend to lose it, how do we tell from this whether an army which combines good equipment with bad leadership will win or not?

There is no doubt that we still speak, in these cases, of one tendency being 'stronger' than another, and we continue to 'weigh' the influence of one factor against that of another. The resultant, we assume, will depend on which influence is the stronger, and the derivation could be represented in the following way:

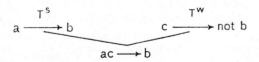

[1] See J. S. Mill—*System of Logic*, Book 3, ch. 6

where the suffixes 's' and 'w' indicate different degrees of strength. It will be clear, however, that this merely leads to a restatement of the problem. For we are still left with the question: what is the criterion for the strength of a tendency?

The answer seems to be that, where we cannot judge the strength of a tendency from the *amount* of effect produced, we judge it from the *frequency* with which it is produced. If the effect attributed to a certain tendency is generally found to occur despite its being associated with various other opposed tendencies in different situations, we conclude that considerable weight must be given it in any further combination. Whereas, if it is constantly being effectively counteracted, we minimize its importance. Thus someone may conclude that the banking reform will not occur because the effects of press agitation on government policy are counteracted in far fewer combinations of circumstances than are the effects of the advice of experts. And in the same way, someone may argue that superior leadership usually tells.

It will be realized that when we use this criterion for the strength of tendencies we revert to considerations of chance. They are, however, chance considerations of a new kind. In particular, there is no attempt here to re-introduce the illegitimate form of argument in which the chance of an *ac* being *b* is derived from a more-than-even chance of *a* being *b* and a less-than-even chance of *c* being *b*. The chance-statement introduced is of a higher order, being about tendency statements themselves and their relations to resultants. To illustrate this symbolically, suppose that *a* is a factor telling in favour of *b* and *d, e, f* and *g* are adverse factors. And suppose that in the following combinations—*ad, ae, af, ade, aef*, the result is *b*, whereas in the combinations *adf* and *ag*, the result is not-*b*. We would then say that *a* had not been counteracted in 5 out of 7 of the tried combinations. If this figure held for larger numbers, it would support the view that there was an approximately $\frac{5}{7}$ chance of *a* not being countereacted in any further combination. Using the simple principle for the application of chance-statements, we would take this as fairly good evidence for saying that *a* would not be counteracted by the further factor *c*. Similarly, if the adverse influence of *c* was found to be frequently counteracted when in combination with other favourable factors—say, *h, i, j, k*, etc.—this would be evidence in favour of *c* being counteracted by *a*. And all this would be summed up by saying that the influence of *a* is stronger than that of *c*.

We see then that even in these circumstances we have a rule for combining different tendency statements to derive a resultant. Though it may appear elaborate when exposed for logical examination, it is nevertheless one which we constantly use for estimating the relative importance of causal factors in social situations.[1] It will be clear, however, that

[1] For further discussion of the 'importance' of different factors, see Ch. XV pp. 190–192. An additional criterion of 'importance' is there pointed out.

once we have to fall back on rough-and-ready chance-statements for relating tendencies to resultants in a theoretical system, we are very far removed from the ideal of the factor theory of physical dynamics.

Finally, whatever kind of rule we use there is one general point which must be borne in mind. Such rules of combination are not logically necessary principles. Even in the simple case where all factors are favourable, it does not *follow* that the combination of them will be favourable. The only justification for adopting any such rule as a constituent principle in a factor theory is that the theory so constituted has numerous verifiable consequences.

Judged by these standards, the principle of the composition of forces is a firmly established law of physical dynamics. But once we move outside this field, we have to recognize that there are types of case in which the corresponding rules of combination do not appear to hold. These are the types of case in which we say that a reaction takes place to a situation 'as a whole'. Suppose that there are various factors present in a social situation which taken separately would each have a specifiable influence on what happens. When they are present together, these factors may be said to form a qualitatively distinct 'pattern', and there appear to be cases where the influence of such a pattern is not deducible by any rule from the influences of the separate factors.[1] It is possible, for example, that when an increase in the price of beer is combined with persuasion that it is bad for the health, its consumption may increase, the reaction to such an accumulation of sorrows being that they must be drowned.

When John Stuart Mill spoke of the composition of causes, he was well aware that there were cases of this type. He pointed to chemistry and biology as fields in which effects could often not be compounded. In discussing the social sciences, however, he was prepared to assume that the principle of the composition of causes was the universal law.[2] This enabled him to visualize social theories generally as theories of the factor type based on certain theoretical laws of individual human nature.

Now there is no doubt that this principle has been assumed successfully in economics, and we have in this fact a further reason why it has been possible to develop a body of economic theory which bears at least some resemblance to the model of physical dynamics. But even here we cannot rely on the principle when we ask about such things as the factors influencing demand, as is shown by the illustration we have just given.

[1] For earlier comment on 'patterns', see Ch. IX, pp. 98–99. In speaking here of 'patterns of factors' we are stretching the 'pattern' metaphor further than was done in the previous context. For 'factors' are features of a situation, not its parts. A 'pattern' of factors is of course entailed by the presence of the factors, just as a pattern of parts is entailed by the positions of the parts. But it does not follow from this that laws about the effects of the pattern are entailed by laws about the effects of the different factors.

[2] J. S. Mill, op. cit., Book 3, Ch. 6. and Book 6, Ch. 7, Sect. 1.

And this suggests in general that, in considering the impact of various social influences on individuals, we cannot accept without further investigation the procedure of analysing factors and using factor theories.

We must conclude then that resort to tendency statements, though necessary for the theoretical development of social enquiries, is not a universal panacea, the application of which will create a revolution in the social sciences, similar to the Galilean revolution in mechanics.[1] It is not just that social enquirers have not been clever enough so far to devise theories which measure up to the standards of physical dynamics. Our considerations will have shown that the difficulty lies rather in the nature of their subject-matter. What is important is that we should recognize the limitations which this subject-matter imposes, and see what can be done within them.

[1] Cf. K. Lewin—*The Dynamic Theory of Personality*, Ch. 1, on Galilean versus Aristotelian modes of thought in psychology. When Lewin advocates the adoption of a 'Galilean' approach, the use of factor theories is one of the main things he has in mind.

XIV

THE ASSUMPTION OF RATIONALITY

WHEN upholding the scientific character of social enquiry, in Part I, we were made to recognize the significance of the fact that human beings are to some extent rational in their actions and beliefs. This fact, we pointed out, does not relieve the social enquirer of the necessity of making use of general statements or of relying on empirical evidence.[1] But nevertheless it has specially important consequences for the procedure of social enquiry. These consequences we must now examine.

To act rationally, or to have a good reason for acting, it is necessary not merely that we should believe the action the most suitable for achieving an end, but also that this belief should itself be rational. That is to say, the belief itself should be the result of a recognition that there is sufficient evidence in its favour. Thus if someone puts super-phosphate into his soil because he recognizes that, on the available evidence, this is the best way of preserving its fertility, he may be said to be acting rationally. Whereas, if someone performs a first-fruit ritual because he thinks it preserves soil fertility without taking account of any evidence there may be for or against this supposition, this would be a case of irrational action.[2]

The peculiar feature of the former case—that of rational action—is that the very same facts which provide evidence for a belief constitute at the same time one of the factors which help to explain its being held, and hence also to explain the action which ensues. Where the evidence is taken account of, then, given certain other conditions, the use of super-phosphate will ensue. The fact that in such cases the evidence has a dual role has, as we have seen, often caused discomfort to those who wish to defend the scientific character of social enquiry. We have claimed that this discomfort is unjustified. Furthermore, we have pointed out that

[1] Ch. IV, pp. 45–46, and Ch. V, pp. 53–54.

[2] For this illustration, used in a somewhat different context, see S. F. Nadel—*Foundations of Social Anthropology* (Cohen and West 1953), p. 274.

if the dual role of evidence were denied in the crucial case of the beliefs of social enquirers themselves, we would be involved in absurd consequences and social enquiry would itself become impossible.[1] Now we must take a further step and follow up the point already foreshadowed,[2] that the admission of the rationality of human beings is not only possible and necessary for social enquiry, but also of considerable assistance in the development of a body of scientific social theory.

THE USE OF THE WORD 'RATIONAL'

We must start with some words of caution about terminology.

Rational Action and Rational Belief

In the first place we have assumed, in speaking of rationality, that the rationality of actions is always dependent on the rationality of beliefs. This is natural enough, since to be rational is to take account of evidence, and evidence is relevant primarily for deciding what to believe—not what to do. But it may be objected that this is to limit the field of rational action unduly, including within it only those actions in which we have thought out beforehand the most suitable means to our ends. If someone applies the brake and swerves to avoid an accident, he could surely be said to have acted rationally, yet we might feel uncomfortable about giving an account of this incident in terms of what he believes about ways of avoiding accidents and the evidence he has for these beliefs.

Such objections, however, need not worry us if we remember that a belief, in the sense in which we are using this word, is a *dispositional* feature of a person. Someone may *hold* a belief—and a rational belief—without continually assessing evidence and drawing conclusions. It is enough that, either all at once by systematic enquiry or gradually through trial and error, he has found out that certain things are necessary, or sufficient, if certain consequences are to follow.

Thus the car-driver who applies the brake and swerves may be said to hold rational beliefs about the best way of avoiding accidents, even though he does not think out a plan on the spur of the moment. The beliefs are, as it were, already there, ready to be manifested when appropriate circumstances arise such as the approach of an oncoming car.

Furthermore, such beliefs may be manifested directly in action, without the making of statements. Not only is it unnecessary for the car-driver to assess evidence on the spot, it is also unnecessary for him to reaffirm his belief on the spot, saying to himself 'This is the best way of

[1] Ch. VII, pp. 75–76.
[2] Ch. IV, pp. 45–46 and Ch. V, p. 53.

157

avoiding an accident'. Part of what is meant by saying he believes that applying the brake helps to avert accidents is that he is disposed actually to apply the brake at the appropriate time. When this kind of manifestation of the belief predominates we are inclined to say that he 'knows how' to avert accidents rather than that he 'knows that' the best ways of avoiding accidents in these circumstances are such and such. This may suggest that the term 'rational' should in such cases be applied directly to actions, without mentioning beliefs. But to accept such a suggestion would be to confuse the belief, considered as a disposition which may manifest itself both in assertion and action, with one of its manifestations, namely, assertion.

Means and Ends

We now come to our second word of caution, this time about the terminology of means and ends. Here in fact four distinct points need to be made.

Firstly, in assuming that the rationality of actions depends on the rationality of beliefs about the most suitable means to desired ends, we must keep in mind that at any given time a person may desire many different things. We can therefore never speak in terms of one single end and of the simple estimation of the most suitable means of achieving it. Much of the rationality of any action consists in considering means for reconciling different ends, and, where they cannot all be achieved at a given time, in considering which is likely to be most satisfying in the long run, which can be postponed till later, and so on. The situation is further complicated by the fact that the means to any given end are rarely neutral. They may themselves be either desired or not desired, whether for their own sakes or for other consequences which follow from them. In almost anything we do there are in fact disadvantages as well as advantages, and to be rational we must count the cost, or—to put it another way—consider whether our ends on balance justify the means. If superphosphate were very expensive, it might well be irrational to use it.

Secondly, however complicated the relation between means and ends, it must be made clear that it is no more rational, in our sense of the word, to pursue one end than another. The term 'rational', in other words, is not applicable to motives in dissociation from beliefs. We could not say, for example, that it was more rational to seek to improve fertility than to seek to destroy it, to aim at general happiness than to aim at general misery, or to promote good causes rather than bad ones. In each case a person would be acting rationally if he had soundly based beliefs about how to achieve the end, but this would apply, whatever the end might be.

Thus when economists define rational behaviour as that in which the best available means are selected for maximizing profits, there is a considerable danger of confusion. For it is suggested here that for a man to act rationally two things are required; firstly, he must make an estimate, justified by the evidence at his disposal, of the best means for achieving his end, and secondly, his end must be the maximizing of profits. In our use of 'rational' he would be acting rationally if he satisfied the first condition alone, and this would be the case even if he preferred to maximize his losses. Anyone who adds that it is rational to maximize profits is clearly giving a wider use to the word 'rational', and one which has the defect of obscuring a vital distinction.

Thirdly, however, there is one respect in which rationality may be said to have something to do with ends. Though it is no more rational to pursue one end than another, a person may believe one end to be better than another. He may, that is to say, hold what we have called moral beliefs about the goodness or badness of ends as well as factual beliefs about the means of achieving them.[1] If, having such beliefs, he is inclined to do what is good, and if the beliefs themselves are well grounded, he may be said, in a broad sense, to be acting rationally quite apart from any considerations about means.[2] Though we would not say it was rational to promote good ends, we might well say that, given the inclination, it was rational to promote those which, with sufficient reason, we believe to be good.

We have seen that there are reasons for being cautious about extending the use of the word 'rational' in this way. For there is some difficulty in deciding what is involved in a moral belief being well grounded, or maintained with sufficient reason. Whether the extension is convenient in fact depends largely on the use which we give to ethical words like 'good', 'right', or 'ought'. In so far as they are used expressively, the extended use of 'rational' would be very misleading, since statements such as 'Individual initiative ought to be promoted' would in this case more properly be said to express attitudes than to express beliefs and the question whether evidence for them has been properly assessed would not arise. Where the use is naturalistic on the other hand, moral beliefs become a species of the factual, and may be graded as more or less rational in exactly the same way as beliefs about means to ends. It is thus the remaining possibility—that in which moral beliefs are taken to be about irreducible ethical features of states of affairs—that creates the real difficulty. For the discovery of such features has commonly been spoken of as the work of reason, and beliefs which arise from such discovery as rational. Yet the evidence for such beliefs must be of a peculiar kind, one person not being able to check the evidence offered by another in the same way as is done with evidence for factual beliefs. One thing is certain and that is that, in view of this difficulty in comparing evidence, the assumption that anyone is acting on the basis of

---

[1] See Ch. IV pp. 39–40. On the use of the word 'moral' see Note 1, p. 40.
[2] See Ch. VI, pp. 63–64.

rational moral beliefs will be very difficult to check, and hence of no special assistance to a social enquirer. In what follows, therefore, we can afford to ignore such moral rationality except in those cases where the ethical words used have an unambiguously naturalistic meaning.

Fourthly, to return from ends to means, we must keep in mind that there may be various alternative ways of achieving an end. To act rationally, we have suggested, is to select what on the evidence is *the best* way of achieving it. This implies not only that there may be various ways but also that they may be graded for effectiveness, it being rational to adopt that which is at the top of the list. And it may be said that this is to give an unduly strict meaning to the word 'rational'. It may be that in certain circumstances compost would be more effective than superphosphate, but we would still consider the use of superphosphate rational in a sense in which the performance of a ritual was not. It would at least be *a* way of achieving the end.

This of course must be admitted. But we can avoid ambiguity if we recognize that this is one of the respects in which rationality may be said to vary in degree. So far we have assumed that variations in degree of rationality depend entirely on the extent to which a person makes mistakes in assessing evidence for any statement, so that we would count his belief as *perfectly* rational if he simply made no mistakes. We must now add, however, that if he is to act in a perfectly rational way, he must make no mistakes, not only about possible means to his ends, but about what are *the best* means to his ends. Anything short of this may be regarded as rational, but as a departure from perfect rationality. It is after all not unnatural to regard it in this way, since to desire to achieve an end is *ipso facto* to desire to achieve it in the most effective possible way. Anyone who says that the second best will do is merely being influenced by a further motive—that of saving trouble.

Rationality, Intelligence and Objectivity

A final word of caution is needed when rationality is attributed to a *person* rather than to an action or a belief. To say of anyone that he *is* rational is presumably to say of him that he is *disposed* to acquire rational beliefs. Yet if this is so, we must be careful not to identify the rationality of a person with his intelligence. For, as we have seen,[1] two things at least are necessary if a person is to acquire rational beliefs—intelligence and objectivity. However intelligent a person may be, we cannot argue directly from this fact to the rationality of any of his beliefs. We have also to be assured that he is not prevented from paying a proper regard to evidence by any counteracting factors such as arise from motive, custom, and so on. It follows that a person may be intelligent without being rational, and if this sounds odd, we must

---

[1] Ch. VII, p. 77. We do not include availability of evidence here, because it is not relevant for the *rationality* of a belief.

remember that the consequences of identifying rationality with intelligence would be even more odd. For we would then have to say that a rational person might be disposed (through persistent failure of objectivity) to hold irrational beliefs. And there is a lack of symmetry in this which might well lead to confusion.

THE IMPORTANCE OF RATIONALITY
FOR SOCIAL ENQUIRY

With this clearing of the ground, we are now ready to ask what advantage the social enquirer gains from having as his subject-matter people who act in a rational way.

The answer, to put it shortly, is that where the evidence for a belief is in question, the enquirer, being himself rational, can consider the evidence for himself. Where there is evidence bearing on a particular problem, then we know that if *anyone* takes proper account of that evidence, he will be inclined by it as a consequence—that is, as a causal consequence—to give a particular answer. This is a general principle which holds both for the enquirer himself and for the people whose conduct he is studying. Hence the enquirer, starting from the fact that he himself would come to a given conclusion after taking account of certain evidence, may argue that the people he is studying would come to the same conclusion, so long as they had the same evidence and were sufficiently rational to take account of it.

Let us suppose, for example, that information about the observed effects of various substances on plant growth is sufficient to establish the view that superphosphate is best for improving the fertility of a certain kind of soil. Taking account ourselves of this evidence for the view, we may argue that wheat-farmers working on this kind of soil, having the same information—and being rational—will take the same view, and guide their actions accordingly. Similarly, we may explain their use of superphosphate by pointing out that there are good reasons for supposing it is best for improving fertility and that they, being rational, will be aware of this.

This is the procedure, we have seen, which is somewhat misleadingly, though colourfully, expressed as that of re-thinking people's thoughts.[1] It would be more suitably described as a procedure in which the enquiry is divided into two parts. In one of its parts we study our subject-matter directly, seeking to find out what people's ends are, in what circumstances they are placed, what information is available to them, and the extent of their rationality. In the other part, we study the problems with which these people are presented, seeking to find out what beliefs would be adopted by a rational person as a solution to them. The relevance of this second part of the enquiry depends on the extent to

[1] Ch. V, p. 53.

which we and the people we are studying are rational. If we could assume that both we and they were perfectly rational, the connection between the two parts of the enquiry would be complete. For we would then know that we had the correct solution and that they had the correct solution, hence that their solution would be the same as ours.

It will be seen that this procedure relies on an elementary logical point—namely, that, given certain evidence, there can only be one correct solution to the problem as to the best way of achieving a given end, whereas there will be an indefinitely large number of incorrect solutions. It must be noted that the situation would be different if the problem were to find *a* way of achieving an end, for in this case there may well be a number of possible alternatives. If someone, while departing from our standard of 'perfect' rationality, were yet sufficiently rational to adopt *some* sound way of increasing fertility, we could not infer from this that he would do anything in particular—say, use superphosphate. But it would still be true that the control imposed by the evidence would place a very great restriction on the possible ways of acting. For there would still be only a limited number of correct solutions, and these would stand out from among the indefinitely large number of incorrect ones.

Whether it is applied in the stronger or the weaker way, however, it must be realized that this logical point is not in itself sufficient to justify the procedure. For it is conceivable that a person might see that the evidence points to a given conclusion and yet fail to believe the conclusion true. If this were to happen it would be extremely queer, but it is logically possible. Hence we need also the causal principle that, whenever anyone takes account of evidence, he will believe the conclusion to which it points. There is very good empirical evidence for this. If we were to come across any exceptions to it, we would immediately attribute them to the fact that the influence of prejudice or of custom was in these cases extremely strong and dismiss the cases as being so abnormal as to have no appreciable effect on the value of the procedure.[1] If a person is rational enough to see the force of an argument, we can rely on him being rational enough to accept the conclusion. And it is only because we rely on this that we can infer a person's beliefs from the fact that he takes account of evidence.

The great advantage gained by this procedure will become clear if we compare rational beliefs with those which arise from mistakes in judgment or from the effect of prejudice or custom. It is most obvious where the alternative is the simple making of mistakes. Consider the case of a monopolist who wishes to maximize his profits. If we know that he acts rationally and has information about how costs and demand vary with

---

[1] Our first reaction would, of course, be to doubt the genuineness of the exception and ask whether the person in question had really seen the significance of the evidence. We would only be prepared to be pushed further if we were quite sure that he had done this.

increase in production, then we will be able to say something about the price of his product; it will be the price which, with all goods sold, will be equal to his marginal cost. But, if we have reason to suppose that he miscalculates, we will not be able to say anything at all about the price. For, while there is only one correct solution to this problem, there is, as we have said, a very large number of incorrect ones, hence the number of possible mistakes which the monopolist might make will be very large. He might, for example, under-estimate the elasticity of demand, or wrongly assume constant marginal cost, or simply go on producing as much as he could without reorganization and hope for the best. Which mistakes he actually makes may depend on all sorts of factors, often of a quite incidental kind, and it would take a hopelessly detailed investigation to disentangle them.

Where mistaken beliefs can be shown to arise from prejudice or custom, the position of the enquirer is admittedly very much better. For to show that they arise in this way is at once to restrict the enquiry to assessable factors of a definite kind, and it is by no means hopeless to attempt to establish that some such factor has a predominant influence on a person's belief.[1] Thus we may explain a monopolist's mistake about how to maximize profit by pointing to his philanthropic tendencies or to current practices, and if we know of his philanthropy or conservatism we may even infer from this what sort of non-rational beliefs about price policy he will form. It may be asked, then, what advantage the appeal to a person's ascertained rationality has over an appeal to his ascertained prejudice or ascertained conformity?

We may point out that the advantage is still considerable. For, in the first place, prejudices and current practices vary from person to person and group to group, while rationally drawn conclusions do not. If we know that a monopolist acts rationally we know that, whoever or wherever he may be, his policy will be determined by the available evidence, which anyone can consider for himself. There is no need for us to enquire further into his mental make-up or social background. But if we know him to be prejudiced we are still left with the need to discover what his particular prejudices are. And if we know him to be influenced by custom, we must still find out what beliefs are customary among the members of his group. In particular, we cannot assume at the outset that the prejudices and customary beliefs will be the same as our own.

Secondly, even if prejudices and customary beliefs did not vary in this way, they would still be different for different subject-matters. The philanthropic motives which might explain a businessman's economic miscalculations would not explain, let us say, his refusal to employ

---

[1] The point of Freud's account of error (*Introductory Lectures on Psycho-Analysis* Chs. 2–4) is that it attributes all error to a kind of prejudice, and thus restricts the field of possible explanations to manageable proportions. Cf. comment in note to p. 77.

foreign workers, and different distorting factors would be needed again to explain the performance of a first-fruit ritual. Whereas, if the businessman is rational, we may infer, in the light of the evidence at his disposal, what conclusions he will draw on any subject whatsoever. And if people generally are rational, we may similarly infer what conclusions anyone may draw on any subject, whether it be the fixing of prices, the efficiency of different kinds of workers, or the improvement of land fertility. We thus have one single general principle which can be used in the explanation and prediction of an indefinitely large number of human actions, occurring at all times and places, and in all kinds of circumstances.

In all this, it must be remembered that rationality is a matter of degree, and that the principle, despite its fruitfulness, only applies to the extent that people in fact do not make mistakes about the best means of achieving their ends. It could only be completely relied on if people *never* made mistakes about this—that is, if they were *perfectly* rational. And it is clear enough that we cannot accept the simple statement that men are rational—that is, perfectly rational—as a straightforward law. This is a matter for regret, since it is a statement which would have served admirably as the key principle of a subsumptive theory about human action. If we could have accepted it as a law, we would have been able to deduce from it, as special cases, innumerable more or less specific statements about what a person would believe or do if he had certain ends, circumstances, and available evidence. Even if we could only accept it, on some given occasions, as a restricted general statement about the invariable rationality of a particular individual we could deduce a similarly large number of statements about that individual. But unfortunately this is not possible. We would soon find that some of our deductions did not conform to the facts, just as some deductions from the principle that people seek to maximize their money-gains do not conform to the facts. The 'rational man' like the 'economic man' is after all only an ideal.[1]

What we must do, therefore, in order to make use of the procedure, is to treat the rationality of men as an 'unrealistic assumption'.[2] We may continue to deduce what men would do if they were perfectly rational, thus retaining all the advantages of a flexible subsumptive theory. But we must recognize that its key principle is itself a theoretical law. Men *tend* to be rational, but this is a tendency which may be offset, in any specific case, by all those other factors which lead to the making of mistakes. We may regard our first task as that of finding out what the rational action would be; we may then correct our result by a consideration of distorting influences. In other words, when we make use in our procedure of the fact that men are rational, we must remember that

[1] Cf. Ch. XI, p. 120.
[2] Cf. Ch. XIII, pp. 146–47.

we are working all the time within a framework of theory which is of the factor type.

LIMITATIONS OF THE ARGUMENT FROM RATIONALITY

Now that the general character of the procedure has been made clear, it will be seen that, despite its advantages, it cannot be regarded as a simple and universal panacea for the troubles of social enquirers. There are various difficulties in the way of applying it which commonly lead to restrictions on its application, and furthermore there are kinds of enquiry in which it cannot be applied at all. Let us consider these difficulties and restrictions in turn.

Deviations from Rationality

The most obvious difficulty arises from the need to correct deductions from the assumption of rationality, in any specific case, by a consideration of other factors. Since the statement that men act rationally is a tendency statement, nothing whatsoever can be inferred from it when it is taken by itself. An estimate has to be made of the extent of the influences leading to error, and if the enquiry is to be taken further, something must also be known of their character.

These are requirements which it is often not easy to fulfil. But it is much easier to find out about the extent of the influences than to find out about their character. There are ways of judging whether someone is going to make a mistake, but it is quite another matter to predict what sort of a mistake it is going to be. And even if we know about the mistake it will be a difficult matter to explain how it came about. To do so we would need to re-introduce, alongside the influence of evidence, a consideration of all those other influences which, in using the assumption of rationality, we had hoped to avoid. And this means we would be little better off than before.

For this reason, the effective use of the procedure is in fact limited to those cases where it has been ascertained that departures from rationality are not great. Our task is not so much to correct deductions from the assumption in the light of other factors known to be operating, as to exclude those cases where these intractable factors cannot be ignored. It is an empirical fact of considerable importance for social enquiry that there is a substantial range of cases in which human beings show some approximation to the rational ideal. But to apply the procedure to these cases we have to be able to distinguish them from the rest.

There are no doubt occasions when there are no effective counteracting factors. On such occasions, we may say, people act in a perfectly rational manner. There are many simple actions of daily life, such as turning on taps and running for trains, when one of the alternative ways of achieving an immediate end stands out as obvious and is most unlikely to be ignored. Even where the rational choice requires more effort, as in the case of someone buying an article at the cheapest possible price for the quality, there will be occasions when it is found in its pure form. But we know that some of the actions of any person depart in varying degree from the standard, and we know that different people may themselves be graded as more or less rational according to the range and the extent of these departures. The question then is how we can tell, in any given case, whether such a departure has occurred, and, if it has, how greatly it will affect the belief and consequent action.

Where we have to explain an action which we already know of, the test for rationality is relatively simple and effective. It is most effective of all when we are in a position to ask the person concerned what his reasons were, or have some record of reasons set down in books or documents. For in this case all we need to do is to decide for ourselves whether the stated reasons are good reasons. If they are, we can generally rely on explaining the action in terms of them. The stated reasons might of course be made up after the event as a rationalization, but, if this were so, their happening to be good reasons would be an unlikely coincidence.

Where we do not have stated reasons, the test is admittedly not as sure. But if we find that an action is appropriate, this in itself is good evidence in favour of its having been done as a result of a recognition that it is appropriate. Whenever someone does the right thing, it is at least likely that he has had good reasons for doing it, even if he has not stated them. The trouble in this case is that the field of plausible alternatives is left more open. People sometimes do the right thing for the wrong reasons. A monopolist may decide on the correct economic price because one miscalculation offsets another. And in particular, where a belief happens to be consoling or orthodox, then, however sensible it is, we may well suspect the influence of motives or of custom and allege a failure of objectivity.[1] Hence even when we are explaining an action it is as well to have some other evidence for its rationality.

When we pass from explanation to discovery, this other evidence is obviously essential. For in this case we have no stated reasons and no action before us; hence we cannot start by asking whether the stated reasons are good reasons, or the action appropriate. We have to infer what a person does from a prior knowledge that he has a good reason for doing it.

One way to proceed in such circumstances is to argue from the rationality of the *person* to the rationality of the specific action. If we consider that someone has a general disposition to take account of evidence, this will support the view that he will take account of evidence, or has taken account of it, on some given occasion. And we judge of a person's dispositional rationality by applying to his other actions the

[1] Cf. Ch. VII, pp. 84–85.

procedure we have just described as suitable for explanation. If a person's actions have been consistently appropriate in various circumstances, this provides cumulative support for saying that he has, on each occasion, been influenced by the evidence. In so far as his record in this respect is a good one, we are then justified in inferring what he will do when faced with a new problem. We rely here on a restricted generalization about the chances of an individual acting rationally, reinforced by the unrestricted general principle that there is only a very slight chance of there being a sudden break in any individual's dispositional make-up.

It should be observed that this argument from a person's disposition would be much more effective if his rationality were a mere matter of intelligence and did not also require objectivity. For intelligence—the capacity, that is to say, to judge of the sufficiency of evidence—is a general disposition, in the sense that it shows no great variation from subject-matter to subject-matter. Hence, if a person is found to avoid mistakes on one subject, this is good evidence that he will avoid mistakes on all. But we cannot so safely rely on a general disposition to be objective. It is well known that a specialist who is a model of objectivity in his own field may be full of prejudices and socially-instilled beliefs on questions which lie outside it. There is thus always a danger that someone who has been shown to be rational, and therefore objective, in the past may prove to have his judgment sadly distorted on the question under consideration, and hence to act in a way which we had not foreseen.

This last point suggests another way in which we may estimate the likelihood of rational action. As well as appealing to the records of individuals, we may appeal to general considerations about subject-matter. Thus we know that there are some subjects concerning which people are more likely to be objective than others; it is safer, for example, to assume objectivity, and hence rationality, when they are concerned with their natural than with their social environment. Again, we know that people are more likely to act rationally when they are faced with simple than with complex problems. This is why it is safer to assume rationality when a few immediate and obvious moves are needed than when a complicated plan has to be worked out. It is also why it is safer to assume rationality when the problem is one of achieving some single and definite end than when the achievements of various ends have to be balanced one against another. Thus the fact that the end of maximizing gains is definite and relatively isolated from others is one of the things which justifies a special reliance on the assumption of rationality in economics.

We see from all this that the tests for rationality are various, and that some are very much less reliable than others. We must now point out, however, that they all have one fundamental feature in common. They all rest on the presupposition that we ourselves—the social enquirers—are rational. If it were not taken for granted that *we* could discriminate for ourselves between good reasons and bad, this whole kind of argument in favour of, or against, others having good reasons for their actions would fall to the ground. Once we begin to doubt our own intelligence or objectivity we become involved in circularity. We saw this in Chapter VII, where general doubts were raised about the objectivity of social enquirers themselves.[1]

Reliance on our own rationality is of course essential not only for testing the rationality of others, but also for applying the procedure once their rationality has been established. If we, as economists, for example, were to be mistaken about the optimum monopoly price, we would draw the wrong conclusions about the price fixed by the monopolist, even though we already knew that he was rational. The assumption of the enquirer's rationality is thus all along of equal importance with the assumption of the rationality of those he is studying. In so far as the enquirer has reason to suppose that his solution to their problems is defective, he ceases to be justified in arguing from his solution to theirs.

If it is asked how the enquirer can establish his own rationality, the answer, of course, is that primarily he can only do so by checking his own work, making sure he has taken account of all relevant evidence and drawn no unjustfied conclusions. If his conclusions differ from those of others, this may be a much needed stimulus for him to look again. But this is all that can be said.

Differences in Ends, Circumstances and Availability of Evidence

In laying stress on the need to estimate the extent of people's rationality, we must not forget the other conditions which are required for the application of the procedure. Before we can start rethinking people's thoughts there are various things we must know about them. The discovery of these things is included along with the discovery of the extent of their rationality in what we have called the first part of the enquiry, and the point that must now be made is that this discovery, which is essential, is sometimes difficult.

Before we can consider what it would be reasonable for a person to do, we must know at least three different kinds of fact about him. We must know what ends he is seeking to achieve, we must know in what circumstances he is placed, and we must know what information is available to him when he makes his judgments about the best thing to do in these circumstances. We cannot tell, for example, what price a

---

[1] Ch. VII, pp. 85–86. It will be remembered that in that passage (pp. 84–85) we also discussed direct tests for the objectivity of social enquirers which did not presuppose our own. These were the tests of noting whether a belief was in fact consoling or customary or in conflict with others. But we saw that such evidences of lack of objectivity were inconclusive. They are therefore not relevant here. We would not be justified in excluding a belief as irrational simply on these grounds.

rational monopolist will fix unless we know what he is aiming at; it will be one price if his aim is to maximize profits, and another if it is to provide service to the public with a small margin for himself. Again, we cannot tell about the price unless we know whether it is physically possible for him to increase production, and whether there is danger of a competitor entering the market. And, finally, we cannot tell about the price unless we know whether he is aware of the cost and demand schedules for his product; if he has no evidence on which to base an estimate of these, the most rational thing for him to do might well be to hold on to an existing profit-margin and avoid the blind risk of experimentation.

It is clear from this that there may have to be a great deal of direct enquiry into people's characters and circumstances before we can begin to infer their actions from their rationality. The procedure will therefore be applied most easily where this part of the enquiry can be cut to a minimum. This can be done best where it is already known what ends people are likely to be pursuing and where their circumstances and information are known not to vary greatly or to differ greatly from our own. The procedure is thus much more suited to the economist studying modern market conditions than it is, say, to the anthropologist studying the actions of men in a primitive society. Even if it is assumed that primitive men act rationally, their actions may still be misinterpreted because of uncertainty about their motives, their conditions, and the extent of their knowledge.

Diffusion of Subject-Matter

We come now to a different kind of difficulty—one which concerns the second part of the enquiry rather than the first. If part of our task is to consider what a rational man will do to achieve his end, in a given situation, the problems we will have to solve may be of many different kinds, and many of them will be right outside the normal field of social enquiry. For people's ends are various, and many at least of their proximate ends will have to do with the altering not of their social but of their natural environment. They may be concerned, for example, to improve soil fertility or build bridges or to travel into outer space. And even if their ends are social, the means required to achieve them will involve manipulation of their natural environment. To avoid city congestion, roads may have to be built. To complete with a business rival, new manufacturing processes may have to be devised. In all such cases the knowledge that is needed to tell us what people will do will be knowledge not so much of social processes as of soil chemistry, structural engineering, aeronautics, and the like.

We see here a special difficulty in the way of making a social enquiry self-contained. In any social enquiry, of course, attention must be paid at one point or another to the influence of natural environment. But where people act rationally, this influence takes the special and acute form of their taking account of their natural environment and acting in the light of what they discover about it. They thus engage in all sorts of technical activities designed to alter it, and, although it is the presumed task of a social enquirer to understand the actions of human beings, there are in fact many of such actions that can only be understood by those who have the required technical knowledge about the subject-matter in hand. Let a social enquirer loose on a farm or on a construction job or in a physics laboratory and his own specialized knowledge will not help him to explain many of the things that go on. So long as the general knowledge which people acquire remains at the level of common sense the social enquirer may, of course, refer to it without trouble in giving an account of their actions. But as soon as it becomes at all specialized, he can do little more than draw on information acquired from specialists in other fields.

This is well illustrated by the extreme case in which natural science is considered as a social activity. No social scientist can hope to give a full account of the development of science. He has to restrict himself to the non-rational factors which affect this development—those, for example, which influence the selection of scientific problems, the unreflective presuppositions of scientists, the opportunities provided for research, and so on. To do more he would have to master the natural sciences himself and understand the arguments which have led scientists to hold the theories they do. To deny that this was necessary would be in effect to deny that science was a rational activity.

The limitation referred to here is of course absent where the suitable means for achieving an end are themselves social in character. To build a bridge, a government may have to be induced to provide the finance; to avoid congestion, parking laws may have to be enforced; to compete with a business rival, prices may have to be lowered or a selling campaign started. In such cases the social scientist can explain the rational actions of the people concerned without requiring technical knowledge of the natural-scientific kind. The problems these people have to deal with are of the same kind as the problems of the social scientist himself, hence the two parts of the enquiry will both remain within the same field.

Thus it is, for example, that the social scientist is in a position to give a full account of the development of social science, even though he cannot do this for the development of science generally. For in this case the rational factors which bring about changes in the views of the social scientists he is studying are of the kind which it is his special business to study.

Again, it is for this reason that students of politics and of economics are in a peculiarly favourable position for using the assumption of rationality. It is not merely that people who seek political or economic ends are specially likely to act in a rational way, though it may well be that this is so. It is rather that the means available to these people are to a large extent political and economic means. Thus the understanding of political relationships is of importance for those who engage in politics as well as for the political scientist. And economic reasons affect the decisions of businessmen as well as the conclusions of economists. Hence there is nothing to stop political scientists and economists using their own specialized knowledge when considering issues from the point of view of the politicians and businessmen whose activities they are studying, judging what would be the best thing for them to do, and inferring from this that they will do it. Whereas a student of military strategy who wishes to consider issues from the point of view of a general may well have to know something about ballistics, and a historian who asks what reasons people might have for building Gothic cathedrals with flying buttresses will have to know something of the principles of building construction. And this means that they have to spread their enquiries into subjects with which they are not specially equipped to deal.

Uncertainty and Risk

So far, in speaking of belief and evidence, we have failed to take account of two facts. The first is that a person may hold a view about the outcome of his action with varying degrees of confidence. And the second is that the evidence he has before him may vary in its cogency. If he is rational, we may assume that the better the evidence, the greater his confidence will be. And where the evidence is such as to put the outcome beyond all reasonable doubt, we who appreciate the evidence will have no difficulty, as far as this point is concerned, in deciding what he will do.

But where the evidence is not so good, and the man has doubts, further problems arise. How much confidence must he have if he is to be said to believe that a proposed action will lead to what is on the whole the desired result? And how good must the evidence be in order to justify that degree of confidence?

The first of these questions is concerned only with the definition of 'belief', and for our purposes it can be answered quickly. We will say that a person *believes* an action will have a desired result, taking into account all its relevant consequences, if his confidence is sufficient to make him ready to perform the action on the appropriate occasion. His acting in line with a given view about means to ends is a sign that he has committed himself to that view, even though he does not feel certain of success.[1] And so our second question becomes: how good must the evidence be to justify a person in thus committing himself?

[1] There is danger of misunderstanding here. It must be made clear that 'desired result' means 'total desired result'. A person may be very confident about the best

(Continued at foot of next page)

To this question there is unfortunately no straight answer. Where the evidence leaves room for uncertainty, we cannot tell, simply by considering it for ourselves, whether it is sufficient to make a rational man act or not. We have to take account of at least two other factors.

The first of these is the extent of the risk. We have to consider not only how much evidence there is that a proposed action will have a given outcome. We must also consider how much the agent stands to gain in the way of fulfillment of desired ends if he is right about the outcome, and how much he stands to lose if he is wrong. We say he runs a risk if it is the case both that the evidence leaves room for legitimate doubt, and he loses if he is wrong. The risk in this sense[1] increases either as the evidence becomes weaker or as the potential loss becomes greater. Similarly, what we may call his 'legitimate expectations' increase with the increase either of the cogency of the evidence or the potential gain.[2]

[1] The word, of course, has other, though less common uses. Cf. F. H. Knight, *Risk, Uncertainty and Profit*, where risk is taken as that kind of uncertainty which can be largely eliminated by the application of well-supported chance-statements to large sets of instances, as for example, though insurance. See pp. 19–21 of 1948 reprint, (Houghton Mifflin),—also p. 233.

[2] There is no suitable term for the positive correlate of this composite notion of risk. Our 'legitimate expectation' resembles the statistician's 'mathematical expectation', except that the latter term (*a*) is used for the result where risk has been deduced, and (*b*) is used only in the special case where the evidence consists of statistically-supported chance-statements. For a clear presentation of the importance of considerations of gain and loss when making a rational choice between chance-statements ('statistical hypotheses') on the basis of given statistical evidence, see Braithwaite—*Scientific Explanation* (Cambridge, 1953) Ch. 7, pp. 196–210.
'Expectation' is commonly used simply for a 'feeling of confidence that something will happen', and economists commonly use it in this commonsense way. Cf., G. L. S. Shackle—*Expectation in Economics* (second edition, Cambridge 1952) Shackle is concerned with the effect on action of different 'degrees of belief' or of 'potential surprise', when these are taken together with envisaged gains and losses arising from success or failure. He doesn't discuss adequacy of evidence which might or might not justify different amounts of surprise felt at different outcomes. In other words, he is not concerned with our problem about what a *rational* man will do. The use of the word 'legitimate' in 'legitimate expectation' goes some way towards averting confusion between our problem and his.

---

thing to do to achieve some *given* end, and yet not do it because he would thereby be prevented from achieving other ends. In such a case we would certainly speak of belief, though the person in question would not have committed himself in action. Thus we may say of a farmer that he believes superphosphate should be used to improve fertility, and yet he may not act on this belief because he is too lazy or too busy, i.e., gives priority to his desire for relaxation or for other things. His *not* using superphosphate may here be regarded as a sign of his belief that its use will *not* conduce to what he wants *on the whole*. But why do we still say he believes that superphosphate is best for fertility? The answer indicates a further complication. We may commit ourselves theoretically as well as practically. We may wish to find out the truth, about means to hypothetical ends or any other matter, and when our confidence in having done so reaches a certain point, we decide to incorporate the statement in question into the body of statements we accept as true. This commitment, as well as commitment in action, may be spoken of as 'Belief'. It is however the criterion of action that concerns us in this context.

Now it will be clear that a rational man, deciding whether to adopt a course of action about the outcome of which there is ground for uncertainty, will take account of risks on the one hand and legitimate expectations on the other, thus including a consideration of what he will gain if right, and lose if wrong. Where he loses nothing if he is wrong, there will be no risk, and he will therefore commit himself on relatively slender evidence. Further he will commit himself on more and more slender evidence, the greater the gain that will come from his being right. On the other hand, the smaller the gain that comes from success and the greater the loss that comes from failure, the more he will raise his standards and require solid evidence for the connection between proposed action and desired end.

Thus, if someone is deciding whether to invest a given sum in capital equipment, and his aim is to make a certain level of profit, he will consider not only how likely it is on the evidence that he will achieve this aim. He will also take account of the importance to him of achieving the aim, assuming he is successful, and the severity of the loss assuming he fails. If he stakes all he has in the venture and the profit is small or in other ways unimportant for him, it will be reasonable for him to minimize his risk and maximize his expectation by investing only if the venture is very likely to be successful. Whereas, if the possible loss is negligible and the profit aimed at is of great value to him, we might well try it out even though there is little likelihood of success.

We see then that in estimating what a rational man will do (or in explaining what he has done) in conditions of uncertainty, we must take account of more than the evidence at his disposal. The fact of his being rational, however, will still give us a guide since it is rational to minimize risks and maximize expectations. This unfortunately cannot be said when we come to the other factor which we have to take into account. Even where potential gain and potential loss are allowed for, it is still the case that two people who agree entirely about the amount of evidence in favour of there being a given outcome for an action, may yet disagree about whether it is sufficient to justify the action. They could only settle this disagreement if there were a standard of sufficiency which could itself be rationally determined. And there would seem to be no such standard. All we can say is that some people are prepared to take greater risks than others. Hence to find out whether even a perfectly rational person will act on the basis of given evidence, we have not only to consider the issues from his point of view, but also to ask ourselves a further important question about his character—how cautious is he?

It should be noted that these difficulties which arise when people act on limited evidence are especially acute when they use social means to achieve their ends. For they then have to estimate what influence their proposed actions will have on the future actions of other people. And such social predictions, we have seen, are very rarely capable of being established beyond reasonable doubt. Hence economists, political scientists and other social enquirers who are concerned with actions designed to have social effects are faced with difficulties which offset to some extent the advantage they gain through not having to consider problems outside their own field. The businessmen, politicians, and other economic and political agents whose actions they study are hardly ever in a position to regard the outcome of any course of action as a foregone conclusion. In social life perfect rationality does not imply perfect foresight; hence, however rational people may be, we cannot predict or explain their socially-directed actions without considering such other factors as risks and their preparedness to take them.

Mutual Anticipations

When we are concerned with such socially-directed action there is a further problem which arises. One person, in estimating the social consequences of his action, has to take account of the fact that others may also be acting rationally. In deciding what to do, he will clearly have to consider, among other things, what *they* will decide to do in the light of the situation created by his action, and what they do will depend on *their* estimate of what *he*, and still others, are likely to do next in the light of the situation created by their action—and so on. This complication, which in extreme cases would involve a person in working out an indefinite number of steps, is particularly evident in conflict-situations. One competitor, in considering whether to make a move, must consider how others will react to the move, and to do this he must look at their problem from their point of view, judging what they think he will do as a result of their move.

This mutual use of the assumption of rationality by social agents, which is to be found in some degree in many economic and political situations, makes the complete solution of their problems peculiarly intricate.[1] The trouble here is not merely that each may be acting on insufficient evidence. Even if two people know all about each other, and each has all the relevant information—as, for example, in a game of chess—the mutual repercussions will still be difficult to work out. And

---

[1] It does not make the solution *logically* impossible. The suggestion that it does has been made. See e.g. T. W. Hutchison—*The Significance and Basic Postulates of Economic Theory* (Macmillan, 1938) pp. 97–99. This would only be the case, however, if each person were supposed to work out what the others would do if they took no account of his proposed action. On the assumption that the situation confronting them would be one which would be altered by his proposed action, the neglect of it would lead to absurd results. Perfect foresight of what others will do, irrespective of what you do, is impossible. But this is not the situation we are discussing.

For detailed treatment of the solution of problems where there are mutually intereacting rational agents, see Von Neumann and Morgenstern—*Theory of Games and Economic Behaviour* (2nd Ed. Princeton, 1947). Ch. 1 contains a non-technical introduction; see esp. Section 2.

what is difficult for the participants is equally difficult for the social enquirer who puts himself in the place of any one of them. With difficult problems, we have pointed out, departures from rationality become more likely. And since *all* participants must be rational if the calculations of any one of them as to the outcome are to hold, the likelihood that allowances for such departure will have to be made increases with the number of participants. In practice no one who works out social consequences in this way is likely to pursue the calculation beyond one or two steps. Hence a persistent need to allow for other factors and to make uncertain estimates.

So far we have discussed difficulties in applying the procedure and the restrictions which arise from these. We must now point to further restrictions which arise from the fact that there are certain kinds of social enquiry in which the application of the procedure is not so much difficult as simply inappropriate.

Unintended Consequences

The first of these is that in which we seek to trace the unintended consequences of people's actions. We do not have in mind here merely those consequences which occur when people fail in their intentions, either through insufficient rationality or insufficient evidence.[1] Even if a person acts with perfect rationality and has evidence enough to guarantee success, his action may have all sorts of further effects which have nothing to do with the achievement of his ends. From his point of view, these will be by-products, but from the point of view of a social enquirer they may be of considerable importance. Every action a person performs produces a change in the situation in which other people have to act. And even though their actions do not concern him at all, they will nevertheless be influenced by the change.

Thus, if someone breaks a way through scrub with the sole purpose of reaching a certain point, other rational people seeking the best way to get to the same destination will choose the same route. If someone, motivated by scientific curiosity, succeeds in revealing the possibilities of atomic fission, military strategists will reconstruct their policies in the light of the discovery. If a number of people—buyers and sellers of a commodity, each seeking the maximum gain—settle after a series of adjustments on a uniform price, other potential buyers and sellers will adjust their production or consumption in the light of this price.[2] In all such cases, we may be able to estimate what each individual will do by

[1] Cf. Ch. IX, p. 94 where our illustration of an unintended social influence (that of an orator producing in his audience a reaction against his policy) was of this first kind.

[2] The first and third of these illustrations are similar to those used by F. A. Hayek who, as we have seen (Ch. IX, p. 107 Note 2) regards the forms of order arising from the undesigned results of human action as the basic subject-matter of the social sciences. Cf. F. A. Hayek, op. cit., pp. 40–41.

looking at his situation from his point of view, but this will tell us nothing about the ways in which the actions of one will influence the situations of another.

Rationality and Social Structure

Finally, we must recognize that the assumption of rationality is only relevant at all so long as we are concerned with the action of individuals. For it is only individuals who are rational in the sense of holding beliefs about the suitability of actions based on evidence. Hence if we keep on the level of the study of institutions and concern ourselves with generalizing about group structure and changes in group structure, we cannot make use of any considerations about what would be rational or not. And yet this kind of study, as we have seen, includes a considerable part, though not an independent part, of social enquiry.[1]

Those who have wished to give an independent status to the study of social structure have often found this simple conclusion unwelcome. Some have thought to avoid it by supposing that in addition to the rationality of individuals there is an 'objective reason' working within institutions. The main trouble with this supposition, as it is found for example in the writings of Hegel and his followers, is that it is hard to understand what could be meant by reason being manifested in society without its being the reason of any individual. If we consider what we normally mean by an institution or a form of social organization being rational, we will in fact see at once that such rationality is derivative from the rationality of individuals, and does not in any way make possible the direct application of the procedure to institutions.

One obvious case in which we could describe an institution as rational would be that in which it is 'instituted' by certain individuals with certain ends in view, and, when established, is successful in securing those ends. It may be doubted whether there have ever been cases of this kind, though the setting up of such basic sets of laws as the American Constitution might be cited as possible examples. In such cases, however, whether real or alleged, it is clear that to test the rationality of the institution would be to test the rationality of its founders and the explanation of the institution would be similar to the explanation of any other of the intended consequences of their actions.

Though institutions may never be 'instituted' in this clear-cut way, we might still speak of them as rational in the same general sense if we conceived of them as having arisen gradually out of the rational activity of many people in the past, all of them admittedly seeking certain specific ends, but yet all having some pervasive end in view. Thus Edmund Burke may be said to have defended the rationality of the English political system of his day when he conceived of it as the

[1] See Ch. IX, pp. 103–4

embodiment of the wisdom of the ages.[1] If the social enquirer could put himself in the place of these many people and appreciate the general drift of their activities in gradually modifying the institutions, he could be said to be using the assumption of rationality in order to explain the institutions and the changes which occur in them. But in doing so, he would at the same time be showing how they are derived from the actions of individuals.[2].

It must be admitted that we sometimes attribute a rationality to institutions in cases where we cannot trace their origin to the rational actions of any human beings. This is done when we point to the *function* they perform in a given society and say they are rational if they effectively perform their function. A first-fruits ritual, for example, is evidently irrational if we take it to arise from a desire to improve fertility. Yet we may claim for it a functional rationality in that it ensures a control over harvesting which prevents the premature dissipation of food stocks and the danger to health caused by eating unripe crops.[3]

It is easy to see why the word 'rational' is used in these circumstances. For, as we have pointed out,[4] to give a functional explanation of an institution is to show that it is, in a sense, an effective means to certain ends. But it must be remembered that the 'ends' here are not ends envisaged and desired by any of the people whose actions we are studying; they are simply certain kinds of states of affairs which we, the enquirers, ourselves select as the focal points for our enquiry. We select them for different reasons, one main one being that we note that there are certain states of affairs to which many different institutions all appear to contribute. Such, for example, are the stability and survival of the group, 'ends', it should be noted, to which conservation of food crops and preservation of health are themselves evidently means. Given such ends, we may proceed to judge of the rationality of institutions in terms of the effectiveness with which they contribute to them. But since the ends are selected by the enquirer and the means to them not devised by anybody, we clearly go no way towards establishing the occurrence of these means by pointing out in a merely hypothetical way

---

[1] See the opening passages of his *Reflections on the Revolution in France* esp. pp. 29–31 (Everyman edition, 1951 reprint).

[2] Burke in fact denied that any social enquirer could do this. He did so on the ground that any individual's 'private stock of reason' was small compared to the 'general bank and capital of nations and of ages' (op. cit., p. 84). In other words, he accepted without question the collective rationality of his predecessors, and assumed that, if a present-day individual disagreed with their conclusions as embodied in existing institutions, he must be wrong. This would make the procedure inapplicable. We could not infer anything from the rationality of an institution unless we ourselves could pass reliable judgment on what is rational and what is not.

[3] Cf. S. F. Nadel, op. cit., pp. 274–5.

[4] Ch. IV, p. 37.

that they are what *would* have been devised by rational people *if* they had had these ends in view. Unplanned tendencies towards end-states may be discovered in human affairs, but not inferred from what it is reasonable for people to do.

It appears then that there is no discoverable sense of 'rational', as applied to institutions, which will enable us to use the procedure of assuming rationality in making a study of them. Hence we have to recognize here a final and important limitation on the use of the procedure.

Our list of difficulties and restrictions has been formidable, and it shows that we need to use the assumption of rationality with caution. But it does not show that we can do without it. Men are perpetually acting in ways which are at least approximately rational. If we seize on this point and treat their rationality as a factor the operation of which can be examined in a great variety of circumstances, we at once provide ourselves with a framework in terms of which we can sort out many of the complexities of social life. It may be said, in fact, that it is the possibility of using a factor theory of this type which compensates the social enquirer in some degree for his inability to construct theories measuring up to the standards of physical dynamics.

XV

THE STUDY OF HISTORY

A LL social enquirers are concerned to discover and explain what happens in the social life of men, and all use general statements and theories of various kinds for this purpose. Historians, we have seen, are no exception.[1] From the point of view of any given enquirer 'what happens' may be in the past, the present or the future. To be an historian is simply to be concerned with what has happened in the past.

It is for this reason that we have made no attempt so far to distinguish history from the social sciences as a special field of enquiry. In discussing the use of general statements, many of our illustrations have in fact been historical ones, and these illustrations have been interspersed at random with others which would not normally be considered historical. The time has now come, however, to consider some of the special features of the study of the past.

We must keep in mind here that every enquiry has its historical side. People study the history of the stars, the sun, the earth, plant and animal life, and so on. What we call 'history' without any explanatory adjective is no more than the historical side of one special kind of enquiry—social enquiry.

We do, however, have a special interest in the social past for its own sake, and this no doubt is the reason why we single out the history of human society by calling it 'history' *simpliciter*. We like finding out how people have lived at times removed from our own. Moreover, there are many different things to find out, because of the exceptional swiftness of social change.

For such reasons there is a tendency to make history into a separate field of study, alongside those others, such as politics and economics, which are normally spoken of as 'social sciences'. It is not that it in any way fails to be scientific, in our sense of the term, or to be interdependent with these sciences. The difference consists solely in the kind of statement which the historian and the social scientist are more especially concerned to establish. It is assumed that to be a social

[1] See Ch. III, p. 25.

scientist one must be interested in establishing general statements, developing theories, and where possible predicting in terms of these. Whereas to be a historian one must be interested in establishing statements about particular past events in their temporal sequence. This means that the historian, though he must use general statements, will use only those general statements which are required for his purpose; while on the other hand, the social scientist will use only those statements about particular past events which are required for *his* purpose.

Accepting this difference in aim, let us consider the special features of the procedure of the person who seeks to answer the specifically historical questions: What happened? and Why? The answering of the first of these questions may be called 'retrodiction',[1] the answering of the second is historical explanation. Though they are closely related, we will consider them in turn.

RETRODICTION

There is a certain lack of symmetry between prediction and retrodiction, even though they both embody the general principle of applying general statements to particular cases.

To begin with, there is the obvious point that a historical statement can never be tested directly by observation as can a statement about the future. When the time comes, we can check up on a prediction and see whether it comes true, whereas it might be said of the historian that he can never be found out.[2] And this, from the point of view of enquiry, is a disadvantage.

It would be a mistake, however, to lay too much stress on this. For, despite the impossibility of such a direct test, it is clear that present evidence for past events is generally very much better than present evidence for future ones. It is a sign of this that enquirers constantly use their retrodictive knowledge of past events for supporting statements about the future, but they never think of using their predictive knowledge of future events for supporting statements about the past. They thereby accept the superiority of retrodiction. If we consider the character of retrodictive arguments we will realize their reasons.

We must start with the fact of memory. Here, even below the level of

---

[1] The word 'retrodiction' is a coined one, which has not et passed into general use. See, e.g. W. H. Walsh—*An Introduction to Philosophy of History* (Hutchinson, 1951) p. 41. Walsh attributes the original suggestion of the erm to G. Ryle. It provides us with a convenient short way of referring to the establishing of what has happened in the past, and we adopt it in what follows.

[2] The phrase is Santayana's—see *The Life of Reason* (Revised one-volume edition, Constable & Co.–1954) Part 5, Chapter 2, p. 399. Santayana lays unwarranted and paradoxical stress on this point, as the context shows: 'Inferred past facts are more deceptive than facts prophesied, because while the risk of error in the inference is the same, there is no possibility of discovering that error; and the historian, while really as speculative as the prophet, can never be found out.'

argument, we have a source of information about past events to which nothing corresponds in the case of future ones. Along with memory we may include for practical purposes direct testimony given to us by other people who we have good reason to suppose also remember. As we know only too well, neither of these sources of information about the past is infallible, but they are undoubtedly sources. The trouble with them is that the information so gained is very limited and does not take us far back into the past. For most retrodiction we still need argument.

Records, Interpretation and Reconstruction

For such argument, however, we are fortunate in having an important general principle of which we invariably make use. It is an ascertained fact that many kinds of physical objects are durable. We may therefore argue from their existence in the present to their existence in the past. We know furthermore what the earth's surface would be like in its natural state, and hence which among the enduring physical objects we find around us have been produced by human beings. Thus we observe such objects as houses, roads, utensils, tools, coins, parchment scrolls and printed books. Recognizing the durability of these objects, we infer that human beings were active in making them in the past. But if they invariably crumbled and dissipated immediately after use, our knowledge of the past would be reduced to very little.

In contrast, the recognition of the durability of these artefacts is of little use for the making of social predictions. We may, it is true, infer from it their continued existence in the future, and their future existence may be one of the factors influencing future human behaviour. If it is likely that a bridge will still be standing or a book still legible in fifty years' time, we know that people will be likely to act then in such a way as to take account of these things. But we will not be able to infer from this that they will perform specific actions like those we infer to have been performed in the past—the building of bridges, for example, or writing of books. A footprint in the sand tells us that someone has walked in a given direction over it in the past; it will tell us nothing comparable about the future.

Such records, as we may call them, tell us not only that something has happened in the past, but also, within narrower or wider limits, *when* it has happened. This is because there are established general statements not only about their durability but also their rate of decay. We know that footprints in the sand must be recent, whereas stone walls are not necessarily so, the age of their construction being judged by extent of weathering, amount of silt deposited over them, and the like. It is in such ways that we give dates and a chronological order to past human activities. Recently introduced processes such as that of testing the extent of disintegration of carbon-14 in dead organic substances do no more than bring refinements to the same kind of argument.

In using records we rely only on the durability of physical objects which human beings have made. There are, of course, other kinds of durability, such as that of customs and institutions. It is for this reason that we can speak of social traditions. Languages endure, for example, as well as scrolls and books. And we may therefore argue from the present state of a language to its past state. But the information so gained will only be of a very general character. Starting with existing institutions we will not be able to infer in any detail what happened at particular times and places. Thus, for our knowledge of dead languages we rely not on any principle of language continuity, but on the survival of the written word.[1]

It is clear then that it is records which provide us with the decisive break-through into the past. It is largely because of them that the historian has an advantage over the social scientist who seeks to predict the future. By making use of physical and chemical laws he can fix the times and places of occurrence of various describable kinds of human action.

But this, we know, is only the beginning. For one thing, once we have ascertained what has been done, and where and when, we need to find out further what were the motives and beliefs of the people concerned, and what were the customs and institutions in the context of which the actions took place. In other words, the records have to be interpreted. If a building is excavated we ask what we can tell from its general character about the aims, convictions and accepted practices of those who built it or used it. Was it, for example, a dwelling-house or a monastery? To answer such questions we need to use generalizations of the social kind about motives, reasons and customs, and various kinds of human action which arise from them, generalizations which must themselves depend in the last resort on the evidence of what has been observed of the actions of people in our own time, taken together with what has been inferred about their states of mind. If the building had large rooms with benches round the walls, we infer that it was not a family dwelling, but a place of meeting or communal living.[2] We infer this because we know that family dwellings in general do not contain rooms of this kind. If it were asked how we know this, we might say that it is a matter of common observation, or, more likely, that it would be unreasonable to construct such rooms for small numbers of people. If we give this last reply we would be making a simple use of the assumption of rationality, and it will be clear that a judicious use of this assumption plays a large part in our interpretation of the records of the past. We are constantly asking for what ends reasonable people would do such-and-such things.

[1] We neglect oral traditions here. These rely not on argument but on the memories of a series of individuals.

[2] This illustration, though simplified and artificial, is suggested by accounts of the recent excavation of the Qumran Monastery on the Dead Sea. See, e.g. J. M. Allegro—*The Dead Sea Scrolls* (Pelican, 1956) Ch. 5, pp. 82 et. seq.

There is one kind of record which is of especial importance here, and that is the written document. The writing of words, like the building of a wall, is a human action which requires interpretation. The difference is that the interpretation in this case is more complicated and more fruitful. In the case of words we need to ascertain their accepted meaning at the time of writing, something which demands, for languages very different from our own, an elaborate deciphering procedure. We have then to infer the beliefs and also the motives of the author in the light of generalizations about human behaviour. Where the documents contain statements of fact about the author's own time, we must estimate their truth by considering his objectivity, intelligence and access to evidence. In these ways we are often able to gain a great deal of information about the past which would never be yielded by non-verbal artefacts. For this reason, 'history' has sometimes been identified with written history and undocumented periods spoken of as prehistoric. And a consideration in detail of the procedures involved in interpreting documents has always formed the major part of what has been called historiography.

Interpretation, however, even where there are documents, still leaves us with only fragmentary information. From this information a complete historical narrative has to be reconstructed. This, of course, does not mean finding out everything about what happened in a given period and region; this is manifestly impossible in practice. But historical statements are made about much more than the motives, customs and ways of life of those who brought the records into existence, and much more than what is found in reliable documents. Suppose, for example, that we know from documents that an invading army occupied one town at one time and another some time later, and that we know also from the state of the ruins of a settlement in the intervening area that it was unoccupied from that time on. This will at least suggest to the historian that the settlement was deserted for fear of the invading army, though there is no indication of this either in the documents or in the ruins. This suggestion will be supported by an appeal to established general statements about movements of armies and reasons for evacuation. Thus the filling-in which any historical narrative requires depends, like the interpretation of records, on the use of general statements about what goes with what in social life.

The Principle of Cumulative Evidence

The general statements used in such arguments may be of various kinds. In the first place they may be to the effect that whenever something occurs something else will occur later, or to the effect that whenever something occurs something else must have occurred earlier. Where the statements are laws we express this by saying that they assert either the sufficient or the necessary conditions of the later event. Moreover, these two kinds of statement may be used in two different ways. They may be used as a basis for direct argument from some known event to the occurrence of another, or as a basis for confirming the occurrence of an event by inferring known consequences from it. Where it is available, the direct form of argument is undoubtedly to be preferred,[1] and since every retrodictive argument taken as a whole is from the present to the past, the most effective type of statement for the historian to use is one which asserts a preceding necessary condition of some known event. But it must be recognized that sufficiently well-established statements of this kind are not always available.

Furthermore, it must be recognized that the general statements used are not normally laws but rather chance-statements, or spatio-temporally restricted statements, or both. For established social laws, being rare, are no more easily available to the historian than to any other social enquirer. Thus we frequently couch the relevant generalizations in terms of what we would expect to happen in certain circumstances. We would expect a family dwelling not to have large rooms with benches. We would expect an invading army to occupy intervening settlements along its path. By saying that we would expect something in these cases, we clearly mean that it is normal—that is, that there is a good chance of it happening but not that it always happens. When we do make statements about invariable rather than normal occurrence, we are careful to restrict ourselves to given periods, as when we say 'When buildings of this kind were built in *Ancient Egypt*, they were always intended as tombs'. Thus the only laws of which any considerable use is made are those which enable us to fix the times and places of past actions, and these, as we have seen, are laws of physics and of chemistry.

This general inability to use laws, taken together with the need to fall back at times on confirmation as a substitute for direct argument, might be thought to detract very seriously from the effectiveness of the whole retrodictive procedure. If each piece of argument were taken in entire separation from others, this would indeed be the case. But to assume this would be to neglect an important point about retrodiction which we must now proceed to bring out. Historical evidence is cumulative, and where a number of retrodictive arguments converge and reinforce each other, they can become very powerful. Let us see how this comes about.

The simplest case is that in which the occurrence of one single event or state of affairs[2] is supported by various independent pieces of evidence.

---

[1] Note that it is never available for the establishing of the general statements themselves.

[2] Though for simplicity we speak here mainly of 'events', we must remember that an historian may equally well wish to establish the existence of some enduring condition of an individual or group, such as a motive, a belief, a custom, or an institution.

Consider, for example, the statement that the Sectarians of the Qumran Monastery by the Dead Sea deserted it in A.D. 68.[1] This is supported by the fact that coins were found among the ruins dating from before that time but not after it (there being a good chance of a building of this kind being occupied during periods for which such coin deposits are found). It is also supported by documentary evidence from Josephus to the effect that the Roman Tenth Legion left a garrison in the area that year and that the Roman approach was heralded by a general panic (there being a good chance of the members of any settlement in an occupied area joining in such a panic). Though each piece of evidence might not be very good taken by itself, the coincidence of their both pointing to the same date of evacuation makes the total argument very strong. For we may argue that if the event had not taken place at that time, the occurrence together of two separate indications that it did would be very unlikely. The chance of such an event occurring, in other words, given the *combination* of these indications, may well be taken to be very high. In this way historical evidence may on occasions accumulate very quickly to the point where it becomes virtually conclusive.

This principle of cumulative evidence takes a more complex form when we are concerned with the evidence for the occurrence not of a single event but of two or more different events. If we have independent evidence for various events, and they can all be shown to fit in as parts of one historical narrative, then the evidence for each one of them is immediately enhanced. The 'fitting in' may take a weaker or a stronger form. In its weaker form, two events may be said to fit in if their joint occurrence is not inconsistent with any established general statement, social or physical. No army marching on foot can be at two different places 100 miles apart on two successive days; politicians will not normally advocate radically different policies in two successive speeches. If our story of events is 'consistent' in the sense of avoiding such unlikely juxtapositions, each item in it receives thereby support additional to what it would have had if taken by itself.

This additional support will be greatly increased if the 'fitting in' takes the stronger form. It takes this form when the joint occurrence of two events, each supported by its own evidence, is not only consistent with established general statements but is made positively likely by them. If an army sets out on foot from a given place in a given direction, it is likely that it will be somewhere about twenty miles away in that direction on the following day, hence reports of its presence in these two places on two successive days will confirm each other. If, to develop our previous illustration, we take the advance of the Tenth Legion as one event and the flight of the Qumran community as another, we see that these would fit in, in the sense that given the one we would expect

[1] See J. M. Allegro—op. cit., p. 86.

185

the other, and hence, to that extent, the evidence for each would become evidence for both.

It will be clear then that an historical narrative in which the items all fit in together fulfils a function for historians somewhat similar to that of a theory for other social scientists. Just as the logical connections between sets of general statements in a theory enable the evidence for them all to be pooled, so also is there a pooling of the evidence for a set of statements about particular events when they are connected through the mediation of a heterogeneous series of general statements into a continuous narrative which, as we say, 'makes sense'. In each case, the pooling of the evidence is of great importance for securing reliable results. An historian in fact always relies, in drawing conclusions, on a background of connected narrative in the same way that other social scientists rely on a background of theory.

HISTORICAL EXPLANATION

What happened? and Why did it happen? are very different questions. We may point to the features possessed by some event or state of affairs without in any way attempting to explain them.[1] But the questions have this in common, that in order to answer them we require in each case some mediating general statement. Moreover in some cases the same general statement may serve a dual purpose. It may enable us to infer the occurrence of one event from the occurrence of another, and at the same time it may enable us to explain one in terms of the other. Thus, if it is established that wherever there is an invasion inhabitants of small settlements hostile to the invaders will desert their settlements, this will enable us either to infer the desertion of a particular settlement from the established fact of an invasion or to explain the desertion by reference to the invasion.

Not all general statements, however, are suitable for purposes of explanation. For, in the first place, to explain an event we have to refer to conditions which are sufficient for its occurrence, not to necessary ones. Thus to explain an event of the kind, b, we require a general statement to the effect that whenever some earlier event (say, a) occurs, then b occurs (or, at least, whenever a occurs there is a good chance that b will occur). It would not help us to *explain* an event of the b kind if we said that whenever b occurs, a must have occurred previously (or,

---

[1] R. G. Collingwood's well-known assertion about the historian—'When he knows what happened he already knows why it happened' (*Idea of History*, Oxford 1946, p. 214) is not inconsistent with this obvious point. Collingwood is saying that an historian is not concerned with 'mere events' (physical movements of people) but with the thoughts expressed in them. These, for the historian, are an essential part of 'what happened', and in discovering them he at one and the same time explains another part of 'what happened', the 'mere events' (physical movements). To discover A and to explain B in terms of A are different activities, but often closely related, as we, like Collingwood, go on to point out.

which is its equivalent, that whenever *a* does not occur, *b* does not occur).[1] The case is thus different from that of retrodiction, in which, as we have seen, we make use of both these kinds of statement, and in which the most direct and effective kind of argument is in fact one from a known event to some earlier necessary condition.

In the second place, we regard as unsatisfactory, explanations which make use only of chance-statements. If it is usually the case, or even nearly always the case, that the inhabitants flee from an invading army, a particular invasion would not for this reason be taken in itself as explaining an ascertained departure of inhabitants. It would only do so if the possibility of the case being an exception were excluded.

Given these two limitations, we seem to be left with the position that to explain an event we require a statement of its absolutely sufficient condition, that is, a straightforward law of the form—whenever *a* then *b*. And this would mean that the scope for historical explanation would be very much more limited than the scope for retrodiction, so limited in fact that we could rarely point to any cases of such explanation at all. But at this point we must keep in mind that explanations may be incomplete, and that social explanations are almost invariably incomplete.[2] They mention some factors, but not necessarily all the factors which comprise the absolutely sufficient condition of an event. In other words, the general statements of which they make use are not straightforward laws but tendency statements. Thus a typical historical explanation is one in which we point to certain factors or influences which contribute to the occurrence of an event. If we explain the departure of inhabitants by referring to the fact of an invasion, this is not because such people invariably flee from invaders, nor because there is a good chance of their doing so, but because invasion is one factor which, taken together with others and in the absence of counteracting ones, will ensure that departure will invariably follow.[3]

Given that this is the general pattern of historical explanation, we

[1] Nor would it help us to explain an event of the *a* kind, unless the explanation were to be a functional one.

[2] See Ch. XIII, pp. 148–9.

[3] The invasion, note, is not a necessary condition of departure. But a contributing factor *may* also be a necessary condition. In such a case it remains true that it is as a contributing factor and not as a necessary condition that it is useful for explanation. A confusion on this point appears to underlie the otherwise excellent paper by W. B. Gallie on *Explanations in History and the Genetic Sciences* (Mind, Vol. 64, 1955, pp. 160–180). Gallie speaks of a 'characteristically historical explanation' as one which refers us to 'one or a number of temporarlly prior *necessary* conditions'. But his examples show that he has contributing factors in mind. E.g. the assertion that the spread of Christianity over the Mediterranean world was due to the fact that a proselytizing platform was already provided by the Jewish synagogues. Clearly this was an important factor but not a necessary condition. The presence of the platform could not be inferred from the spread of Christianity.

must go on to raise two questions. One concerns what is explained, the other the explaining factors.

What is Explained

We speak of explaining events or states of affairs, and an event or state of affairs is what happens at a particular place at or during a particular time. But there is danger of confusion here. What happens at a particular time and place may be characterized in a great variety of ways. A particular event, in other words, possesses many features, some more general and some more specific. We may give different descriptions of it, depending on which of these features we refer to. Thus we may describe it in general terms as a war, say, a revolution, a parliamentary debate, or a decision of a general to challenge the political authorities, in which case there are likely to be other events of the same kind occurring at other times and places. Or we may make our description more and more specific, by mentioning more and more features, till we reach the stage at which it will be extremely unlikely that there will be any other event possessing all the features mentioned.

Now it will be clear that when we explain 'an event' we do not explain every feature of what occurs at a particular time and place. We select only certain features and point out what contributed to the particular occurrence having these features. It is these features which are represented by *b* in our formula for the mediating general statement. Thus someone may find out that something took place at a certain spot in Ancient Egypt which may be variously described as carving, carving in stone, carving on a building, carving of certain shapes. If asked to explain it, he will naturally ask *what* we want explained—the bare fact of carving, for example, or the fact of carving on a building of this kind. Similarly, with Europe in August 1914 in mind, it may be asked how we are to account for the outbreak of war, or of an international war, or of a war starting between small states and spreading into a world war, and so on. These are different questions and require different answers.

Thus it is that different explanations can, in a sense, be given of the 'same event', according to the features which we have in mind. Where the feature mentioned is a general one (as when we say, for example, that a war has occurred), the explanation we give may be the same as the explanation we would give of other events of the same kind (that is, other wars).[1] But where the feature is specific, consisting of a combination which to our knowledge is not to be found manifested at any other place or time, the explanation will of course be peculiar to that event.

[1] Even this, however, is not necessarily the case. Instead of trying to find a single set of factors which make up the sole sufficient (and hence also the necessary) condition for the occurrence of war, we may be content to admit various possible sufficient conditions, saying war is sometimes due to one set of circumstances, sometimes to another. Different explanations may be given of different events, even when we have the same feature in mind in each case.

So long as the features we are referring to are explicitly stated this situation will not lead to confusion. This is why there is no trouble in the case of retrodiction. When we try to find out what happened at a particular time and place, our conclusion is always stated in terms of a *description* of what happened. We find out, that is to say, that an event of an explicitly stated *kind* occurred.

With explanation, however, it is different. In this case we often do not state for which of the known features of an event we are demanding an explanation. This is especially evident when we refer to the event by name, speaking for example of the Glorious Revolution of 1688, or the First World War. When asked to explain such events, we are clearly not being asked merely to explain the occurrence at given times and places of a revolution or a war. We are being asked to explain the occurrence of a revolution or a war of a special kind. We take a large number of the features of such an event for granted, and we steadily expand our explanation by making it apply to more and more of them. By filling out the explanation in this way, we soon make it such that it applies to the event in question and no other, since the combination of features which is being made the subject of explanation is likely to belong to this event and no other. We are then inclined to say that we are explaining a unique historical event, and there is no harm in this so long as we recognize that the 'uniqueness' rests solely on the contingent impro- bability of there being other events similar in all the respects included in the scope of our explanation.[1]

This filling out of explanations occurs not only in the case of events to which we give names. We may identify an event by using a general description, and yet proceed to explain much more about it than the features mentioned in the description. If asked, for example, to account for the extension of the franchise in England after 1832, we will be expected to explain not only why there was an extension of the franchise, but also why there was an extension of the special magnitude and character which we know in fact took place. And here again we will tend to leave the way open for considering more and more special features of the event.[2]

It would be pedantic to object to this. What is being explained may generally be understood from the context. Historians are interested in

---

[1] On 'uniqueness' remember what was said in Ch. II, pp. 9–10.

[2] When C. G. Hempel in his well-known paper *The Function of General Laws in History* (Journal of Philosophy, Vol. 39, 1942) speaks of 'explanation sketches', rather than explanations, as typical in the analysis of historical events, it may be that this possibility of continual further filling out of historical explanations is part of what he has in mind. When he speaks, however, of the 'filling-out' required of an explanation sketch, he appears also to be referring to progress towards making an incomplete explanation complete, by including more and more relevant factors. See paras. 5, 4. and 5, 5. It is important that these two quite different kinds of 'filling-out' should be distinguished.

particular events, and hence will naturally be concerned to explain as many of their specific features as possible instead of staying on the level of general features and treating the events as instances of clear-cut types. And yet there is danger of confusion so long as it is not clear what is being done. It must be remembered that the explanation that is given depends on the features of an event which we have in mind, and we should always be able, if need be, to state what those features are.

The Selection of Important Factors

We may now turn to the explaining factors. We start with the supposition that the number of factors is large, especially when the event to be explained is characterized in a relatively specific way, and that we must therefore rest content with incomplete explanations in which only certain of the relevant factors are mentioned. But here the question arises whether we have any reason for discriminating between such factors and paying attention to some rather than to others. There is no doubt that we commonly regard some factors as more important than others, and it is through concentration on the important ones that we thread our way through the maze of influences which contribute to anything that happens in social life. But what is the criterion of 'importance'?

One distinction that can be made is that between the standing conditions which have been in existence for a period of time before the occurrence of the event, and the occasion, or final change which completes the set of factors sufficient for the occurrence. Diplomatic relations, military establishments, economic systems were in a given state in Europe in August, 1914; it was the murder of an archduke at Sarajevo which, given these conditions, finally led to war. Caesar desired power, but it was his perception of the immediate military situation which led him to cross the Rubicon.[1]

This distinction must not be ignored. There is no doubt that there is always a large number of relatively stable conditions which are taken for granted as the background of any historical explanation, and that we often concentrate attention on those changes which, given these conditions, led to the result. But this is only because they are the *new* factors in the situation, and what is new is by no means always considered to be the most important. The crucial point about the outbreak of war in 1914, it may be said, was not the assassination but features of the state of affairs in Europe which lay behind it—the aggressive policy of the German Government, for example, or the need for markets among the capitalistic entrepreneurs of different countries. Again, it

---

[1] Ernest Nagel in a paper on *The Logic of Historical Analysis*, reprinted in Readings in the Philosophy of Science, ed. Feigl and Brodbeck (Appleton-Century-Crofts, 1953), distinguishes five senses of 'importance', applied to causal factors. See pp. 697–700. The selection of the immediate changing factors as important would correspond roughly with his first sense.

may be said that the really important factor explaining Caesar's crossing of the Rubicon was his desire for power, the military situation of the moment merely providing him with the opportunity. In fact, all motive-explanations, as we have seen,[1] stress the enduring state of mind, and tend to pass over without mention the occasioning circumstances of the action.

We must look elsewhere then for a criterion for selecting the more important factors in an explanation. It is here that we must remember what has been said about the relative strengths of tendencies.[2] There is a close relation between saying that one tendency is stronger than another and saying that one factor is more important than another. The more important factors are those which 'carry more weight', or make a greater contribution to the resultant which is being explained. Hence any criterion that we have for 'strength', 'weight', or greatness of contribution will also serve as the criterion of explanatory importance.

We have suggested two ways in which the strength of a tendency may be judged. Where the resultant, or event to be explained, is something which admits of variation in degree, we may judge of it from the amount of effect produced, and where it does not admit of such variation we may still judge of it from the frequency with which it is produced.[3] To these two criteria, however, we may now add a third. In the case of historical explanations, where the event to be explained is of a relatively specific kind, we may judge of the importance of a factor not only by the quantitative difference but also by the qualitative difference produced in the effect.

Events may be arranged on a scale according to their degree of similarity to the specific event we have in mind. We can then say that a factor is important if, after allowing for the effects of other factors, we would still get something substantially similar to what in fact occurred. Certain specific features might be different, but this would be attributable to other 'less important' factors which in themselves contributed nothing to the overall character of the event.

This, for example, is the way in which we might decide which was the more important factor in explaining the American Civil War—the Northern demand for tariffs or the agitation against slavery.[4] In such a case we cannot speak in terms of the amount of effect produced, and

[1] See Ch. IV, pp. 30–31.

[2] See Ch. XIII, pp. 152–3.

[3] These criteria correspond to senses 2 and 4 of 'importance' outlined by Nagel op. cit. His senses 3 and 5 are not relevant for this discussion.

[4] See *Theory and Practice in Historical Study: A Report of the Committee on Historiography* (Bulletin No. 54, of the Social Science Research Council, U.S.A. 1946), Ch. 3, on 'What Historians have said about the Causes of the Civil War' for a general survey by Howard V. Beale, of the various explanations offered. Cf, esp. pp. 63–5 and 70–3, as relevant for the examples here selected.

the frequency with which factors of these kinds are to be found in explanation of such wars is something which no historian would try to assess. Yet someone might well claim that the tariff issue, say, was more important on the ground that while it was there a war of more or less this kind would have broken out sooner or later, whether the slavery issue was there or not, whereas the slavery issue by itself would never have led to war at all. He might of course be wrong, but this in itself shows that a genuine issue would have been raised.[1]

There are then different criteria for deciding the importance of factors in an explanation. They may not always give the same results, but this need not disturb us so long as the criteria can be made explicit when required. What must be emphasized is that a selection made on any of these grounds is neither arbitrary nor dependent merely on the interests of the enquirer. And through making such a selection we can overcome, to some extent, the difficulty involved in being unable to bring in all the relevant factors to give complete explanations.

If it is asked how we find out about the many tendencies appealed to in historical explanations and the different weights to attach to them, we can only refer to what has been said about tendency statements generally. Statements about the effects of different factors cannot be established separately. They form an intricate network, each being used along with others in the giving of large numbers of explanations. They become progressively better supported with every successful explanation made in terms of them. Hence it is a mistake to say that in historical enquiries we make no use of theories. We constantly make use of theories of the factor type, albeit loosely-knit and sprawling ones.

INTERPRETATIONS OF HISTORY

So far, we have been discussing the explanation of particular events. But some social enquirers have wished to do more than give such explanations. They have raised the question whether there is any factor, or kind of factor, which is of predominating importance in the explana-

---

[1] Where concentration is solely on some single specific feature of an event, the important factor may of course be quite different. An interesting case of such a specific feature is the *precise timing* of an event. If it is asked: Why did the American Civil War break out in 1861, and not, say, in 1860 or 1862, we might say that what was important here was the activity of Abraham Lincoln. Note that it is the occasioning circumstances, or 'final changes', which explain precisely *when* an event takes place. But they may do little more than this. It is whenever we recognize that occasioning circumstances of one kind or another would have appeared anyway sooner or later, that we start appealing beyond them, and attributing importance to the stable factors. If we say Caesar's crossing of the Rubicon was due to his desire for power, and fail to mention the specific military situation of the moment, this is because we consider that, given the desire for power, the opportunity would have been sure to present itself within a reasonably short period. It doesn't follow of course that the 'last straw' is never crucial. Whether it is so can only be decided by empirical enquiry.

tion of social events generally. The assertion that there is, is the main point of those who offer a general 'interpretation of history'. Thus some assert the importance of economic factors, others the competition of men for political power, others changes in scientific knowledge, and so on. What are we to say of such assertions?

The Character of an Interpretation of History

The first thing to notice about them is that they have often been discredited by overstatement. They have been presented as though they were assertions to the effect that all social events could be entirely explained in terms of some single kind of factor. It is easy enough to show, by quoting particular cases of historical explanation, that this is not the case. In the first place, there is, as we have seen, a large number of factors entering into the explanation of any given event and historians rarely do more than deal with the important ones. It follows that no general interpretation of historical events could possibly do more than assert the greater *importance* of some factor among others in the explanation of all historical events. When it was said by Marx, for example, that all history was the history of class-struggles, it could not have been supposed that a reference to class-struggle would give a *complete* explanation of the repealing of the British Corn Laws or Hitler's decision to invade Russia, let alone of the discovery of the spinning jenny or of Michelangelo's sculpturing of David. An interpretation of history must therefore be regarded not as a simple law of a general kind to be used at first-hand in explaining anything that happens in the social life of men; it is at most a law of a second order, about the relative importance of different kinds of factors which contribute to such explanation.

But further, it would be quite implausible to suggest that some given kind of factor was the most important for the explanation of all social events. There are numberless events of specific kinds which it would be easy to quote as exceptions to any such straightforward law. Certain passages in a politician's speech may be due mainly to his moral beliefs, while others can be traced back to competition for power. The timing of the American Civil War might depend on the character of Abraham Lincoln, though the occurrence of the war in the general period may have been largely the result of the incompatibility of economic systems. No exceptionless principle will here be found to hold. At best, we will be able to say that some kind of factor is the most important for *most* events, and that there is a good chance that in the case of any further event we will find an explanation of this kind. In saying this, we are making an interpretation of history into an approximate generalization, stating what we should *expect* to be the important factors in any explanation.

Even this, however, will not do. For 'events' are not isolable units occurring side by side like ninepins or one after another like beads on a temporal chain. There are events within events, and these within other events. What we call an event depends on what parts of an ever-changing situation we have in mind. The sinking of such and such a battleship is an event, so is, say, the Battle of the Coral Sea, so is the Second World War. And further, what we offer as an explanation depends on which features of any event we are paying attention to. Hence it becomes necessary to introduce a distinction between large-scale and small-scale events, and at the same time to keep in mind that any event has both general and specific features. The man who frames an interpretation of history may be said to be pointing out the type of factor which is more important in explaining in their more *general* features the *large-scale* changes which occur in social life.

If it asked what is meant by a change being 'large-scale', we have to point out that the phrase covers two different features of a change. To put it briefly, a large-scale change is one which is both extensive and radical. That is to say, it must be one which involves a large number of people or a widely accepted institution, and it must also be one in which the final state of affairs is very different in character from the initial state of affairs. The death of one individual, though radical enough if one considers only that individual, is not an extensive change, and therefore would not be counted as one of the large-scale changes of history. But neither would a slight rise in income-tax, since this, though payable by a whole population, would not be counted as sufficiently radical.

It will be clear from this that 'large-scaleness', like importance, is a matter of degree, and, again like importance, is measurable on a two-fold scale. Hence it is not possible to frame an interpretation of history such that we can read off from it, in a clear-cut way, whether a given type of factor will predominate in a particular case. There will be clear cases, but there will also be borderline cases. It does not follow from this, however, that such broad generalizations are empty and incapable of disproof. If an exponent of one of them could not show the un-doubted importance of his selected kind of factor in the case of un-doubtedly large-scale changes, his particular interpretation would have to be discarded.

'Laws of Historical Development'

It must be said at once that those who have discovered a 'pattern' in history or have formulated what have been misleadingly called 'laws of historical development' have often committed themselves to much more than the general statements we have here described. It is one thing to say that when large-scale changes occur they are susceptible to some general kind of explanation, and another to say that large-scale changes of certain kinds, explained in the way specified, do in fact recur at more or less regular intervals throughout the course of history. We must distinguish, for example, between saying that revolutionary changes in social structure depend largely on the conflict between economic classes, and saying that such changes, brought about by these conflicts, occur in a recurrent sequence with periods of relative stability in between. Statements of this latter kind—let us call them statements of recurrent sequence—are general statements, and when the recurrence is asserted to be invariable, in all periods, they may be called laws.[1] They may be expressed in the form 'Wherever there is human society (or wherever there is private property, or whatever it may be), events of a certain kind will recur at certain intervals'. Where the recurrence is exact in respect of certain stated features, we say that the course of change is cyclical; where it is recurrence with a difference in certain respects (a similar difference being found on each occasion) we say that there is a trend or a development. Both types of sequence have been asserted by those who have speculated about the general course of human history, and both have been used for making predictions about the main features of the future course of events.

The obvious trouble about such laws is that they are very difficult to establish. It is not merely that there is some uncertainty as to what is to count as a large-scale change of a certain kind—the rise of a civilization, for example, or the rise to power of an economic class. It is also that at best there will be only a few ascertainable instances of such large-scale changes constituting any given sequence, and the number of independent sequences, if any, is likely to be fewer still.[2] These may be sufficient to suggest a rough generalization, but further support is needed, and this can only be obtained if we can derive the statement of recurrent sequence from more general statements in some theoretical system, thereby showing *why* we should expect the sequence to recur. It is

[1] K. R. Popper in *The Poverty of Historicism* (Routledge, 1957) Sections 27–8, denies this on the ground that such statements are statements about trends and that these are singular historical statements, not laws. There is no doubt that those who make such statements usually have in mind their application to some particular series of large-scale social changes—the 'stages of evolution' of some given society over the last few thousand years. But the statements themselves contain no reference to any particular item in the series, nor need they contain a reference to any particular series. They may be compared with such statements as 'Stars gradually grow cooler'. They are existential only in the sense that they presuppose the existence of large-scale social changes, just as this other statement presupposes the existence of stars. They may admittedly be stated not as laws applying to any changes but as restricted general statements applying only to changes occurring in a particular period and place. Thus we may say that there are such and such recurrent sequences in the history of *European* society, just as we may say *the Sun* grows gradually cooler. But even in this case they remain as general statements applicable to *any* item in the sequence.

[2] Arnold Toynbee in his study of the rise and fall of civilizations (see *The Study of History*) refers to twenty-one instances of 'civilizations'. The major economic revolutions specifically referred to by Marxists can be numbered on the fingers of the hand.

among such more general statements that we find, figuring largely, what we have called interpretations of history. But assertions that certain factors are of greater explanatory importance are not by themselves sufficient for deriving the regular recurrence of any special kinds of change. Insistence on the importance of class conflict, for example, will not in itself show us why capitalist economic institutions replaced the feudal, or why the socialist should replace the capitalist. For this, much more detailed explanation is needed.[1] And since circumstances vary greatly at each stage in a sequence, there is ample opportunity for neglecting factors which may make all the difference to the case. There is therefore much to justify those historians who regard generalization about large-scale sequences as nothing more than tentative speculation.

With interpretations of history, however, as we have described them, it is different. It is true, as we have pointed out, that there is fluidity in the borderline between the important and the unimportant and between the large-scale and the small-scale. It is true also that different social enquirers have held firmly to different interpretations without being able to resolve their disputes. But there is no reason to suppose that the attempt to resolve these disputes is lacking in scientific value. An interpretation of history, unlike a statement of recurrent sequence, is not a speculative addition to the study of history. In so far as any interpretation can be established, it will give theoretical support to large numbers of specific explanations and predictions—all those in fact, which are concerned with large-scale changes, of whatever kind. And any interpretation will be progressively confirmed by the success of those explanations and predictions which are carried on within its framework.

It is always possible, of course, that no kind of factor, however general, has the overall importance which any interpretation of history ascribes to it. But whether this is so or not is something which can only be discovered in the course of enquiry. Furthermore, *if* it is the case that there is no predominating kind of factor, it is most necessary that this should be made clear. For, as has often been pointed out, social enquirers in general and historians in particular are prone to concentrate on certain kinds of explanation on the assumption that certain kinds of factor have the greater influence. It is vital that such assumed interpretations should be recognized openly and their soundness considered. If they cannot be supported in any way, then they should be carefully eliminated as distortions which, however satisfying, have no place in the body of social theory.

[1] It is explanation of this kind, it should be noted, and not broad generalizations about historical sequences, which fills most of the pages of Marx's *Capital*.

XVI

SOCIAL ENQUIRY AND SOCIAL PRACTICE

THOSE who engage in social enquiry may, as we have pointed out, have two very different kinds of end in view, the theoretical and the practical. Their aim, that is to say, may be simply to discover and explain what happens in social life, or it may be to produce changes in it, influencing the states of mind and the actions of other people and the character of their groups and institutions.[1]

The aim is very commonly a practical one. To be disinterested, in the sense of having an exclusively theoretical interest, is rare. People concern themselves for the most part not so much with what happens as with how to achieve certain results. Their practical motives may be various. They may be concerned to help their fellow-men or to increase their own reputations, to prevent unemployment or to make profits, to establish a just society or to retain power. When they have no particular end in view themselves, they may still be employed to give advice to those who have. Thus it is that studies such as economics and politics have often been regarded as 'arts' rather than 'sciences', and compared to engineering and medicine rather than to physics and biology. Some general end is assumed, such as government, or getting a living out of scarce resources, and the job of the political scientist or the economist is thought of as working out how to achieve the end, as studying the art of government or the art of getting a living. Social enquiry thus comes to be regarded as social technology.

We have emphasized that the presence of a practical interest on the enquirers' part need in no way vitiate the enquiry.[2] The establishing of true conclusions is a means to practical success, and those who seek a practical end will endeavour to secure the means. Hence, apart from the

[1] When theory is distinguished from practice, the word 'theory' is, of course, being used in a broader sense than that adopted in Ch. X. (See Note 1 to p. 114). It is equivalent to 'enquiry', and makes no reference to the distinction between those enquiries which, in our earlier sense, use 'theories', or are 'theoretical', and those which are not.

[2] See Ch. VII, p. 77.

distorting effects of prejudice and bias, there is no general reason to expect an enquiry undertaken for practical ends to be less efficiently conducted than one undertaken for its own sake.

There are, however, certain features of the relation between social enquiry and practical social activity to which it is important to draw attention.

Reciprocity Between Enquiry and Practice

When we aim at producing social changes, this is often in order to achieve further non-social ends, and one of these ends is the theoretical one of testing the truth of statements about social life. Hence it comes about that the relation between enquiry and practice is in a sense reciprocal. On the one hand we may utilize the results of an enquiry for the practical purpose of producing desired social changes. On the other hand the producing of social changes may itself help to further the end of social enquiry. Well-established conclusions help to ensure successful action. But action—successful or unsuccessful—also helps to establish the conclusions.

A person who acts merely in order to test his theories may be said to be conducting an experiment. He is to be contrasted with the person who has a merely practical motive and uses well-established results to enable him to achieve his end. The important point to notice here is that the normal case lies somewhere between these two extremes. With practical ends in view we act on beliefs for which there is some evidence, but which we recognize not to be conclusively established. In doing so we take a greater or a lesser amount of risk. But whether we succeed or fail, we at the same time test the truth of the beliefs on which we act. It is in this way that everyone is constantly learning by practical experience how to live with other people. Hence it might be said that a great deal of social practice is in some degree experimental.

It must be admitted that when people speak of using experimental methods in social enquiry, they are frequently using the word 'experiment' in a narrower sense. They would not, that is to say, regard mere learning by trial and error in the normal course of life as satisfying the conditions of a properly conducted experiment. For this they would require that we also have control over the conditions in which we act, and arrange these conditions so as to eliminate the influence of factors other than our action. It is this control which we have in its most developed form in a laboratory, and action under 'real life conditions' rarely attains it, even when there is a merely theoretical end in view. In any discussion of experiment, therefore, the distinction between the narrower and the wider sense should be kept in mind.

In each case, however, experiment involves action on the part of the enquirer, and when people stress the importance of practice for social enquiry, it is often the value of such experimental action that they have in mind. That it has this value is beyond question. It enables the enquirer to choose the time at which his observations are made; and if, further, he is able to control the conditions under which he acts, he can isolate the effects of different factors with much greater ease, thus laying the basis for the construction of theories. The beneficial effect of practice on enquiry is to that extent easily vindicated. All that has to be remembered is that experiment is frequently not possible. Even where social enquirers are able to produce social changes and control social conditions,[1] there are special difficulties in the way of their doing these things for theoretical purposes. They will commonly be prevented from producing any changes which are held socially undesirable, even if they themselves are willing to produce them. They cannot, for example, test their theories by artificially creating poverty or pain, however illuminating the theoretical results might be. Furthermore, the people affected by any experimental action will commonly become aware of its purpose, and their reactions will be altered accordingly.[2] The enquirer may thus find out only how people react to being experimented upon, and this after all is only of passing interest. Hence it comes about that, however valuable experimental practice may be for social enquiry, there are considerable limitations on its use.

Those who stress the importance of practice for social enquiry, however, often have in mind something quite different from the value of experiment. They are often wanting to say that, for the progress of enquiry, what is important is not so much that practice be engaged in for theoretical purposes as that theory be engaged in for practical purposes. The very fact of having practical problems to solve, it is suggested, serves to stimulate enquiry, and this is so whether or not the enquiry is itself carried on by means of experiment.

It will be clear that to stress the importance of practice in this sense is to raise quite a separate question. It is the sort of question people have in mind when they ask whether it is better for social enquiry to be conducted by practical men of affairs or by academic experts, in the market-place or in the ivory-tower.

To this question there is no simple answer. There are clearly considerations on both sides. To have a practical problem to solve may well give one a greater sense of urgency in pushing the enquiry forward. It may also bring one into more immediate contact with the subject-matter which it is one's business to investigate. And again it may help in the avoidance of the danger of constructing social theories without paying due attention to the complexity of the situations in which they are applied.

---

[1] Difficulties in the way of their doing these things are discussed later. See pp. 204 et. seq.

[2] Difficulties of this kind are well illustrated by the famous 'Hawthorne experiment' on the output of workers in a Chicago factory. For a brief account of this, see J. Madge—*The Tools of Social Science* (Longmans, Green & Co., 1953) pp. 282–6.

On the other hand, there is the formidable argument from the advantages of the division of labour. To become an expert requires training, skill and time to concentrate on the actual business of enquiry, and these are things we cannot expect of those who are immersed in practical concerns. Again, over against the danger of constructing inapplicable theories, we must put the danger of failing to construct theories at all, and concentrating instead on establishing those lower-level general statements which are required for dealing with immediate practical problems.

How much weight is to be given to these opposed considerations is something which cannot be decided in general terms. There is no reason to suppose that being committed to a policy is a necessary condition of successful social enquiry. On the other hand there are certain kinds of problem on which the best work may be done within the context of practical social activity. What concerns us here, however, is that the possible usefulness of social practice as a context of enquiry should be carefully distinguished from its undoubted usefulness as an experimental test.

Practice and Prediction

We may now turn to the other side of the relation between enquiry and practice, and consider the way in which the results of an enquiry may be used when we seek to bring about social changes.

The first thing to be clear about is the sort of statement which we need to establish if we are to apply our social knowledge to the changing of the world. As we have pointed out,[1] what we need for this is to establish *conditional* statements about what would happen if we were to do this or that, and not statements about actual happenings, past, present or future. When we are deciding what to do, the question at issue is what action, given the existing situation, would lead to a desired consequence. If it is asked, for example, what is to be done to reduce unemployment, the answer may be that in the present circumstances unemployment would be reduced if bank credit were eased. When this answer is given no statement is made about any actual case of reduction of unemployment or any actual case of the easing of bank credit.

One thing, however, which such conditional statements have in common with statements about actual occurrences is that they cannot be established without the use of general statements. If it were asked how we know that in the present circumstances the action of easing credit would be followed by a reduction in unemployment, we would have no alternative but to fall back on the general statement that in circumstances of this kind, an event of the one kind is always followed by an event of the other kind, or at least that there is a good chance of this being so. We appeal, that is to say, to a statement of the form 'Given *s*,

[1] Ch. III, p. 17.

whenever *a* then *b*', (or, 'Given *s*, whenever *a* then, as a rule, *b*'). And this is precisely the same form of general statement that we would require if we were to establish the actual unobserved occurrence of a reduction of unemployment at a given time and place.

That it is the establishing of conditional statements in this way which is needed as a basis for action may seem obvious enough. But there is an important consequence of this which is often insufficiently recognized. It is easy to see that statements about past and present events, taken by themselves, will not help us at all. But the point is sometimes missed that the same applies to statements about future events. Prediction, that is to say, in the simple sense of establishing that something is going to happen in the future, is in itself valueless for practice. From the point of view of an agent—a person who is considering what to do—the issue is what will happen *if* he does this or that, or what will happen *if* he does nothing— never simply what will happen.

This may be put another way by saying that general statements may be applied to the future in one or other of two ways. They may be applied either for purposes of prediction, or for purposes of action. In the former case, another premiss is required, stating that the conditions from which the future consequences will follow do in fact exist now. In the latter case there can be no such premiss, for here the conditions are not complete. There is of course an existing situation, but whether it is so modified that the consequences will follow depends on what the agent decides to do. Thus the work of enquiry comes to an end with the assertion of a particular conditional statement. That is the point at which we pass over into action.[1]

There are, of course, similarities between these two kinds of application. One thing they have in common, for example, is that in each case the general statement used must not be a single theoretical law, or tendency statement. The retention of an 'other-things-being equal' clause will make a statement as useless for action as for prediction. To say, for example, that easing of credit restrictions will, other things being equal, solve the unemployment problem, will not in itself tell us whether credit restrictions should be eased or not. We need to take all factors into consideration, or at least be in a position to say that there is not much chance of there being counteracting factors present. And, as with prediction, this is often not an easy thing to do. When practical men complain about 'abstract theorists' it is the failure to take all factors into consideration that they have in mind. Their complaint is the same as that made by those who require scientists to predict.

Again, the two kinds of application, though distinct, may on occasions

---

[1] K. R. Popper, in *The Poverty of Historicism*, distinguishes these cases as those of 'prophetic prediction' (or 'prophecy') and 'technological prediction'. See pp. 42–3. We have preferred to reserve the term 'prediction' for what he speaks of as 'prophesy'. It would seem that this is the more normal use.

be closely related. Simply predicting what will happen is by itself of no use when we have to choose a course of action. But in the course of making the choice, we may well find that a considerable amount of prediction is involved. In deciding what to do, we have to take into account not only the present situation, but also the future situation in so far as it is outside our control. There are always some things which will happen whatever we do. If we can predict these we can then proceed to work out what action would lead to the best results that are compatible with them. It follows from this that the more the course of events is outside our control, the greater the importance of prediction will be.

A distinction is commonly made between producing social changes and adjusting oneself to changes that will happen anyway. On the one side we might put, say, forcing prices up, and on the other forestalling an anticipated rise in prices by buying in advance. In the one case we appear to be doing something positive, while in the other we appear to be simply swimming with the tide (where the course of events is favourable to our ends) or protecting ourselves against adversity (where it is unfavourable). But it will be clear from what has been said that this is only a distinction of degree. In both cases we engage in social action, and we do so in the light of general considerations about the best way to achieve our ends in the circumstances. The difference is that in the latter case prediction plays a greater preparatory role than in the former. Which is more characteristic of human action generally depends on the extent to which any individual person is in fact able to influence the course of social events. The extent of this influence is thus something which we must go on to discuss.

Before doing so, however, we must issue a warning and dismiss an apparent paradox. It is sometimes maintained that there are social predictions which are inherently self-defeating because of the intimate relation they bear to actions, whether these be our own actions or those of other people. Thus if I predict that I will win a race, on the evidence of my superior physique, training, concentration and so on, this may make me so overconfident that I will lose it. If I predict that because of my temperament and the incitement I have received, I shall do something in the future of which I now disapprove—kill my father, say, like Oedipus in the legend—this is likely to make me take steps to avoid doing it—say, by going to another country. Similarly, if an economist, after examining the behaviour of investors, makes and publishes a prediction that share prices will rise to their highest point at a given time, the investors, on hearing of this, may alter their behaviour in such a way as to make the prices fall earlier than anticipated. If Gallup Poll experts make and publish a prediction that one candidate will be elected, this may galvanize the supporters of his opponents in such a way as to swing the election. In all such cases, it is said, the prediction has effects which ensure its own falsity.[1] And hence, *a fortiori*, it can have no possible value for practice.

Now it is quite true that such predictions have no value for practice. But this is not because they are self-defeating. It is simply because they are not predictions of what lies outside our control. This is obvious in the case in which we predict our own actions. But it holds also in the case where the actions are those of other people, since the effect in this case depends on the publication of the predictions and the publication is something we can withhold. For purposes of practice it will be useful to know what would happen *if* we were to act or *if* we were to publish, but not to know that we will act or that we will publish.

Furthermore, we may add to this that such predictions are not in any real sense self-defeating. The holding of beliefs about the future, especially when they result in public statements, may of course have important social effects, and among these there may well be effects which prove the beliefs false. But it must be remembered that such beliefs are only called predictions in so far as there are good reasons for them; they become predictions rather than mere dogmatic assertions only to the extent that they are based on evidence. And it may be pointed out that they can defeat themselves only in so far as they are defective as predictions; the trouble with them is that the evidence on which they are based is not good enough. To be effective, predictions must clearly take account of the effect —often itself easily ascertainable—which they would have on future actions. Once account is taken of this, prediction and action will fall into line.

Consider the extreme case in which a prediction made by an enquirer about his own action is falsified by its effect on that action. In this case it will be seen that there are two possibilities. On the one hand the enquirer may retain his prediction realizing that its effect on his action will be counteracted once he becomes aware of it. Thus he may continue to maintain that he will win the race, since, having taken account of the fact that the prediction may make him lazy, he may predict further that he will take steps to ensure that it does not do so. And on the other hand he may abandon his prediction, realizing that if he were to continue to uphold it, it would defeat itself. Thus, instead of predicting that he will kill his father, he may instead predict that he will leave the country, arguing that the danger of his killing his father, if he did nothing to avoid it, would be sufficient to make him do something to avoid it.[2]

[1] For comment on such self-defeating predictions, see Popper, op cit., pp. 13–14; also R. K. Merton, *Social Theory and Social Structure* (Free Press of Glencoe, Illinois, 1951.). Introd. to Part 2, pp. 120–3 and Ch. 7. It should be noted that there is a corresponding phenomenon of self-fulfilling predictions. A prediction that a bank will become insolvent may make it insolvent by starting a run on it. A prediction that a revolution will be successful may make it successful by inspiring confidence. In such cases no paradox is involved, but the principle is the same.

[2] Note that in the Oedipus legend, prediction and action are brought into line in a third way. The prediction is retained, but only because of an extra assumption about the intervention of Fate, which makes it come true whatever the acting individual does about it.

What applies in this extreme case will clearly apply also in those much more common cases in which predictions, through their publication, affect the actions of others. In general it may be said that anyone who tries to make a prediction has to take account of any possible effects which the making of the prediction, or its publication, will have either on himself or on other people. Predictions which defeat themselves through having these effects, unforeseen, are in no sense logically absurd, they are merely inadequate.[1]

Knowledge and Power

We may now return to a consideration of the extent to which social knowledge can be applied for the achievement of practical ends. Let us assume that the social enquirer has established conditional statements about the consequences of proposed actions, backed by statements about the existing situation and the future situation so far as it is outside his control. Given that he has this knowledge, how far does it help him to influence the course of social events? As a social technologist, how does his position compare with that of the engineer or the physician?

The Baconian epigram that knowledge is power is sometimes in danger of being taken too literally. It gained currency, understandably enough, with the growth of modern natural science. An antithesis was drawn between 'mankind' on the one hand and the 'forces of nature' on the other. The forces of nature were the situation with which man was confronted; left to themselves they thwarted his ends. He was in fact in a position to exercise a measure of control over them save for one thing; he had no knowledge of their workings. When the natural scientists gave him this, the earth's surface was speedily transformed. The natural sciences produced results, and are still producing them.

This is, however, a deceptively simple account of the matter. When confined to the natural sciences it may not do much harm. But trouble arises when it is transferred to the social sciences, and made the basis for

---

[1] The case of self-fulfilling beliefs may be accounted for in the same way. In this case a prediction, made on the basis of *some* evidence, perhaps quite slender, could have been supported by much better evidence if the predictor had realized that others (or he himself) on believing it would be stimulated to act in ways favourable to it. Thus a prediction of a bank's insolvency would immediately be reinforced once the predictor took account of the effect of its publication on the depositors.

In arguing that the alleged self-defeating character of certain social predictions sets no limit to prediction in social enquiry, we leave open the question whether there is anything else which might do this. For example, assuming it is possible in principle for a social enquirer to predict his own future *actions* and their effects (however valueless this may be for practice), is it likewise possible for him to predict the results of his own future *enquiry*? This raises new issues. It may be argued that prediction by an enquirer of his own future results is really impossible in principle, since it requires that he knows the evidence which will lead him to adopt those results, and, if he has this evidence now, he will be led to adopt the results now, and not in the future.

Cf. R. R. Popper—*The Poverty of Historicism*, Preface, pp. ix-xi, for an argument that the prediction of future discoveries is impossible, and that this disproves the possibility of predicting the future course of history.

a contrast between them and the natural ones. Since the growth of natural science, it is said, has given man control over the forces of nature, what is now required is a corresponding growth of the social sciences which will give him control over the forces of society. Knowledge of our natural surroundings has given us electric light, refrigeration, fast transport and so on. But we are still left with poverty, hunger, crime, domestic unhappiness, destruction of life and property. If only the social sciences could catch up, we would learn to manage our own affairs as we have learnt to manage our environment.[1]

To make clear what is wrong with this, we must point out that even in the case of natural science, knowledge is only a necessary, and not a sufficient, condition for control. Two other things are required.

In the first place, the laws or other general statements established in the science must be such that some human action which is practically possible will lead to the desired results. It might have been that, because of the way things worked, even the greatest development of natural science would have left men powerless to increase their control over nature. Knowledge of astronomy has not enabled, and may never enable, men to redirect the planets, however much they might wish to do so. If the structure of the atom had been different, atomic research might never have enabled them to utilize atomic energy. The subject-matter of the science must conform to certain kinds of general order, before action can lead to control.

In the second place, those who have the knowledge must not only know what possible human actions would lead to the desired results, but must also have sufficient social influence to enable them to perform them. The vague reference to what can be done by 'mankind' obscures this point. Taken individually, men may know perfectly well what to do and yet not have the resources to do it. An inventor, for example, may know how to construct a machine, yet be unable to construct it because he lacks access to materials which are under the control of others.

Natural scientists, in their engineering ventures, have in fact been fairly fortunately placed with regard to both these conditions, and this is why the growth of their knowledge has been so easily accepted as the important thing. In medical practice there has been trouble with the first condition but not so much with the second. Social scientists on the other hand appear to fall well behind on both counts, and it is because of this rather than the lack of maturity of their sciences, that a contrast has to be drawn with natural scientists, in respect of practical results. Let us consider these two conditions of control in turn.

[1] For good examples of a presentation of the contrast in these terms, see the final pages of C. D. Broad's *Mind and its Place in Nature* (Kegan Paul, Trench, Trubner & Co. 1925, pp. 665–6) and, more recent, the opening pages of Barbara Wootten's *Testament for Social Science* (George Allen & Unwin, 1950, Ch. 1). 'The contrast,' writes Mrs. Wootten in her opening sentence, 'between man's amazing ability to manipulate his material environment and his pitiful incompetence in managing his own affairs is now as commonplace as it is tragic.'

In engineering projects, the first condition is fairly well satisfied, because the materials are not only available in the earth's crust, but are relatively inert. They are not subject to many influences which tend to change them of their own accord. There are of course always some influences which must be allowed for or guarded against, such, for example, as changes in wind, water and temperature when a bridge is being built. But the principal change is that produced by human agents, and for that reason it is under their control. It is therefore natural to speak of 'designing' and 'constructing' such things as bridges. The materials are there to be put together, to conform to a blue-print, and the engineer can rely on their not changing of themselves in the course of construction.

This is not the case in social—or in medical—practice. The social scientist is confronted not with raw materials, but with existing situations, constantly changing as a result of many influences. He has to deal with men in action, all perpetually striving to achieve their ends, and affecting one another. It is thus the interconnectedness of the social subject-matter, as compared with the physical, which makes the difference.[1] It means that social scientists cannot simply put materials together while guarding against outside influences; they can only intervene in what is already in process of change, thereby adding a further influence to the many already operating.

It is this which accounts for the artificiality of the terminology of 'designing' and 'constructing' when applied to social institutions. It is more natural to speak of a plan of action in terms of intervention, re-direction, or strategy, than of construction.[2] And it is somewhat misleading to speak of blue-prints at all. It will always be possible in principle so to intervene that the course of events will lead to a state of affairs envisaged beforehand in the blue-print manner. But it may be doubted whether it is possible in practice. The effects of intervention are difficult to estimate in any detail, because of their combination with other influences, both present and future. Hence in social practice the plan of action assumes increased importance. It must be flexible, so as to meet the contingencies that continually arise, and though directed towards certain general ends it cannot be regarded as the simple implementation of a preconceived design. It is a commonplace that

[1] It must be remembered that this contrast is to be found in some degree among physical occurrences themselves. The weather is also constantly changing of its own accord as a result of many influences, and the meterologist is thus in a position somewhat similar to the social scientist and the medical man in respect of control. The case of astronomy is different. The lack of control in this case is due simply to the size and distance of the objects studied.

[2] See Karl Mannheim—*Man and Society in an Age of Reconstruction* (Routledge and Kegan Paul 1951) pp. 191–3, for the use of the military metaphor of 'strategy', when he seeks to emphasize the distinction between social planning and invention. Marx used a medical metaphor when he spoke of his task as a practising social scientist as being that of shortening and lessening the birth-pangs of a new social order. For Marx, social practice was mid-wifery rather than engineering.

anyone who starts off with a social blue-print ends up with something very different from what he intended, although he may well have achieved something. And this applies just as much to small-scale projects for welfare centres and model factories as it does to grandiose blue-prints for a new social order.

The greater the number of change-producing factors outside our control, the greater the need, as we have pointed out,[1] for prediction. Such prediction is often not possible; the contingencies that arise frequently remain unforeseen. But it is clearly desirable, and of especial importance for social practice. If we know what other people whom we cannot influence are going to do, we can prepare to adjust ourselves to it. If it is something which makes the realization of our ends easier, we can make use of it, co-operating with the favourable 'social forces', and doing our bit to help them along, just as the doctor makes use of disease-resisting forces in the body. If on the other hand it is something which gets in our way, we may attempt to counteract its effect on our plans, as a doctor does when he uses antiseptic, or modify our plans to bring them in line with what is possible.

That these are the typical kinds of social policy is sometimes obscured by the fact that in most communities there are governments which hold a central position of political power. One way in which social scientists engage in practice is by advising governments on matters of policy. A simple picture of the situation is to think of the economists, or other social enquirers, making the plans, and the government implementing them by making laws and regulations. This naïve picture, however, is deceptive. What advice is accepted by governments depends on all sorts of influences playing upon them. And when laws are made there is always a large number of factors determining whether they have the effect intended.

This brings us to the second condition of control. The interconnected and changing character of the social subject-matter, we have said, makes it in itself relatively insusceptible to control. And this would apply even if social scientists were themselves in key positions in society, suitably placed for exerting influence on others by means of force, wealth, or persuasion—or, if not in such positions themselves, did really have their advice unquestioningly accepted by governments or other bodies which held such key positions.

Such conditions are in fact seldom realized. Social scientists, as well as being limited in the possibilities of control by the nature of their subject-matter, are hardly ever in key positions of social power, and are by no means always listened to by those who are. This is the second respect in which they are not so well placed as natural scientists.

Natural scientists, though they have not been themselves in key social positions, have nevertheless shared their ends, on the whole, with those

[1] This chapter, p. 202.

who have, and have had no great social opposition to overcome. It is true that their researches have often been thwarted by the upholders of dogmas, machines have been broken by displaced workers and inventions pigeon-holed by monopolists. And on the other hand some of them have been loath to co-operate in developing weapons of destruction such as the atomic bomb. But on the whole, those who have had the access to resources have been prepared to use scientific knowledge for the achievement of their ends, and scientists have been content to supply it. This is why they can so easily be regarded as the representatives of 'mankind', advising it what to do to gain control over nature. This applies equally to biological scientists who can be regarded as supplying their advice about the maintenance of health.

This attitude is eloquently expressed by the use of the first person plural. 'If we are to construct a bridge (or to cure tuberculosis)' someone may say, 'we must do so and so.' Who 'we' are is irrelevant for the propositions of applied physics or biology which follow. But the use of the word assumes co-operation between the scientist and the firm or government for whom he is working, or the readers of his textbook, or whoever it may be, for the purpose of modifying the natural world or the condition of human bodies. The scientist works out the plans, and the others, it is assumed, will help him carry them out.

In the case of social scientists, however, this assumption becomes most unplausible. In social practice—in this respect unlike medicine—there is no agreement on ends. 'We', in the sense of men in general, have no common purpose on the achievement of which we may ask for a social scientist's advice. And the powers-that-be are not likely to accept advice on how to achieve ends they do not share. Given a policy, an economist may, for example, advise a government or a business corporation on the best strategy to adopt. But this will not help those who are in disagreement with this policy. An economist may say 'If we are to nationalize the banking system, we must do so and so'. But the 'we' here is not 'mankind'; at most it is a political party, and not necessarily one which has much influence.

For this reason, those who wish to put their knowledge to practical use may well be pushed one step further back. They may have to set themselves as a practical social problem not merely how to carry out a given policy, but also how to obtain power. It must be emphasized that for a social enquirer this is simply one problem among others, but from the point of view of practice it is crucial. Its importance is not lessened by the fact that, owing to the variety of circumstances, there are few explicitly formulated general rules to apply to the solution of it. Those who have social reforms in mind must know not merely how to implement them but how to fight for them. This is again—and in this case almost literally—a problem of the strategical kind. The danger is that, because securing power for oneself or for those who support one's aims is such an important and difficult part of the task, it may make those who undertake it lose sight of the aims themselves, and restrict themselves to the more limited end of simply obtaining power.

It will be seen then that it is not the immaturity of the social sciences which is responsible for the continuance of those features of social life which we consider objectionable. And we must not suppose that more social science is the only thing needed to save mankind. It would be a pity, however, if we were to be led by this realization to the conclusion that persistence with social enquiry was not worth while. We should be led rather to achieve as much as we can achieve, practically as well as theoretically, while avoiding an unscientific arrogance about our results.

INDEX

210

INDEX

INDEX

INDEX

The International Library of
Sociology
and Social Reconstruction

Edited by W. J. H. SPROTT
Founded by KARL MANNHEIM

ROUTLEDGE & KEGAN PAUL
BROADWAY HOUSE, CARTER LANE, LONDON, E.C.4

CONTENTS

PRINTED IN GREAT BRITAIN BY HEADLEY BROTHERS LTD
109 KINGSWAY LONDON WC2 AND ASHFORD KENT

GENERAL SOCIOLOGY

Brown, Robert. Explanation in Social Science. *208 pp. 1963. (2nd Impression 1964.) 25s.*

Gibson, Quentin. The Logic of Social Enquiry. *240 pp. 1960. (2nd Impression 1963.) 24s.*

Goldschmidt, Professor Walter. Understanding Human Society. *272 pp. 1959. 21s.*

Homans, George C. Sentiments and Activities: Essays in Social Science. *336 pp. 1962. 32s.*

Jarvie, I. C. The Revolution in Anthropology. *Foreword by Ernest Gellner. 272 pp. 1964. 40s.*

Johnson, Harry M. Sociology: a Systematic Introduction. *Foreword by Robert K. Merton. 710 pp. 1961. (4th Impression 1964.) 42s.*

Mannheim, Karl. Essays on Sociology and Social Psychology. *Edited by Paul Keckskemeti. With Editorial Note by Adolph Lowe. 344 pp. 1953. 30s.*

Systematic Sociology: An Introduction to the Study of Society. *Edited by J. S. Erös and Professor W. A. C. Stewart. 220 pp. 1957. (2nd Impression 1959.) 24s.*

Martindale, Don. The Nature and Types of Sociological Theory. *292 pp. 1961. (2nd Impression 1965.) 35s.*

Maus, Heinz. A Short History of Sociology. *234 pp. 1962. (2nd Impression 1965.) 28s.*

Myrdal, Gunnar. Value in Social Theory: A Collection of Essays on Methodology. *Edited by Paul Streeten. 332 pp. 1958. (2nd Impression 1962.) 32s.*

Ogburn, William F., and **Nimkoff, Meyer F.** A Handbook of Sociology. *Preface by Karl Mannheim. 656 pp. 46 figures. 38 tables. 5th edition (revised) 1964. 40s.*

Parsons, Talcott, and **Smelser, Neil J.** Economy and Society: A Study in the Integration of Economic and Social Theory. *362 pp. 1956. (3rd Impression 1964.) 35s.*

Rex, John. Key Problems of Sociological Theory. *220 pp. 1961. (3rd Impression 1965.) 25s.*

Stark, Werner. The Fundamental Forms of Social Thought. *280 pp. 1962. 32s.*

FOREIGN CLASSICS OF SOCIOLOGY

Durkheim, Emile. Suicide. A Study in Sociology. *Edited and with an Introduction by George Simpson. 404 pp. 1952. (2nd Impression 1963.) 30s.*

Socialism and Saint-Simon. *Edited with an Introduction by Alvin W. Gouldner. Translated by Charlotte Sattler from the edition originally edited with an Introduction by Marcel Mauss. 286 pp. 1959. 28s.*

Professional Ethics and Civic Morals. *Translated by Cornelia Brookfield. 288 pp. 1957. 30s.*

Gerth, H. H., and **Mills, C. Wright.** From Max Weber: Essays in Sociology. *502 pp. 1948. (5th Impression 1964.) 35s.*

Tönnies, Ferdinand. Community and Association. *(Gemeinschaft und Gesellschaft.) Translated and Supplemented by Charles P. Loomis. Foreword by Pitirim A. Sorokin. 334 pp. 1955. 28s.*

SOCIAL STRUCTURE

Andrzejewski, Stanislaw. Military Organization and Society. *With a Foreword by Professor A. R. Radcliffe-Brown. 226 pp. 1 folder. 1954. 21s.*

Cole, G. D. H. Studies in Class Structure. *220 pp. 1955. (3rd Impression 1964.) 21s.*

Coontz, Sydney H. Population Theories and the Economic Interpretation. *202 pp. 1957. (2nd Impression 1961.) 25s.*

Coser, Lewis. The Functions of Social Conflict. *204 pp. 1956. (2nd Impression 1965.) 18s.*

Glass, D. V. (Ed.). Social Mobility in Britain. *Contributions by J. Berent, T. Bottomore, R. C. Chambers, J. Floud, D. V. Glass, J. R. Hall, H. T. Himmelweit, R. K. Kelsall, F. M. Martin, C. A. Moser, R. Mukherjee, and W. Ziegel. 420 pp. 1954. (2nd Impression 1963.) 40s.*

Kelsall, R. K. Higher Civil Servants in Britain: From 1870 to the Present Day. *268 pp. 31 tables. 1955. 25s.*

Marsh, David C. The Changing Social Structure in England and Wales, 1871-1961. *288 pp. 2nd edition 1965. In preparation.*

Ossowski, Stanislaw. Class Structure in the Social Consciousness. *212 pp. 1963. 25s.*

SOCIOLOGY AND POLITICS

Barbu, Zevedei. Democracy and Dictatorship: Their Psychology and Patterns of Life. *300 pp. 1956. 28s.*

Crick, Bernard. The American Science of Politics: Its Origins and Conditions. *284 pp. 1959. 28s.*

Kornhauser, William. The Politics of Mass Society. *272 pp. 20 tables. 1960. (2nd Impression 1965.) 28s.*

Laidler, Harry W. Social-Economic Movements: An Historical and Comparative Survey of Socialism, Communism, Co-operation, Utopianism; and other Systems of Reform and Reconstruction. *864 pp. 16 plates. 1 figure. 1949. (3rd Impression 1960.) 50s.*

Mannheim, Karl. Freedom, Power and Democratic Planning. *Edited by Hans Gerth and Ernest K. Bramstedt. 424 pp. 1951. (2nd Impression 1965.) 35s.*

Mansur, Fatma. Process of Independence. *Foreword by A. H. Hanson. 208 pp. 1962. 25s.*

Martin, David A. Pacificism: an Historical and Sociological Study. *202 pp. 1965. 30s.*

Myrdal, Gunnar. The Political Element in the Development of Economic Theory. *Translated from the German by Paul Streeten. 282 pp. 1953. (4th Impression 1965.) 25s.*

Polanyi, Michael, F.R.S. The Logic of Liberty: Reflections and Rejoinders. *228 pp. 1951. 18s.*

Verney, Douglas V. The Analysis of Political Systems. *264 pp. 1959. (3rd Impression 1965.) 28s.*

Wootton, Graham. The Politics of Influence: British Ex-Servicemen, Cabinet Decisions and Cultural Changes, 1917 to 1957. *320 pp. 1963. 30s.*

FOREIGN AFFAIRS: THEIR SOCIAL, POLITICAL AND ECONOMIC FOUNDATIONS

Baer, Gabriel. Population and Society in the Arab East. *Translated by Hanna Szöke. 228 pp. 10 maps. 1964. 40s.*

Bonné, Alfred. The Economic Development of the Middle East: An Outline of Planned Reconstruction after the War. *192 pp. 58 tables. 1945. (3rd Impression 1953.) 16s.*

State and Economics in the Middle East: A Society in Transition. *482 pp. 2nd (revised) edition 1955. (2nd Impression 1960.) 40s.*

Studies in Economic Development: with special reference to Conditions in the Under-developed Areas of Western Asia and India. *322 pp. 84 tables. 2nd edition 1960. 32s.*

Mayer, J. P. Political Thought in France from the Revolution to the Fifth Republic. *164 pp. 3rd edition (revised) 1961. 16s.*

Schlesinger, Rudolf. Central European Democracy and its Background: Economic and Political Group Organization. *432 pp. 1953. 40s.*

Thomson, David Meyer E., and **Briggs, A.** Patterns of Peacemaking. *408 pp. 1945. 25s.*

Trouton, Ruth. Peasant Renaissance in Yugoslavia 1900-1950: A Study of the Development of Yugoslav Peasant Society as affected by Education. *370 pp. 1 map. 1952. 28s.*

CRIMINOLOGY

Ancel, Marc. Social Defence: A Modern Approach to Criminal Problems. *Foreword by Leon Radzinowicz. 240 pp. 1965. 32s.*

Cloward, Richard A., and **Ohlin, Lloyd E.** Delinquency and Opportunity: A Theory of Delinquent Gangs. *248 pp. 1961. 25s.*

Downes, David. The Delinquent Solution. A Study in Sub-cultural Theory. *304 pp. 1965. 42s.*

Dunlop, A. B., and **McCabe, S.** Young Men in Detention Centres. *192 pp. 1965. 28s.*

Friedländer, Dr. Kate. The Psycho-Analytical Approach to Juvenile Delinquency: Theory, Case Studies, Treatment. *320 pp. 1947. (5th Impression 1961.) 28s.*

Glueck, Sheldon and **Eleanor.** Family Environment and Delinquency. *With the statistical assistance of Rose W. Kneznek. 340 pp. 1962. 35s.*

Mannheim, Hermann. Group Problems in Crime and Punishment, and other Studies in Criminology and Criminal Law. *336 pp. 1955. 28s.*

Comparative Criminology: a Textbook. *Two volumes. 416 pp. and 360 pp. 1965. 42s. each.*

Morris, Terence. The Criminal Area: A Study in Social Ecology. *Foreword by Hermann Mannheim. 232 pp. 25 tables. 4 maps. 1957. 25s.*

Morris, Terence and **Pauline,** assisted by **Barbara Barer.** Pentonville: a Sociological Study of an English Prison. *416 pp. 16 plates. 1963. 50s.*

Spencer, John C. Crime and the Services. *Foreword by Hermann Mannheim. 336 pp. 1954. 28s.*

Trasler, Gordon. The Explanation of Criminality. *144 pp. 1962. 20s.*

SOCIAL PSYCHOLOGY

Barbu, Zevedei. Problems of Historical Psychology. *248 pp. 1960. 25s.*

Blackburn, Julian. Psychology and the Social Pattern. *184 pp. 1945. (7th Impression 1964.) 16s.*

Fleming, C. M. Adolescence: Its Social Psychology: With an Introduction to recent findings from the fields of Anthropology, Physiology, Medicine, Psychometrics and Sociometry. *271 pp. 2nd edition (revised) 1963. (2nd Impression 1964.) 25s.*

The Social Psychology of Education: An Introduction and Guide to Its Study. *136 pp. 2nd edition (revised) 1959. 11s.*

Fleming, C. M. (Ed.). Studies in the Social Psychology of Adolescence. *Contributions by J. E. Richardson, J. F. Forrester, J. K. Shukla and P. J. Higginbotham. Foreword by the editor. 292 pp. 29 figures. 13 tables. 5 folder tables. 1951. 23s.*

Halmos, Paul. Towards a Measure of Man: The Frontiers of Normal Adjustment. *276 pp. 1957. 28s.*

Homans, George C. The Human Group. *Foreword by Bernard DeVoto. Introduction by Robert K. Merton. 526 pp. 1951. (4th Impression 1965.) 35s.*

Social Behaviour: its Elementary Forms. *416 pp. 1961. 30s.*

Klein, Josephine. The Study of Groups. *226 pp. 31 figures. 5 tables. 1956. (4th Impression 1965.) 21s.*

Linton, Ralph. The Cultural Background of Personality. *132 pp. 1947. (5th Impression 1965.) 16s.*

Mayo, Elton. The Social Problems of an Industrial Civilization. With an appendix on the Political Problem. *180 pp. 1949. (4th Impression 1961.) 18s.*

Ridder, J. C. de. The Personality of the Urban African in South Africa. A Thematic Apperception Test Study. *196 pp. 12 plates. 1961. 25s.*

Rose, Arnold M. (Ed.). Mental Health and Mental Disorder: A Sociological Approach. *Chapters by 46 contributors. 654 pp. 1956. 45s.*

Human Behaviour and Social Processes: an Interactionist Approach. *Contributions by Arnold M. Ross, Ralph H. Turner, Anselm Strauss, Everett C. Hughes, E. Franklin Frazier, Howard S. Becker, et al. 696 pp. 1962. 60s.*

Smelser, Neil J. Theory of Collective Behaviour. *448 pp. 1962. 45s.*

Spinley, Dr. B. M. The Deprived and the Privileged: Personality Development in English Society. *232 pp. 1953. 20s.*

Wolfenstein, Martha. Disaster: A Psychological Essay. *264 pp. 1957. 23s.*

Young, **Professor Kimball**. Personality and Problems of Adjustment, *742 pp. 12 figures, 9 tables, 2nd edition (revised) 1952. (2nd Impression 1959.) 40s.*
Handbook of Social Psychology. *658 pp. 16 figures. 10 tables. 2nd edition (revised) 1957. (3rd Impression 1963.) 40s.*

SOCIOLOGY OF THE FAMILY

Banks, J. A. Prosperity and Parenthood: A study of Family Planning among the Victorian Middle Classes. *262 pp. 1954. (2nd Impression 1965.) 24s.*
Chapman, Dennis. The Home and Social Status. *336 pp. 8 plates. 3 figures. 117 tables. 1955. 35s.*
Klein, Josephine. Samples from English Cultures. *1965.*
   1. Three Preliminary Studies and Aspects of Adult Life in England. *447 pp. 50s.*
   2. Child-Rearing Practices and Index. *247 pp. 35s.*
Klein, Viola. Britain's Married Women Workers. *176 pp. 1965. 28s.*
Myrdal, Alva and **Klein, Viola.** Women's Two Roles: Home and Work. *238 pp. 27 tables. 1956. (2nd Impression 1962.) 25s.*
Parsons, Talcott and **Bales, Robert F.** Family: Socialization and Interaction Process. *In collaboration with James Olds, Morris Zelditch and Philip E. Slater. 456 pp. 50 figures and tables. 1956. (2nd Impression 1964.) 35s.*

THE SOCIAL SERVICES

Ashdown, Margaret and **Brown, S. Clement.** Social Service and Mental Health: An Essay on Psychiatric Social Workers. *280 pp. 1953. 21s.*
Hall, M. Penelope. The Social Services of Modern England. *416 pp. 6th edition (revised) 1963. (2nd Impression with a new Preface 1965.) 30s.*
Hall, M. P., and **Howes, I. V.** The Church in Social Work. A Study of Moral Welfare Work undertaken by the Church of England. *320 pp. 1965. 35s.*
Heywood, Jean S. Children in Care: the Development of the Service for the Deprived Child. *264 pp. 2nd edition (revised) 1965. 32s.*
   An Introduction to teaching Casework Skills. *192 pp. 1964. 28s.*
Jones, Kathleen. Lunacy, Law and Conscience, 1744-1845: the Social History of the Care of the Insane. *268 pp. 1955. 25s.*
   Mental Health and Social Policy, 1845-1959. *264 pp. 1960. 28s.*
Jones, Kathleen and **Sidebotham, Roy.** Mental Hospitals at Work. *220 pp. 1962. 30s.*
Kastell, Jean. Casework in Child Care. *Foreword by M. Brooke Willis. 320 pp. 1962. 35s.*
Rooff, Madeline. Voluntary Societies and Social Policy. *350 pp. 15 tables. 1957. 35s.*
Shenfield, B. E. Social Policies for Old Age: A Review of Social Provision for Old Age in Great Britain. *260 pp. 39 tables. 1957. 25s.*

Timms, Noel. Psychiatric Social Work in Great Britain (1939-1962). *280 pp. 1964. 32s.*
Social Casework: Principles and Practice. *256 pp. 1964, 25s.*

Trasler, Gordon. In Place of Parents: A Study in Foster Care. *272 pp. 1960. (2nd Impression 1965.) 30s.*

Young, A. F., and **Ashton, E. T.** British Social Work in the Nineteenth Century. *288 pp. 1956. (2nd Impression 1963.) 28s.*

SOCIOLOGY OF EDUCATION

Banks, Olive. Parity and Prestige in English Secondary Education: a Study in Educational Sociology. *272 pp. 1955. (2nd Impression 1963.) 28s.*

Bentwich, Joseph. Education in Israel. *224 pp. 8 pp. plates. 1965. 24s.*

Blyth, W. A. L. English Primary Education. A Sociological Description. *1965.*
1. Schools. *232 pp. 30s.*
2. Background. *168 pp. 25s.*

Collier, K. G. The Social Purposes of Education: Personal and Social Values in Education. *268 pp. 1959. (2nd Impression 1962.) 21s.*

Dale, R. R. and **Griffith, S.** Downstream: Failure in the Grammar School. *112 pp. 1965. 20s.*

Dore, R. P. Education in Tokugawa Japan. *356 pp. 9 pp. plates. 1965. 35s.*

Edmonds, E. L. The School Inspector. *Foreword by Sir William Alexander. 214 pp. 1962. 28s.*

Evans, K. M. Sociometry and Education. *158 pp. 1962. 18s.*

Foster, P. J. Education and Social Change in Ghana. *336 pp. 3 maps. 1965.*

Fraser, W. R. Education and Society in Modern France. *150 pp. 1963. 20s.*

Hans, Nicholas. New Trends in Education in the Eighteenth Century. *278 pp. 19 tables. 1951. (2nd Impression 1965.) 25s.*
Comparative Education: A Study of Educational Factors and Traditions. *360 pp. 3rd (revised) edition 1958. (4th Impression 1964.) 25s.*

Holmes, Brian. Problems in Education. A Comparative Approach. *336 pp. 1965. 32s.*

Mannheim, Karl and **Stewart, W. A. C.** An Introduction to the Sociology of Education. *208 pp. 1962. (2nd Impression 1965.) 21s.*

Musgrove, F. Youth and the Social Order. *176 pp. 1964. 21s.*

Ortega y Gasset, Jose. Mission of the University. *Translated with an Introduction by Howard Lee Nostrand. 88 pp. 1946. (3rd Impression 1963.) 15s.*

Ottaway, A. K. C. Education and Society: An Introduction to the Sociology of Education. *With an Introduction by W. O. Lester Smith. 212 pp. Second edition (revised). 1962. (3rd Impression 1965.) 21s.*

Peers, Robert. Adult Education: A Comparative Study. *398 pp. 2nd edition 1959. 35s.*

Pritchard, D. G. Education and the Handicapped: 1760 to 1960. *258 pp. 1963. 28s.*

Samuel, R. H., and **Thomas, R. Hinton.** Education and Society in Modern Germany. *212 pp. 1949. 16s.*

Simon, Brian and **Joan** (Eds.). Educational Psychology in the U.S.S.R. *Introduction by Brian and Joan Simon. Translation by Joan Simon. Papers by D. N. Bogoiavlenski and N. A. Menchinskaia, D. B. Elkonin, E. A. Fleshner, Z. I. Kalmykova, G. S. Kostiuk, V. A. Krutetski, A. N. Leontiev, A. R. Luria, E. A. Milerian, R. G. Natadze, B. M. Teplov, L. S. Vygotski, L. V. Zankov. 296 pp. 1963. 40s.*

SOCIOLOGY OF CULTURE

Fromm, Erich. The Fear of Freedom. *286 pp. 1942. (8th Impression 1960.) 21s.* The Sane Society. *400 pp. 1956. (3rd Impression 1963.) 28s.*

Mannheim, Karl. Diagnosis of Our Time: Wartime Essays of a Sociologist. *208 pp. 1943. (7th Impression 1962.) 21s.*
Essays on the Sociology of Culture. *Edited by Ernst Mannheim in co-operation with Paul Kecskemeti. Editorial Note by Adolph Lowe. 280 pp. 1956. (2nd Impression 1962.) 28s.*

Weber, Alfred. Farewell to European History: or The Conquest of Nihilism. *Translated from the German by R. F. C. Hull. 224 pp. 1947. 18s.*

SOCIOLOGY OF RELIGION

Argyle, Michael. Religious Behaviour. *224 pp. 8 figures. 41 tables. 1958. (2nd Impression 1965.) 25s.*

Knight Frank H., and **Merriam, Thornton W.** The Economic Order and Religion. *242 pp. 1947. 18s.*

Watt, W. Montgomery. Islam and the Integration of Society. *320 pp. 1961. (2nd Impression.) 32s.*

SOCIOLOGY OF ART AND LITERATURE

Beljame, Alexandre. Men of Letters and the English Public in the Eighteenth Century: 1660-1744, Dryden, Addison, Pope. *Edited with an Introduction and Notes by Bonamy Dobree. Translated by E. O. Lorimer. 532 pp. 1948. 32s.*

Misch, Georg. A History of Autobiography in Antiquity. *Translated by E. W. Dickes. 2 Volumes. Vol. 1, 364 pp., Vol. 2, 372 pp. 1950. 45s. the set.*

Schucking, L. L. The Sociology of Literary Taste. *112 pp. 2nd edition, 1965. 18s.*

Silbermann, Alphons. The Sociology of Music. *224 pp. 1963. 28s.*

SOCIOLOGY OF KNOWLEDGE

Hodges, H. A. The Philosophy of Wilhelm Dilthey. *410 pp. 1952. 30s.*

Mannheim, Karl. Essays on the Sociology of Knowledge. *Edited by Paul Kecskemeti. Editorial note by Adolph Lowe. 352 pp. 1952. (3rd Impression 1964.) 35s.*

Schlesinger, Rudolf. Marx: His Time and Ours. *464 pp. 1950. (2nd Impression 1951.) 32s.*

Stark, W. America: Ideal and Reality. The United States of 1776 in Contemporary Philosophy. *136 pp. 1947. 12s.*
The Sociology of Knowledge: An Essay in Aid of a Deeper Understanding of the History of Ideas. *384 pp. 1958. (2nd Impression 1960.) 36s.*
Montesquieu: Pioneer of the Sociology of Knowledge. *244 pp. 1960. 25s.*

URBAN SOCIOLOGY

Anderson, Nels. The Urban Community: A World Perspective. *532 pp. 1960. 35s.*

Ashworth, William. The Genesis of Modern British Town Planning: A Study in Economic and Social History of the Nineteenth and Twentieth Centuries. *288 pp. 1954. (2nd Impression 1965.) 32s.*

Bracey, Howard. Neighbours: Neighbouring and Neighbourliness on New Estates and Subdivisions in England and the U.S.A. *220 pp. 1964. 28s.*

Cullingworth, J. B. Housing Needs and Planning Policy: A Restatement of the Problems of Housing Need and "Overspill" in England and Wales. *232 pp. 44 tables. 8 maps. 1960. 28s.*

Dickinson, Robert E. City and Region: A Geographical Interpretation. *608 pp. 125 figures. 1964. 60s.*
The West European City: A Geographical Interpretation. *600 pp. 129 maps. 29 plates. 2nd edition 1962. (2nd Impression 1963.) 55s.*

Dore, R. P. City Life in Japan: A Study of a Tokyo Ward. *498 pp. 8 plates. 4 figures. 24 tables. 1958. (2nd Impression 1963.) 45s.*

Jennings, Hilda. Societies in the Making: a Study of Development and Redevelopment within a County Borough. *Foreword by D. A. Clark. 286 pp. 1962. 32s.*

Kerr, Madeline. The People of Ship Street, *240 pp. 1958. 23s.*

Mann, P. H. An Approach to Urban Sociology. *240 pp. 1965. 30s.*

Morris, R. N., and **Mogey, J.** The Sociology of Housing. Studies at Berinsfield. *232 pp. 4 pp. plates. 1965. 42s.*

Rosser, C., and **Harris, C.** The Family and Social Change. A Study of Family and Kinship in a South Wales Town. *352 pp. 8 maps. 1965. 45s.*

RURAL SOCIOLOGY

Bracey, H. E. English Rural Life: Village Activities, Organizations and Institutions. *302 pp. 1959. 30s.*

Infield, Henrik F. Co-operative Living in Palestine. *With a Foreword by General Sir Arthur Wauchope, G.C.B. 170 pp. 8 plates. 7 tables. 1946. 12s. 6d.*

Littlejohn, James. Westrigg: the Sociology of a Cheviot Parish. *172 pp. 5 figures. 1963. 25s.*

Saville, John. Rural Depopulation in England and Wales, 1851-1951. *Foreword by Leonard Elmhirst. 286 pp. 6 figures. 39 tables. 1 map. 1957. 28s. (Dartington Hall Studies in Rural Sociology.)*

Williams, W. M. The Country Craftsman: A Study of Some Rural Crafts and the Rural Industries Organization in England. *248 pp. 9 figures. 1958. 25s. (Dartington Hall Studies in Rural Sociology.)*

The Sociology of an English Village: Gosforth. *272 pp. 12 figures. 13 tables. 1956. (3rd Impression 1964.) 25s.*

SOCIOLOGY OF MIGRATION

Eisenstadt, S. N. The Absorption of Immigrants: a Comparative Study based mainly on the Jewish Community in Palestine and the State of Israel. *288 pp. 1954. 28s.*

SOCIOLOGY OF INDUSTRY AND DISTRIBUTION

Anderson, Nels. Work and Leisure. *280 pp. 1961. 28s.*

Blau, Peter M., and **Scott, W. Richard.** Formal Organizations: a Comparative approach. *Introduction and Additional Bibliography by J. H. Smith. 328 pp. 1963. (2nd Impression 1964.) 28s.*

Jefferys, Margot, with the assistance of Winifred Moss. Mobility in the Labour Market: Employment Changes in Battersea and Dagenham. *Preface by Barbara Wootton. 186 pp. 51 tables. 1954. 15s.*

Levy, A. B. Private Corporations and Their Control. *Two Volumes. Vol. 1, 464 pp., Vol. 2, 432 pp. 1950. 80s. the set.*

Levy, Hermann. The Shops of Britain: A Study of Retail Distribution. *268 pp. 1948. (2nd Impression 1949.) 21s.*

Liepmann, Kate. The Journey to Work: Its Significance for Industrial and Community Life. *With a Foreword by A. M. Carr-Saunders. 230 pp. 40 tables. 3 folders. 1944. (2nd Impression 1945.) 18s.*

Apprenticeship: An Enquiry into its Adequacy under Modern Conditions. *Foreword by H. D. Dickinson. 232 pp. 6 tables. 1960. (2nd Impression.) 23s.*

Millerson, Geoffrey. The Qualifying Associations: a Study in Professionalization. *320 pp. 1964. 42s.*

Smelser, Neil J. Social Change in the Industrial Revolution: An Application of Theory to the Lancashire Cotton Industry, 1770-1840. *468 pp. 12 figures. 14 tables. 1959. (2nd Impression 1960.) 40s.*

Williams, Gertrude. Recruitment to Skilled Trades. *240 pp. 1957. 23s.*

Young, A. F. Industrial Injuries Insurance: an Examination of British Policy. *192 pp. 1964. 30s.*

ANTHROPOLOGY
(*Demy 8vo.*)

Crook, David and **Isabel**. Revolution in a Chinese Village: Ten Mile Inn. *230 pp. 8 plates. 1 map. 1959. 21s.*

The First Years of Yangyi Commune. *288 pp. 12 plates. 1965. 42s.*

Dube, S. C. Indian Village. *Foreword by Morris Edward Opler. 276 pp. 4 plates. 1955. (5th Impression 1965.) 25s.*

India's Changing Villages: Human Factors in Community Development *260 pp. 8 plates. 1 map. 1958. (2nd Impression 1960.) 25s.*

Fei, Hsiao-Tung. Peasant Life in China: a Field Study of Country Life in the Yangtze Valley. *Foreword by Bronislaw Malinowski. 320 pp. 14 plates. 1939. (5th Impression 1962.) 30s.*

Firth, Raymond. Malay Fishermen. Their Peasant Economy. *420 pp. 17 pp. plates. 2nd edition (revised and enlarged 1965.) 55s.*

Gulliver, P. H. The Family Herds. A Study of two Pastoral Tribes in East Africa, The Jie and Turkana. *304 pp. 4 plates. 19 figures. 1955. 25s.*

Social Control in an African Society: a Study of the Arusha, Agricultural Masai of Northern Tanganyika. *320 pp. 8 plates. 10 figures. 1963. 35s.*

Hogbin, Ian. Transformation Scene. The Changing Culture of a New Guinea Village. *340 pp. 22 plates. 2 maps. 1951. 30s.*

Hsu, Francis L. K. Under the Ancestors' Shadow: Chinese Culture and Personality. *346 pp. 26 figures. 1949. 21s.*

Lowie, Professor Robert H. Social Organization. *494 pp. 1950. (3rd Impression 1962.) 35s.*

Maunier, René. The Sociology of Colonies: An Introduction to the Study of Race Contact. *Edited and translated by E. O. Lorimer. 2 Volumes. Vol. 1, 430 pp. Vol. 2, 356 pp. 1949. 70s. the set.*

Mayer, Adrian C. Caste and Kinship in Central India: A Village and its Region, *328 pp. 16 plates. 15 figures. 16 tables. 1960. (2nd Impression 1965.) 35s.*

Peasants in the Pacific: A Study of Fiji Indian Rural Society. *232 pp. 16 plates. 10 figures. 14 tables. 1961. 35s.*

Osborne, Harold. Indians of the Andes: Aymaras and Quechuas. *292 pp. 8 plates. 2 maps. 1952. 25s.*

Smith, Raymond T. The Negro Family in British Guiana: Family Structure and Social Status in the Villages. *With a Foreword by Meyer Fortes. 314 pp. 8 plates. 1 figure. 4 maps. 1956. (2nd Impression 1965.) 28s.*

DOCUMENTARY
(*Demy 8vo.*)

Meek, Dorothea L. (Ed.). Soviet Youth: Some Achievements and Problems. *Excerpts from the Soviet Press, translated by the editor. 280 pp. 1957. 28s.*

Schlesinger, Rudolf (Ed.). Changing Attitudes in Soviet Russia.

1. The Family in the U.S.S.R. *Documents and Readings, with an Introduction by the editor. 434 pp. 1949. 30s.*

2. The Nationalities Problem and Soviet Administration. Selected Readings on the Development of Soviet Nationalities Policies. *Introduced by the editor. Translated by W. W. Gottlieb. 324 pp. 1956. 30s.*

Reports
of the Institute
# of Community Studies

(*Demy 8vo.*)

Cartwright, Ann. Human Relations and Hospital Care. *272 pp. 1964. 30s.*

Jackson, Brian. Streaming: an Education System in Miniature. *168 pp. 1964. 21s. Paper 10s.*

Jackson, Brian and **Marsden, Dennis.** Education and the Working Class: Some General Themes raised by a Study of 88 Working-class Children in a Northern Industrial City. *268 pp. 2 folders. 1962. (3rd Impression 1965.) 28s.*

Marris, Peter. Widows and their Families. *Foreword by Dr. John Bowlby. 184 pp. 18 tables. Statistical Summary. 1958. 18s.*
Family and Social Change in an African City. A Study of Rehousing in Lagos. *196 pp. 1 map. 4 plates. 53 tables. 1961. 25s.*
The Experience of Higher Education. *232 pp. 27 tables. 1964. 25s.*

Mills, Enid. Living with Mental Illness: a Study in East London. *Foreword by Morris Carstairs. 196 pp. 1962. 28s.*

Runciman, W. G. Relative Deprivation and Social Justice. *344 pp. 1966. 40s.*

Townsend, Peter. The Family Life of Old People: An Inquiry in East London. *Foreword by J. H. Sheldon. 300 pp. 3 figures. 63 tables. 1957. (2nd Impression 1961.) 30s.*

Willmott, Peter. The Evolution of a Community: a study of Dagenham after forty years. *168 pp. 2 maps. 1963. 21s.*

Willmott, Peter and **Young, Michael.** Family and Class in a London Suburb. *202 pp. 47 tables. 1960. (2nd Impression 1961.) 21s.*

Young, Michael. Innovation and Research in Education. *192 pp. 1965. 25s.*

Young, Michael and **Willmott, Peter.** Family and Kinship in East London. *Foreword by Richard M. Titmuss. 252 pp. 39 tables. 1957. (3rd Impression 1965.) 25s.*

The British Journal of Sociology. *Edited by Terence P. Morris. Vol. 1, No. 1, March 1950 and Quarterly. Roy 8vo., £2 10s. p.a.; 12s. 6d. a number, post free.*

All prices are net and subject to alteration without notice